P9-CAA-620

Stalin's Silver

Stalin's Silver

The Sinking of the USS John Barry

John Beasant

St. Martin's Press
New York

PICTURE SOURCES
Asharq Al Awsat: page 3 *bottom*
Brian Shoemaker: page 4
John Ferguson: pages 5, 6
Catherine Bailey Ltd: page 7
All remaining pictures supplied by the author.

Library of Congress Cataloging-in-Publication Data

Beasant, John.
Stalin's silver : the sinking of the USS John Barry / John Beasant.
p. cm.
Originally published: London : Bloomsbury, 1995.
Includes index.
ISBN 0-312-20590-2
1. John Barry (Liberty ship) 2. World War, 1939-1945—Naval operations, American. 3. World War, 1939-1945—Naval operations—Submarine. 4. World War, 1939-1945—Naval operations, German. 5. Shipwrecks—Arabian Sea. 6. Treasure-trove—Arabian Sea. I. Title.
D774.J63B43 1999
940.54'5973—dc21 99-21627
CIP

First published in Great Britain by Bloomsbury Publishing Plc

First U.S. Edition: May 1999

10 9 8 7 6 5 4 3 2 1

Contents

	Acknowledgements	vii
	Preface	1
	PART ONE	15
1	Wreck Fever	17
2	The Ocean Group	35
	PART TWO	47
3	Buddy Can You Spare a Dime?	49
4	A Paw for the Bear	63
5	For Freedom and Liberty	71
6	The Maiden Voyage of No Return	85
7	Voyage to the Deep	101
8	In the Straits of Malacca	121
	PART THREE	141
9	A Surfacing of Facts – A Dive to the Deep	143
10	Silver Galore!	161
11	Secrets from the Top – Secrets from the Deep	171
	Appendix I: The Significance of *U859*'s Secret Cargo	185
	Appendix II: The Key Documents	191
	Index	213

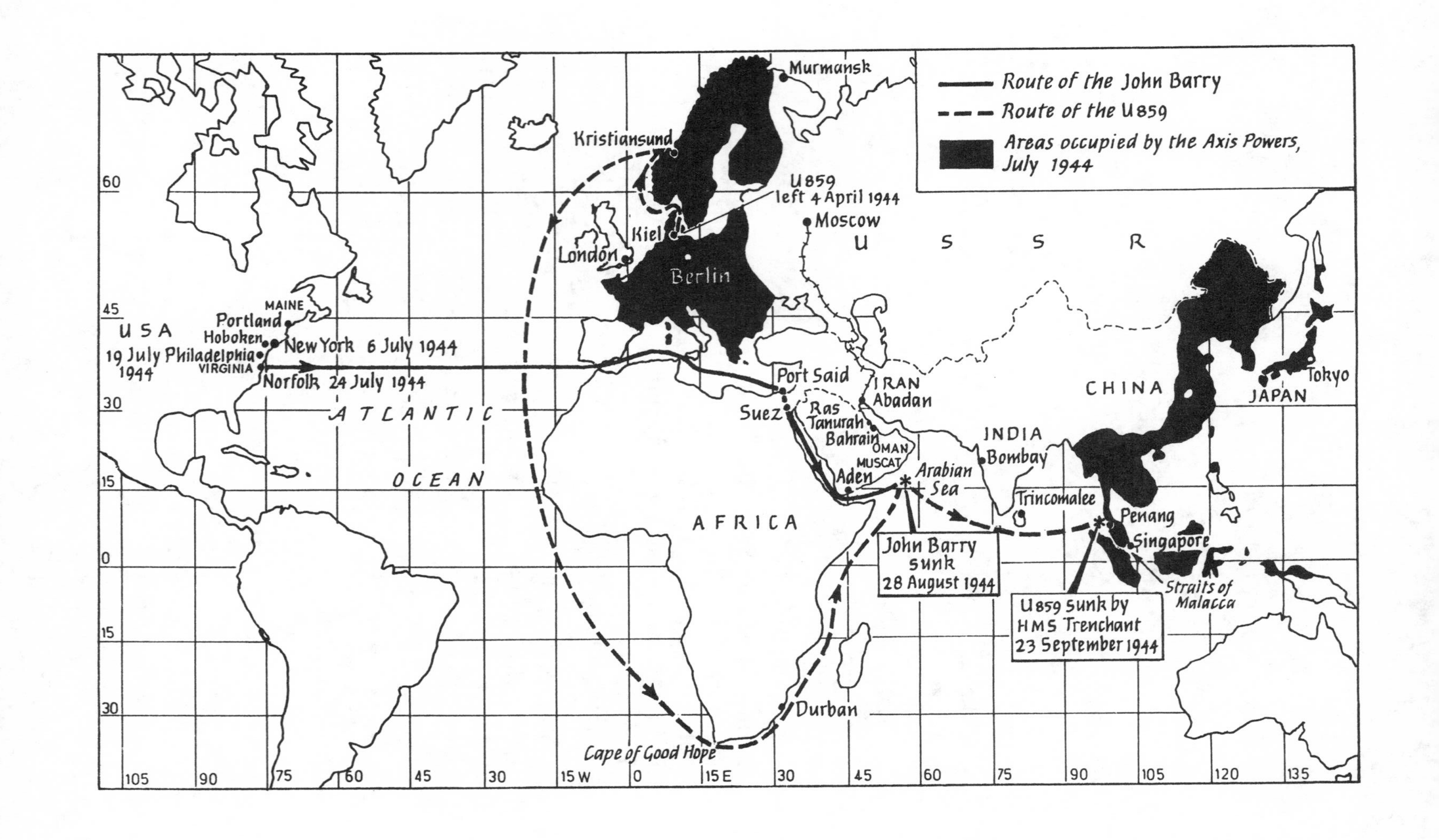
Route of the John Barry
Route of the U859
Areas occupied by the Axis Powers, July 1944
Murmansk
Kristiansund
U859 left 4 April 1944
Moscow
U S S R
Kiel
London
Berlin
MAINE
Portland
U S A
Hoboken
New York 6 July 1944
19 July 1944 Philadelphia
VIRGINIA
Norfolk 24 July 1944
Port Said
IRAN
Abadan
CHINA
JAPAN
Tokyo
Suez
Ras Tanurah
Bahrain
OMAN
MUSCAT
INDIA
Bombay
ATLANTIC
OCEAN
Aden
Arabian Sea
Trincomalee
AFRICA
Penang
Singapore
John Barry sunk 28 August 1944
U859 sunk by HMS Trenchant 23 September 1944
Straits of Malacca
Durban
Cape of Good Hope
60
45
30
15
0
15
30
105
90
75
60
45
30
15 W
0
15 E
30
45
60
75
90
105
120
135

Acknowledgements

Among the many people who gave invaluable assistance during the writing of this book, I would initially like to mark my gratitude to His Highness Sheikh Ahmed Farid al Aulaqi, Prince of the Yemen, who answered my many questions with patience and courtesy and made available to me his private papers for research. Similarly, I appreciate the help of Captain Brian Shoemaker, whose own research papers were of pivotal importance. The staff at the national archives in the USA, Britain and Germany afforded professional assistance of the highest quality. I am also particularly grateful to Igor Lebedev of the Foreign Ministry Archives in Moscow. His Excellency Alexander Patsev, the Ambassador of the Russian Federation to the Court of His Majesty the Sultan Qaboos of Oman at Muscat, also gave essential assistance, as did his Third Secretary at the Embassy, Elmir Tagirov.

I would like to thank Ekaterina Noor for valuable help with Russian translation, and Brigitta Veen-Miklauschina for her constant help with German research and translation. For research and administrative assistance in the United Kingdom I would like to thank Michael and Barbara Williams and Robert Hudson, and in Germany Volker Mayer. I thank Christopher Ling for research assistance into various aspects of World War II, and Commander M. R. Wood for research into naval history. I am truly grateful to Clive Ponting of Swansea University, author of *1940* and *The Right to Know*, who generously allowed me to compare my conclusions with his own pre-eminent research material. I am also very grateful to Professor John Charmley of the University of East Anglia, author of *Churchill – The End of Glory* and *Churchill's Grand Alliance*, for his kind guidance at a particularly difficult stage in my research, and to Martin Garnett, Curator at London's Imperial War Museum, for his kind and patient help. This book also owes much to Oberleutenant Horst Klatt and to Vice-Admiral Sir Arthur Hezlet, both of whom answered my numerous questions with patience and unfailing courtesy.

Crown copyright is reproduced with the permission of the Controller of Her Majesty's Stationary Office, and I acknowledge in particular kind permission to quote from *The U-boat War in the Atlantic.* I also thank the Naval Institute Press at the United States Naval Institute for permission to quote from John Gorley-Bunker's *Liberty Ships – The Ugly Ducklings of World War II,* Frank Braynard of the American Merchant Maritime Museum Foundation for permission to quote from his foreword to Captain Arthur Moore's *A Careless Word . . . a Needless Sinking*, and Captain Moore himself for allowing me to quote from his work.

I am indebted to Ellen Purvey and Margaret Pike who typed the manuscript, often doing so under great pressure but without ever losing their professionalism and good humour. I extend a warm thanks to Bhanu Joish, Dharma Rajan and Rodondo Gonsalves, the staff of Sheikh Farid's Private Office in Muscat, for their patience and constant assistance. Also in Muscat, I would like to thank Claire Williams, Heide Beal, Richard Simmons, Bruce Carswell and Michael Moore, all of whom were tremendously supportive during the research and writing of this book. At Bloomsbury in London I had the constant support of David Reynolds and Monica Macdonald, and I am especially grateful to my editor, Caroline Taggart, for her skill and professionalism.

Finally, I convey my heartfelt appreciation to all those who rendered invaluable research assistance but who, in honouring past commitments, must remain anonymous.

John Beasant, Muscat, the Sultanate of Oman
September 16 1995

Preface

27 November 1994. The Moon Room of the Intercontinental Hotel, Dubai, on the Arabian Gulf.

It was an appropriate venue for a story of success born of the sea. Dubai, an Arab city on the banks of a creek that sidles out into the waters of the Gulf, has long been a magnet for those who find the element of chance the most appealing aspect of man's insatiable appetite for trade. Once a haven for nineteenth-century pirates and as recently as the 1960s a port of call for consignments of gold from the Indian subcontinent which somehow never appeared on any manifest, Dubai today has to a great extent been tamed by the chartered accountant and the worldwide desire to appear very much like everywhere else in order to be taken seriously by the 'international community'.

Yet, as it panted in the oppressive heat of a late Arabian summer on this day in 1994, Dubai demonstrated that it had not entirely succumbed to the need for respectable restraint. For being unveiled to the city's press corps in the Intercontinental Hotel, whose glass tower looks down upon shoals of wooden sailing boats loading and offloading cargo for and from such exotic ports as Aden and Zanzibar, was a story of modern-day venturers, a multinational breed of men bound together by the promise of fortune and the irresistible attraction of solving a mystery that had held its fascination for over half a century. It was a journalistic opportunity rich in the drama of war, the romance of a desert king's lost riches, the intrigue of international diplomacy and the suspense of an attempt to retrieve a treasure trove from the depths of the Arabian Sea. Indeed, here was a tale with all the elements of an epic film and, like any potential box-office hit, it had an astonishing cast.

Top of the bill was a man born to Arab princehood who had seen his family's realm swept away by the winds of revolution and who, just months before, had ventured into modern warfare in an attempt to regain his birthright (having in the process been declared Governor and Military Commander of the desert realm of Shabwa), and whose personal philosophy represented an admonishment to an anaemic world: 'I abhor the dreary life which lacks the dignity of danger.'

Following on was a California restaurateur who, when not meeting the culinary demands of the rich and famous, was a distinguished cameo actor and celebrated hot-air balloonist. Next in the line-up came a retired American Navy Captain, who had served on Ice Station Zebra in the frozen wastes of the Antarctic.

In quick succession came two former British military officers who, twenty years earlier, had fought a hard guerrilla war for a young Sultan fresh to his throne. And then, crucially, came a taciturn Frenchman who had played a starring role in bringing to the surface artefacts from the wreck of the transatlantic liner *Titanic*.

As if this was not sufficient to excite the most jaded pen, there then came what journalist Neena Gopal described in the next day's *Gulf News* as 'a delicious irony', the former German submarine officer whose U-boat, half a century ago, had been instrumental in sending the subject of the press conference, a World War II US merchant ship – the *John Barry*, one of the so-called 'Liberty Fleet' – down 8,500 feet to the bottom of the Arabian sea.

Such a cast list heralded a journalistic banquet for a corps that for too long had been condemned to a dreary round of product launches disguised as press conferences – automobiles from Japan, perfumes from the fashion houses of Europe and exhibitions by expatriate 'artists' with their production lines of canvases. Today promised to be a departure from the routine and the press had responded in unprecedented strength.

Behind the top stood a row of flags representing the nationalities of those involved in the search for what *The Atlas of Ship Wreck and Treasure* had described as 'one of the most controversial treasure ships of all time and one of the most fascinating underwater mysteries yet to be solved'. To the left of the table, on a black-draped dais, sat an antique Arab chest from which flowed thousands of silver coins, blinking in the glare of a spotlight. Guarding this peep-show of a treasure was a robed and towering figure, recorded in *The Guinness Book of Records* as 'the world's second tallest man' and wielding a period Lee Enfield rifle. Abul Jabbar, from the Pakistani province of Baluchistan, is a doorman at the Dubai Intercontinental Hotel and had been recruited to the press conference for added effect.

While the press had been provided with an outline of the saga about to be unfolded, the central actors had yet to make an appearance in public. As early as 12 January 1991, *Gulf News* had broken the story with a front-page headline, '300 million dollar silver hunt off Oman coast', an exclusive it had followed up on 31 December 1992 with the premature declaration 'Revealed – a King's Ransom – treasure hunt off Oman reaches its climax'. This report had been prompted by the arrival in Oman of the British sea-salvage practitioner Keith Jessop, who was believed to be directing the laying of explosives that would tear away the decks of the *John Barry* to reveal the 'king's ransom'. Jessop had been nicknamed 'Goldfinger' by the British tabloids in recognition of his role a decade earlier in bringing to the surface gold bullion from the British cruiser *Edinburgh*, sunk in the Barents Sea during the Second World War, and his presence in the Gulf provoked much speculation.

The existence of the treasure had always been reported as certain, a king's ransom just waiting to be salvaged, even if at previously untouched depths. The possibility that it might not be there at all had never been mentioned in press reports, in the Gulf or elsewhere.

Gulf News had so far failed in its attempts to identify the leader of the team that hoped to recover the treasure, reporting, 'That still remains a mystery buried as deep as the cargo of treasure lying in the sealed holds of the stricken vessels and is proving just as difficult to bring to the surface.' But following unconfirmed reports in early November that a quantity of silver coins had been retrieved from the wreck – a Reuters bulletin mentioned the figure of $70,000 million – the identity of the man who was leading 'the mother and father of all treasure hunts' was about to be revealed.

The opening remarks of the conference were delivered by the group's spokesman, the author of this book:

The first phase of a multi-million-dollar deep-sea recovery operation has come to a successful conclusion with the raising of one and a half million silver Saudi coins from the holds of an American World War II wreck in 8,500 feet of water off the coast of Oman. The raising of the coins is the deepest heavy-lift recovery operation ever and represents a feat of advanced underwater technology set to astonish the international marine-recovery industry.

The recovery of the silver coins, minted in America for the Saudi monarch King Abdul Aziz ibn Saud, solves to a significant degree an underwater mystery that has puzzled the international treasure-hunting community for almost as many years as the wreck of the American liberty ship the John Barry, *sunk by a German submarine in August 1944, has lain in the depths of the Arabian Sea. For what has made the* John Barry *one of the most controversial treasure ships of all time is the mystery as to the exact nature of her cargo, given that her holds were loaded in America under conditions of great secrecy. According to half a century of persistent theory and rumour, the holds contained, in addition to the coins destined for the Saudi Treasury, silver bars destined for what was then British India which today would be worth hundreds of millions of dollars. The whole exercise represents a personal vindication for Sheikh Ahmed Farid al Aulaqi, Chairman of the Oman-based Ocean Group, who five years ago led his team to Washington and successfully negotiated a transfer of rights to the sunken treasure.*

With the skeleton of the story before them, the assembled journalists were invited to put flesh on its bones by asking questions of the top table. For those who read Arabic, one point demanded immediate clarification. Holding up one of the coins, the Egyptian journalist Asem Rashwan, a reporter with the Gulf-based newspaper *Al Khaleej*, asked, 'If the coins were minted in America, why do they have inscribed upon them "Made in Mecca"?'

Mecca, in Saudi Arabia, is, of course, Islam's holiest place, its name evoking reverence throughout the Islamic world. However, the political nature of Rashwan's question was not lost on his colleagues among the press or indeed on those sitting in front of them. Sheikh Ahmed Farid al Aulaqi, with the Omani flag behind him, plucked at his flowing cream cape before he answered.

'The Second World War gave birth to many mysteries and this is just one further example. But, in view of the certain fact that the coins were designed in the Kingdom, there is a certain truth that cannot be denied in maintaining that they were fashioned in the holy place.'

The author, as anchorman of the proceedings, then invited questions of a technical nature. This focused attention on the salvage master of the recovery operation, former British Marine Officer Robert Hudson, who had spent many years soldiering in the service of Oman's sovereign, His Majesty Sultan Qaboos bin Said al Said. Hudson stared out at the press corps as if sizing up an enemy formation, his ruddy features matching the red in the Union Jack in front of which he sat. He had been on board the recovery vessel, the *Flex LD*, throughout the four-week recovery operation which had drawn to a close only days earlier, and it fell to him to reveal the revolutionary advance in deep-sea operations that had been made during the enterprise. An explanation of the technical details was left to the dark-suited Frenchman sitting in front of the tricolour, Jean Roux.

Roux's reputation flows from his role as an operations director with the distinguished French Marine Institute, Ifremer, which over a three-year period at the Toulon research centre had painstakingly developed the mechanics which had made possible the recovery of the silver coins from the *John Barry*. Jean Roux's pedigree in marine-based endeavours, as sharp as the cut of his Parisian attire, had been given an international dimension in the mid-1980s when he was Ifremer's operations director in an exercise which astonished the world – the bringing to the surface of artefacts lying on the seabed around the wreck of the *Titanic*. The organisation's subsequent film of the liner's grand staircase, with a cut-glass chandelier still hanging as if to light the way of passengers as they made their progress to dinner, filled people around the globe with awe, as did its later recovery from around the wreck of a wealth of personal and company possessions – from a diamond ring to a steward's cotton jacket. But obtaining salvage from the *John Barry* was, Roux told the Dubai press corps, a very different matter:

> *The team that recovered the artefacts from around the* Titanic *did so primarily with manned submersibles. No forced entry was made into the* Titanic, *as it had been with the* John Barry. *Working at such a depth, this required special techniques to be developed. Such a recovery operation as carried out on the* John Barry *had never before been attempted.*

Roux went on to reveal that the *Flex LD* was essentially a drilling ship with the standard rig in its centre, from which 8,500 feet of drill pipe were, over a period of eight hours, lowered into the sea. On the end of the pipe was attached Ifremer's revolutionary, hydraulically powered, remote-control steel 'grab', fitted with a camera that transmitted pictures back to the vessel. Once in place, Roux explained, the 'grab' cracked and then peeled open the upper steel deck of the liberty ship, enabling it to rifle through the vessel's holds in search of its cargo.

While admitting to certain operational problems, such as clarified water having to be pumped down to improve the quality of pictures being sent back to the surface, Roux told the journalists, with a dismissive gesture towards the cascading coins, 'But the equipment is really very intelligent.'

And indeed it was. Even allowing for a bias born of professional pride in what had been achieved, those present were quickly coming to realise that they were witnessing a rare moment, the unveiling of evidence of the boundlessness of man's ingenuity when the incentive is strong enough. In the case of the *John Barry*, this had meant pushing the powers of human invention that little bit further than they had been pushed hitherto, to 8,500 feet beneath the waves of the Arabian Sea, some 127 miles off the eastern coast of Oman.

Yes, this was a moment of good news with an international dimension rare in an increasingly tragedy-stained world, and it was, to many, astonishing that the veil on such a story was being lifted in Dubai. One journalist asked rhetorically, 'Why isn't this press conference being held in Paris, or London, or Washington?' As to the new facility at man's disposal, an 'intelligent grab' which could forage on the deepest seabed and, what is more, lift to the surface 18 tons of silver coins, what was possible now? In one 'grab' alone some 600,000 silver riyals – the Saudi unit of currency – had been deposited on the decks of the *Flex LD*.

In answer to this, Jean Roux spoke with justifiable pride: 'With adaptation for the purpose, the "grab" could recover aircraft and even submarines from the seabed.'

At the mention of submarines, many present turned towards a man seated at the top table whom Sheikh Ahmed Farid was later to describe as 'the star of the show' – a title that showed both modesty and generosity on the Sheikh's part, given that it was some $10 million of his investment that had made the venture possible. And yet no one would have been present in Dubai that day had it not been for a skilled act of warfare exercised half a century before by Oberleutnant Horst Klatt and his comrades aboard the German submarine *U859*. For on 28 August 1944, as the *John Barry* zigzagged its way through the Arabian Sea in an attempt to avoid enemy action, disaster had struck.

Lurking beneath the surface of the water, silently tracking the liberty ship, was *U859*, a German submarine under the command of Korvettenkapitan Jan Jebsen.

At precisely 10 p.m. Jebsen ordered the firing of three torpedoes, one of which struck the *John Barry* amidships on the starboard side, causing the forward section of the vessel to flood. Within ten minutes Master Joseph Ellerwald gave the order to abandon ship. Korvettenkapitan Jebsen, observing through the periscope, saw the crew taking to the lifeboats and rafts, but did not believe the ship was sinking. Mindful of the heavy guns mounted on both prow and stern of the liberty ship and of the bright light cast by the clear moon, he did not surface for another ten minutes, when he judged that there was no one left aboard the target to man the guns. At 10.30 Jebsen ordered the firing of a further torpedo. It scored a direct hit on the *John Barry*'s port-side engine room. The liberty ship promptly broke in two and sank, taking her cargo with her to the depths of the Arabian Sea.

Two of the crew of the *John Barry* were never seen again, apparently swept away when an upsurge swamped their life raft. The survivors were later rescued by two passing ships and taken to safety in Gulf ports.

U859, Horst Klatt told the journalists, one of whom was now slowly tearing his press kit to pieces with the suspense of the narration, did not escape the consequences of its action: it was destroyed by the British submarine *Trenchant* just twenty-six days later, on 23 September 1944, in the Straits of Malacca, twenty miles north-west of Penang Island, in today's Malaysian Federation.

'Out of a total crew of sixty-nine, including Korvettenkapitan Jan Jebsen and five of his brother officers, only nineteen survived. I was the only officer from *U859* to live,' said Klatt quietly, holding up a photograph of his long dead comrades taken on board *U859* on 4 April 1944, the day it set sail from Kiel on its maiden voyage, from which it never returned.

As former Oberleutnant Klatt fell silent the Dubai press corps appeared subdued. The excitement of Robert Hudson and Jean Roux's technical revelations was replaced by a sombre mood, befitting the grim details of death and destruction with which Klatt had concluded his remarks.

Had the press corps assembled in Dubai that day shown more persistence, they could have raised questions that have long hung over the incomplete story of the *John Barry*, and some of them might have been answered. What evidence, for example, did Sheikh Ahmed Farid and his fellow venturers have that silver bullion worth hundreds of millions of dollars was in the holds of the wreck, and where was that evidence obtained? How complete or reliable was it? Why had

America, or Britain for that matter, never laid claim to the precious cargo, given that it was supposed to be being supplied to the British Crown under America's lend-lease programme for use in British India? What of the theory, mentioned in passing in John Gorley Bunker's definitive history of the wartime merchant fleet, that the silver was bound for Russia? Why had Washington for so many years chosen to remain silent as to whether or not the bars of silver had ever been loaded on to the *John Barry*? And, in a world dominated by monetary considerations, did Washington ever bill Britain for the lost silver, as it would normally have done under the terms of the Lend-Lease Act? Nobody seemed interested in reporting on the dramatic historical dimensions of the story, or on the technological advances the search was producing.

The press beyond the Gulf were no more perceptive. They portrayed the group of men Sheikh Ahmed led, and in at least one instance the Sheikh himself, either as gamblers who had struck it rich, or as modern-day Blackbeards who would do well to wear black eye-patches and carry garrulous parrots on their shoulders. As early as August 1991 the British-based *Diver* magazine had headlined its lead story on the discovery of the wreck's location with one word, 'Bingo!' This glib brevity was to set the tone for numerous later press reports. It also set the scene of the hunt for the *John Barry* as if in some sort of water-logged casino inhabited by late twentieth-century pirates. On 6 January 1993, the London *Daily Express*, reporting that the holds of the *John Barry* had been blasted open by the strategic placing of underwater explosives, an exercise observed by Keith Jessop, ran the bold banner headline 'How Mr Goldfinger came to strike silver'. Anyone less like a character from the pages of a James Bond novel than the bluff but brilliant West Yorkshire man would be difficult to imagine.

Nor were such colourful reports confined to the Western press. The Arabic newspaper *Asharq al Awsat*, in a full-page report on 10 November 1994, chronicling the many exploits of Sheikh Ahmed Farid al Aulaqi, ran a cartoon depicting this Prince of the Hadhramaut at the helm of a ship, crashing through the waves, clad in a billowing pirate's blouse.

This approach to the story appeared unstoppable, and seventeen days later reports of the press conference were faithful to the mould. The globe's biggest selling Sunday newspaper, the London-based *News of the World*, which had bought exclusive rights to visit the recovery vessel, published its scoop on 28 November, under the admittedly clever headline 'Splash and Grab'. Robert Hudson, acting as salvage master aboard the *Flex LD* and obviously having decided to play the role the press expected of him, was reported as having told *News of the World* reporter Annette Witheridge about the silver coins raining down on the deck when the grab returned from foraging through the *John Barry*'s holds. When the grab opened it was like watching the world's 'biggest one-armed bandit'.

The German magazine *Der Spiegel*, in a prominently placed report of 28 November, abandoned its usual style to report the Dubai press conference under the curt headline 'Silver Loot'; while the distinguished and internationally respected *Frankfurter Allgemeine Zeitung* the next day summed up Sheikh Ahmed and his group with the headline 'The Hunters of the Silver Treasure'. The night before, television stations around the globe, including the BBC's World Service and CNN in Atlanta, had covered the press conference in reports that clipped across viewers' screens in seconds, one showing a cloaked Sheikh Ahmed in Dubai pouring silver coins through his hands, the other a scene from the recovery vessel of the coins cascading out of the giant grab.

Two days later Tim Wilkinson, the public relations consultant who had advised on the staging of the Dubai conference, summed up the journalists' attitude in a letter to his family in England: 'The press principally focused on Sheikh Ahmed and Herr Klatt, typically demanding details about money, politics and death.'

Money, politics and death had indeed been the dominant theme of the event, although the media's morbid obsession with two of those subjects had led them to neglect the politics of the *John Barry* and its mysterious cargo. While there could have been no guarantees that those at the top table would have revealed that there was more to the *John Barry* saga than the possible surrender by the sea of immense riches, it was a lost opportunity. That canon of journalistic faith, to pursue with greater vigour the 'why' factor, should have been more in evidence.

The writer of this book, it has to be recorded, had an advantage over his press colleagues. As a journalist long resident in Oman, I had first reported the transfer of rights in the wreck of the *John Barry* to Omani-based interests in *Gulf News* on 12 January 1991, and three and a half years later had been appointed press spokesman for Sheikh Ahmed and his Ocean Group. From that privileged position, I had been witness to events that prompted many of these unasked questions. As the conference closed, my conviction that the saga of the *John Barry* was a truly remarkable one strengthened. Here, surely, was a story waiting to be told to a wider world.

Central to the lexicon of questions that could have been asked was why, half a century after her sinking, is the *John Barry* still regarded as 'one of the most controversial treasure ships of all time'? The answer to that is simple, but it lies in another long-unanswered question: was the *John Barry*, in addition to her well-documented cargo of three million silver riyals for the Saudi Treasury, also carrying 2,000 tons of silver bars, and if so what was their destination? At 1995 prices, the market value of such a treasure would be some $300 million, as earlier press reports had suggested. That amount of silver would be equivalent to 90 million Troy ounces, representing an incredible 45 per cent of the 200 million ounces sold in any one year on the international bullion market.

In the spring of 1989, the Washington-based Maritime Administration publicly invited bids from would-be retrievers of the liberty ship's cargo. Following a brief pedigree of the *John Barry* up to the time she was sunk, the invitation to bid continued:

The following US Government-owned cargo is reported to have been aboard the vessel at the time of loss.

750 boxes containing 3,000,000 Saudi Arabian Riyals (minted silver coins)

Silver Bullion

Auto parts	- *11 tons*
Weapons carrier	- *39 tons*
Trucks	- *65 tons*
Cranes	- *108 tons*
Tractor Crawler	- *23 tons*

Beyond employing the term 'reported to have been aboard the vessel at the time of loss', successive Washington administrations, for reasons known only to themselves, have consistently refused either to confirm or deny whether or not silver bullion was loaded into the holds of the *John Barry* in the summer of 1944. Presumably they felt obliged to mention the possibility of its existence in the invitation to bid because of the speculation that has endured for so long and the very real chance that future salvors would eventually locate it. But even so, they declined to specify a quantity or a value. No mention has ever been made by the American authorities of the state-compiled manifest. Yet, as we shall see, one did exist and was known to be in the Maritime Administration Archives as late as November 1967. This crucial document, which bore an annotation stating that the *John Barry* was carrying 'a large quantity of silver bullion', subsequently disappeared from the archives, together with other files containing information on the liberty ship.

No explanation has ever been forthcoming from the American authorities as to why the manifest, together with other *John Barry* documentation, was 'pulled', although it seems reasonable to conclude that they came under some nature of secrecy order. But why fifty years after the end of the Second World War, when matters of far greater confidentiality on the conflict have been declassified on both sides of the Atlantic, is the *John Barry*'s cargo still such a closely guarded secret? All available official documentation from America's National Archives and from the Maritime Administration in Washington is clear and precise as to the nature of the cargo loaded into the holds of the *John Barry* fifty years ago. The coins minted in America on behalf of King Abdul Aziz ibn Saud, the Saudi monarch, were to be offloaded at the port of Ras Tanurah, on the kingdom's eastern Gulf shores, and then trucked across the desert to the capital,

Riyadh, an exercise to be overseen by Washington's Vice-Consul in the kingdom, Parker T. Hart. The Cargo of 'government-owned' goods listed on the 'invitation to bid', 'auto parts, weapons carrier, trucks, cranes and tractor crawler', was, it is known, Russia-bound and, once offloaded in the Gulf, was to be taken overland to the embattled Soviets through Iran.

It is also interesting to record that the public notices inviting bids from potential salvors for the contents of the *John Barry* listed goods which were not government-owned and, therefore, not included in the offering. Amongst the mixed cargo were cedar poles, cement, clay cinders, bare piping and 19 tons of beer! The notice of the bid concluded with the observation: 'It is incumbent upon the Buyer to ascertain ownership of any such cargo and other property and to make all arrangements for appropriate compensation.'

Bids were to close at the Washington office of the Marine Administration at 2.30 on the afternoon of 12 May 1989. However, in an act clearly due to the sort of official unease which has characterised the *John Barry* saga, the invitation to bid was abruptly postponed by Washington. No reason was given, and requests for an explanation were dismissed. It was eventually republished with a new deadline – 11 August 1989.

Curiously, this was not the first time that the government of the United States had invited bids for the cargo of the long-lost liberty ship. In 1978 notices similar to those that appeared in 1989 were published in America, but, for reasons which have never been explained, that invitation to bid was suddenly cancelled, even though several would-be salvors had responded – yet further evidence of the ambiguity displayed over the years in official circles when the *John Barry* and the unknown quantity of its cargo come into the public eye.

PART ONE

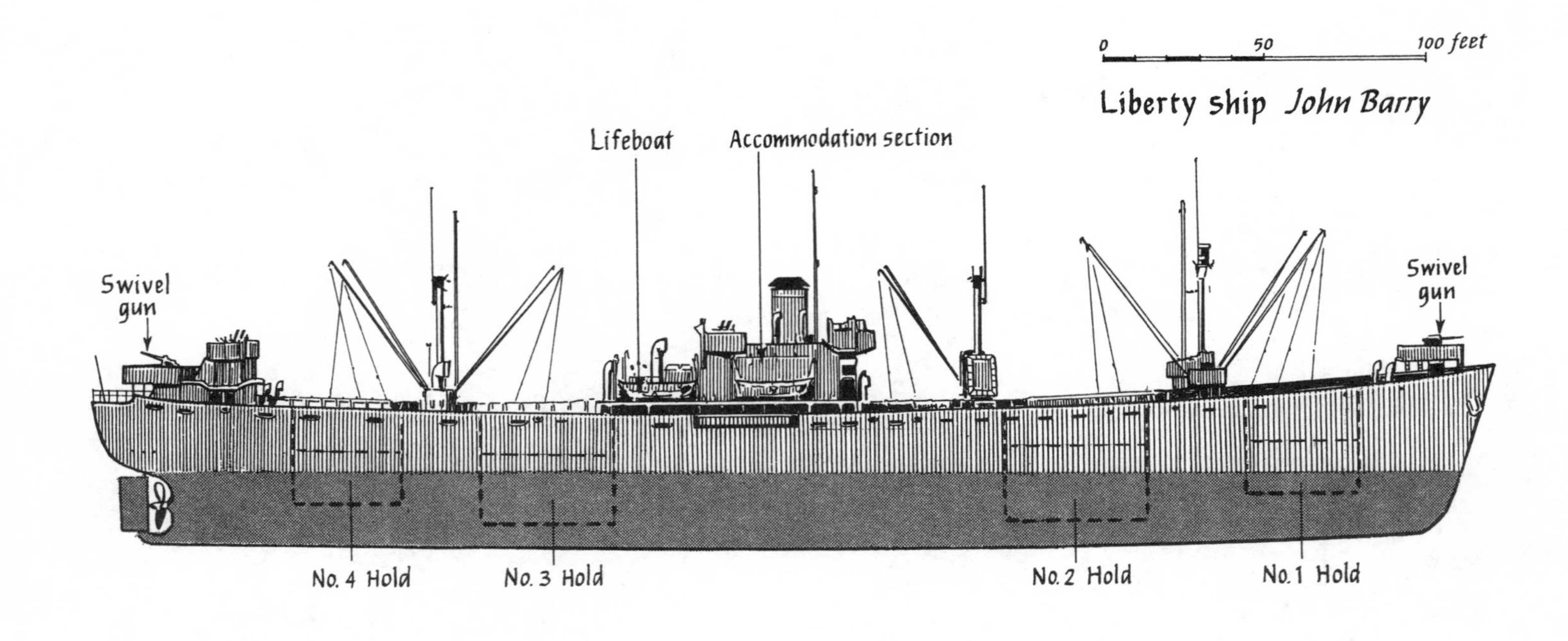
0
50
100 feet
Liberty ship *John Barry*
Lifeboat
Accommodation section
Swivel gun
Swivel gun
No. 4 Hold
No. 3 Hold
No. 2 Hold
No. 1 Hold

Chapter One

Wreck Fever

While successive American governments never forgot the vessel named in honour of the man described as 'the Father of the US Navy', lying in the far-off Arabian Sea, underwater retrieval technology, despite dramatic advances since the end of the Second World War, was incapable of reaching down to such depths. Washington never issued a 'Certificate of Abandonment' of the *John Barry*; under international maritime law, therefore, her remains and cargo remained the sole property and prerogative of 'Uncle Sam'. But, in 1987, in an exercise of initiative and enterprise that John Barry himself would have been proud of, a small band of Americans determined to make an attempt to recover the cargo of the long-lost liberty ship.

The pursuit of treasure, particularly when it is locked away in the sea's safe, attracts people of a particular appetite. For many, the most enticing ingredient is the possibility of fortune; for others the excitement and unpredictability of a sea-based search, allied to the 'time capsule' nature of many wrecks, is the principal magnet. And, on occasions, it is a happy combination of all these aspects of what is commonly regarded as 'treasure hunting'. What is certain, however, is that once one's imagination has been captured by the concept, the ailment described by the California celebrity Jay Fiondella as 'wreck fever' quickly takes hold. And as Fiondella laconically remarks, 'For wreck fever there is no known cure.'

Equally interesting are the circumstances in which these incurable individuals meet and decide to join forces in order to do battle with the sea. The story of how the other founder member of the John Barry Group became enamoured of the possibility of solving the mystery surrounding the liberty ship makes instructive reading.

Captain Brian Shoemaker of Lakeside, Oregon, is a retired US naval officer and the embodiment of the American tradition of self-reliance, initiative and the 'dare to dream' spirit. When it comes to embarking on a venture such as an attempt to retrieve the cargo from a wreck lying in impossible depths in a far-off sea, optimism is perhaps the best ammunition an individual can have in his personal armoury and it is, therefore, relevant that when speaking about his dream of raising the cargo of the *John Barry*, Brian Shoemaker refers to this quality as having played an important part in his early years:

I was raised in the American goldfields, where my father was a mine-manager, and from an early age associated with men who chased rainbows as a way of life. This had the effect of making me receptive to pursuing goals that others didn't even see. It was an environment which taught me not to be timid. This youthful nature of initiative and optimism was only harnessed to the allure of treasure hunting, however, when I read Robert Louis Stevenson's Treasure Island, *at about the age of ten. Not long after, I saw the film based on Stevenson's book. The seduction of my personality was complete. I now had, at a very early age, all the symptoms of 'wreck fever'. But it was not until I joined the American navy that I was able to hone my appetite for the seemingly impractical and to develop still further my incurably romantic nature. While based at Pearl Harbor I went on a scuba-diving course and, consequently, became immersed in the world of underwater exploration.*

In 1964 came a posting which considerably raised Shoemaker's temperature, or in his own words 'heated up my blood'. 'Wreck fever' was definitely on its way.

To be stationed at Key West, in the state of Florida, was to be at the epicentre of treasure hunting in the United States. In the evenings Shoemaker would sit in the bars and listen to the tales and dreams of those who had been chasing 'Spanish Gold' for much of their lives. His imagination was completely captured by their exploits and his weekends were spent exploring the reefs off Key West, searching for hints to any wrecks which might be lying in the depths below. Such weekend excursions were not supported by any archival research; as he says, 'It was hit or miss and throughout my time in Key West was, in actual fact, entirely miss.'

But Brian Shoemaker was now an incurable victim of wreck fever and his subsequent tour of duty aboard the aircraft carrier USS *Intrepid* did little to lower his temperature. For two years the *Intrepid* cruised the Atlantic, Caribbean and the Gulf of Mexico searching for Soviet submarines, moving targets in very deep water. And the thought occurred to Shoemaker, if subs could be located with high technology, why not ships resting on the seabed?

Thus the first seeds were sown and, over the ensuing years, a long series of recovery operations eventually led Brian Shoemaker to that great potential prize in deep-sea treasure trove, the SS *John Barry*.

In the early 1970s the American navy developed equipment which could locate objects both great and small, such as aircraft and missiles, on the seabed, an advance in marine-recovery operations which coincided with Brian Shoemaker's two-year posting to San Diego on a naval flying mission. In the squadron's wardroom was a copy of John Gorley Bunker's book *Liberty Ships – the Ugly Ducklings of World War II*, and it was in this book that Captain Shoemaker first learnt of the existence of the *John Barry* and the belief that silver bullion had been loaded into her holds in abundance. It was a brief account, but it served to whet Shoemaker's appetite.

Fortunately, his time in San Diego was to give him yet more practical experience in the recovery of objects from the seabed. His squadron had lost several helicopters in the sea due to engine failure and he was selected to retrieve them so that it could be determined what had caused the engines to malfunction. They located three: one near San Diego, one in Subic Bay in the Philippines and a third near the Philippines Trench in 8,000 feet of water, using the Klein Smartfish (a later version of which was used to locate the *John Barry*).

The first two helicopters were successfully brought to the surface (from 200 feet of water), but while the new technology enabled Shoemaker to see the third clearly, its capability did not then extend to retrieving it from 8,000 feet beneath the surface of the sea. Brian Shoemaker distinctly remembers thinking at that time of the *John Barry* and the advances that would be required in order to reach down to her.

In 1974 Shoemaker was given a two-year posting to the Arctic, to take command of America's Naval Arctic Research Laboratory, at which techniques were being developed to locate and attack Soviet submarines sailing beneath the ice-cap. It was an area of research and development which made a significant contribution to underwater recovery operations and, as Shoemaker recalls, 'greatly enhanced our ability to locate wrecks in the ocean depths with great accuracy'. And then, in 1976, came a development which for almost twenty years was unknown in the wider world, so secret was it regarded by Washington. In the waters off the Hawaiian Islands, the *Glomar Explorer*, which had been especially adapted for the exercise and used revolutionary technology developed by America's office of Naval Research, lifted a sunken Soviet submarine intact from the Pacific seabed, straight into the salvage vessel, a strategy which concealed the operation from the prying eyes of any space-borne satellite. Crucial to the success of the recovery was the use of a drill pipe with a giant grab attachment.

The *Glomar Explorer* exercise remained a highly classified secret for almost two decades, and accordingly the technology was not made available for commercial salvage operations. But with news, in navy circles, of the success of the *Glomar Explorer* exercise came the realisation that it was now possible to retrieve ships from the deepest ocean. The daunting factor was the huge cost of mounting such an operation and that, consequently, only targets offering very considerable returns could be prosecuted. Nevertheless, the technology to make it possible had at long last arrived. All one had to do was identify a suitable wreck.

Eight years later, while on a return to Antarctica, Shoemaker read Arthur Moore's book *A Careless Word . . . a Needless Sinking*, which, like John Gorley Bunker's earlier work, chronicled the saga of the long-lost liberty ship and its supposed cargo of silver ingots. Then, in April 1985, following his return to the United States from Antarctica, Shoemaker received a telephone call from Jay Fiondella, the proprietor of Santa Monica's celebrated Chez Jay restaurant. A veteran film actor and hot-air balloonist, Jay is a huge, warm bear of a man, a larger-than-life character and a self-avowed victim of wreck fever. Jay wanted to meet Brian and invited him to Santa Monica. The two men were well matched – with Jay's unrivalled contacts to seek financial endorsement for recovery projects and Brian's aptitude for analytical research, a 'team of two' was instantly born. Shoemaker remembers his first meeting with Fiondella well:

Jay's restaurant was a hangout for treasure hunters, Saudi Sheikhs, professional football players, movie stars and astronauts. The bar had been used as the setting for many movies and Jay had acted in many of them. He is a celebrity and people come to his place just to be photographed with him. Chez Jay has a swashbuckling atmosphere right out of Treasure Island, *the story which so captivated my imagination as a child.*

At the time of that first meeting, Jay Fiondella was engaged in a project to recover what was known as 'The Lost Squadron', seven World War II American aircraft – five P–38s and two B–17s – which had ditched in Greenland and were entombed under 200 feet of ice. Having heard of Shoemaker's skills in recovering lost aircraft in difficult conditions, Fiondella wanted to use the naval officer's ski-equipped aircraft in Greenland. Unfortunately, Shoemaker, while keen to work with Fiondella on the project, was unable to obtain official approval. Two years went by before the two met again, this time in San Diego.

'On our second meeting,' Shoemaker recalls, 'I told Jay of my confidence that wrecks could be salvaged from previously undreamt-of depths. All we needed was a target that had proven cargo worth at least five times the cost of the salvage. We agreed there and then that the only wreck we knew of that would meet such a criterion was the SS *John Barry*. The date was 23 July 1987.'

The initial plan of action was that Fiondella would scout for the considerable financial backing that both men knew would be vital to the project, while Shoemaker would embark on the necessary research to attempt to verify from official documents the existence of the rumoured silver bullion. It was a daunting task, as Brian Shoemaker relates:

I had no idea where to begin. The only information I had came from John Gorley Bunker and Arthur Moore's books, but where I went from there to seek confirmation of the two men's claims that the liberty ship had been carrying silver bullion when sunk, I had little notion.

Shoemaker, although approaching retirement, remained a serving officer in the United States navy, so he sought initial guidance from the country's Naval Institute.

The Institute advised me to approach the Navy Historical Centre in Washington, where eventually I was put in touch with Bernard Cavalcante, a senior member of staff there. I first spoke with Bernard on 3 September 1987. It proved to be my first real break.

In addition to making available all his research material on the *John Barry*, Cavalcante also advised Shoemaker to search Washington National Archives, together with those of the United States Coastguard, the Philadelphia Mint, the Treasury Department, the Maritime Administration, the Customs Service and the State Department. Shoemaker's long paper-chase had begun. It was far from easy. Many in positions of authority in the capital were 'discouraging and unhelpful: they had no imagination and appeared reluctant to help, having the attitude that it would take them beyond their routine duties'. Cavalcante's material did, however, contain reports on the sinking of the liberty ship, including statements from survivors that the vessel was carrying $26 million worth of silver bullion.

Exciting as Shoemaker found this information, it did present him with several dilemmas. How should he set about seeking verification of these reports? Were they, for example, based only on interviews with the crew of the *John Barry* or were they given credence by the confirmation of the cargo at the time of sinking? This information, it seemed to him, could only come from such documentation as cargo reports, bills of lading or State Department files. And then, if the bullion was indeed in the wreck, where had it been stowed? Again, this seemed a crucial fact to establish in relation to any eventual salvage operation. And who was the current owner of the wreck and its cargo? Shoemaker had good reason to believe that it was the government of the United States; if so, could they be persuaded to approve a salvage operation? It appeared that the only way to proceed, in a bid to obtain at least some of these answers, was to approach the government directly, and this he did, by letter, on 12 October 1987.

Captain Shoemaker's letter was addressed to the State Department in Washington and proposed a joint venture to salvage the *John Barry* between the governments of the United States and the Sultanate of Oman. The inclusion of Oman was imperative because although the wreck lay some 127 nautical miles off the coast of the Sultanate, its government claimed that it was within its Exclusive Economic Zone.

The result of Shoemaker's initiative was frustrating. No reply was forthcoming; it was only after numerous telephone calls that he was told that the US government had not issued a Certificate of Abandonment of the vessel and that, under international maritime law, both it and its cargo remained the undisputed property of the American nation. This lack of success prompted Shoemaker to take his quest to the navy's Judge Advocate General. On this occasion he was not to be disappointed. Within days of receiving Shoemaker's letter the judge's office had delivered formal letters to the State Department, the Treasury, the US Mint and the Maritime Administration, requesting that an inquiry be held to decide on the status of the SS *John Barry*. The date was 4 December 1987.

But Shoemaker did not let matters rest there. He wrote to Cran Montgomery, the United States Ambassador to Oman, putting the same proposition he had made to the State Department, and further suggesting the participation of both countries' navies in any salvage operation, which would make it a joint goodwill project between the two governments, with Jay Fiondella and himself acting as agents to recover the silver. Shoemaker also asked that Montgomery use his good offices to acquaint the Omanis with the proposal and to put pressure on the Maritime Administration in Washington for a decision. He was later to discover, however, that Montgomery had made a counter-proposal to his political masters in the State Department, that the United States make a gift of the *John Barry* to the Sultanate of Oman, in recognition of the military co-operation agreement between the two states, a strategy that was to be defeated by the Maritime Administration's insistence on putting the vessel up for auction. Indeed, on 5 February 1988, Shoemaker and Fiondella received a letter from the Maritime Administration which confirmed that the SS *John Barry* was to be offered for auction 'in the near future'. (As we have seen, following a postponement for which no official explanation was ever offered, the deadline for bids was finally announced as being 11 August 1989, some two years after Brian Shoemaker and Jay Fiondella had decided to join forces.)

On 1 April 1988, Captain Shoemaker retired from the American navy and, with more time to spare than he had had in decades, set about searching the state archives in an attempt to establish evidence of just what had been loaded into the holds of the *John Barry* in the wartime summer of 1944. He found an early ally in Sally Marks, in the Diplomatic Branch of Washington's National Archives. She took his project to heart and located a State Department file containing correspondence from the US Mission in Saudi Arabia dating back to the time of the Second World War. It contained a folder on the negotiations and delivery arrangements for three million silver Saudi riyal coins, containing a total of one million ounces of silver. The coins, according to the documents in the archives, were packed into 750 wooden boxes and stowed in No. 2 hold aboard the *John Barry*.

Yet, as Shoemaker was quickly to discover, in almost everything associated with the *John Barry* the solving of one question invariably led to another. A quick calculation of the coins' value, at 50 cents per ounce of silver, showed their worth to be about $500,000 at 1944 prices. They were, therefore, definitely not the $26 million worth of silver of which he had read. And there was no documentation in the Saudi file, or among other papers relating to the State Department's 1944 dealings with the Saudi Kingdom, to confirm any transaction involving that amount of silver.

Undaunted, and encouraged by confirmation that the coins at least had been consigned to the liberty ship (although they alone would not make a recovery operation financially viable), Shoemaker then set about a search for surviving crew from the *John Barry*, working through the navy's Armed Guard Association, Merchant Marine Veterans organisations and the archives of the US Coastguard. He was able to locate three seamen and five Armed Guard sailors. While the seamen knew little of their former ship's cargo, two of the Armed Guard had been on duty, on deck, when what they believed to be bullion was loaded into the holds of the *John Barry*. They both gave independent statements in which they recalled seeing boxes, under heavy armed guard, arriving on the quayside from the Philadelphia Mint and then being stowed into a specially built vault made of 2-inch-thick timber planks, measuring approximately 25 feet by 40 feet by 8 feet, situated on the starboard side in hold No. 3, on the second or third deck above the waterline. It was, they said, double layered, with the timbers lying at right angles to one another. It was possible to walk around the vault, although it did take up approximately half the hold.

One of the former Armed Guard, Walter Nendza, told Shoemaker that he saw fourteen 'tractor-trailers' arrive alongside the *John Barry* and load a great number of wooden boxes into the vault. It was completely filled, from top to bottom, and sealed with planks, then steel pipes – 'part of the general cargo' – were placed around it and on top. Nendza also said that it was rumoured by the crew that there were FBI men on board to watch over the vault and its contents.

The most tantalising fact to emerge from these statements is, of course, that a vault of the dimensions the men described would be too big to be filled to the top by the 750 boxes containing the silver coins destined for Saudi Arabia. And as Shoemaker had already seen from the State Department file in the National Archives, which detailed the transaction between the Americans and the Saudis, the coins had been stowed not in hold No. 3, but in hold No. 2. His wreck-fever temperature began to rise.

It was now September 1988. With continuing indecision on the part of Maritime Administration clearly indicating that it would be some time before invitations to bid would be issued, Shoemaker decided to go to Washington, to spend a month researching the nation's archives. Most of the documents he read led nowhere, but a few did support those he already had on the minting and shipment of the Saudi riyals. All the key people involved in America's World War II lend-lease programme featured in the documents he accumulated, including Henry Morgenthau, Secretary of the US Treasury. Through his Washington research Shoemaker also located Parker Hart, who, as a young American diplomat in Saudi Arabia, was to have taken delivery of the silver coins when the *John Barry* docked at Ras Tanurah. He knew nothing about any bullion being on board, but confirmed that he had expected the liberty ship to arrive on about 30 August 1944 and had made arrangements to take the consignment of coins across the desert to the Saudi capital, Riyadh. Towards the end of Shoemaker's month in Washington, while he was going through some Treasury files, in the National Archives, he realised that there were several lend-lease agreements, besides the one with Saudi Arabia. The Dutch, for example, had requested silver with which to mint coins in the post-war period, and the Indian government had made requests to be supplied with silver under lend-lease. There appeared to have been considerable pressure, both from the British, who then governed the country, and the colonial government in India itself, for suppliers of silver, the reason given being that the face value of the rupee was being drastically undermined by hyper-inflation. If the value of the currency had fallen, economic hardship and civil unrest could well have ensued.

These requests made for interesting speculation, particularly when Shoemaker read that the Indian government had asked for 100 million ounces of silver, worth, in 1944, about $50 million. As the government of the United States had met the request, could this, then, be the silver bullion that so many people had for so long believed was loaded into the holds of the *John Barry*? Further research through the State Department's lend-lease files showed that the agreement to supply silver to India had been signed in Washington on 8 June 1944, the signatories being representatives of the United States and the British and Indian colonial governments. Shoemaker also uncovered papers in the archives which confirmed that the *John Barry* had docked at Philadelphia from New York on 6 July. As he put it:

Ally these facts to the size of the specially built wooden vault in hold No. 3 of the vessel, as reported to me by the former Navy Armed Guardsman; that Jay and I calculated that it would have taken about a month to assemble and transport such an amount of silver bullion to Philadelphia; and that the John Barry *had been heading towards the Indian Ocean on what proved to be her final voyage, and it can be well understood when I say that, considering the perfect way in which these pieces of the jigsaw appeared to fit, our collective wreck-fever temperature soared to virtual boiling point.*

While Shoemaker's time in Washington brought him no closer to conclusive documentary proof that the silver bullion had indeed been stowed aboard the *John Barry*, or that the liberty ship had been destined to sail on to India after her voyage up into the Persian Gulf, he and Jay Fiondella were now convinced that they were justified in seeking financial backing for a salvage operation. Once they had successfully bid for the rights to do so from the government of the United States, that endorsement would be sought on the basis that silver bullion, in addition to the silver coins, was almost certainly lying in the wreck in the Arabian Sea. Fiondella's celebrated range of international contacts had earlier led to a tentative approach being made to Sheikh Zaher Hamed al Harthy of Muscat, to join the two Americans, an arrangement that would not only have provided the necessary finance, but that would have met the Shoemaker–Fiondella criterion of bringing an Omani dimension to the enterprise. In the event, Sheikh al Harthy declined to join the project, because of the absence of irrefutable proof that the silver bullion was in the wreck. The two Americans were thus obliged to look elsewhere.

As the summer of 1988 gave way to autumn, and with his Washington search, for the time being at least, all but exhausted, Brian Shoemaker decided to accept an invitation to a sabbatical in England, at the University of Cambridge. His decision was made easier as it had become apparent that the Maritime Administration was unlikely to publish the 'invitation to bid' that year. Before he left for Cambridge he and Jay Fiondella decided that they needed a particularly effective lawyer to push on with the bidding process and to conduct further research in an attempt to find what they had now become convinced did exist – a secret manifest, one that would prove the existence of bullion in the wreck of the *John Barry*.

Shoemaker briefed the Washington-based lawyer Hugh O'Neill, asking him to continue the research and to monitor closely the activities of the Maritime Administration, to ensure they didn't sell the ship before he and Fiondella could make a bid. In the event, Shoemaker was able to keep a closer watching brief on developments than he had originally thought possible: during his Cambridge sabbatical the United States Senate appointed him to an advisory panel on Antarctica and flew him back to Washington on two occasions. On the first visit, in March 1989, he and Fiondella received a tender from the Maritime Administration offering the SS *John Barry* for 'sealed bid' auction, closing on 12 May. But within days the administration announced a postponement of the process, refusing any explanation. They were in limbo yet again.

On 1 May, however, the Maritime Administration issued a statement in which a new date for the receipt of bids was given – 11 August 1989. The race to secure title to the *John Barry* at last appeared to be underway.

Brian Shoemaker's Cambridge orals were held on 27 July. On the 30 July he and his wife hurriedly packed their bags and flew home to the States. Within a week of returning he was back in Washington, where he met with Hugh O'Neill to discuss the mechanics of making the bid. O'Neill recommended that they bid $50,010, with a commitment to pay to the United States government 10 per cent of the value of any silver raised from the wreck. They needed a 10 per cent down payment as evidence that they were earnest – $5,001. On 11 August 1989, they secured a draft for $5,001 and very carefully went over the bid form. Shoemaker was particularly anxious that it should not be disqualified on a technicality. He and O'Neill then walked from the lawyer's office to the Maritime Administration building, handing the bid in just hours before the afternoon deadline. 'We were nervous before we delivered the bid,' Shoemaker remembers, 'but once we had done so a feeling of confidence swept over us. For some indefinable reason we just knew that we had won!'

And they had. The team of three, soon to be joined by a fourth as an investor, Heman McGuire Riley, had secured title to the liberty ship. It was a moment of triumph, yet it seemed appropriate to Brian Shoemaker that the closing moments of their attempt should be tense:

The bids were opened by Mrs Jesse Fernanders of the Maritime Administration, assisted by a junior colleague. The room fell silent. The only sound to be heard was the rustling of paper as the sealed bids were opened and scrutinised. There were five, two of which were frivolous, being ridiculously low. One was for $15,526 and 15 per cent of any proceeds of the salvage to the US, the other for $20,000 and 12 per cent. With our bid of $50,010 and 10 per cent we were declared the holders of the title to the world's most controversial shipwreck!

One financial hurdle remained. The group had just one month in which to raise the additional $45,009 with which to complete a transfer of funds to the full value of their bid to the Maritime Administration. Failure to do so would have meant that the bid would be declared null and void and that they would lose their investment.

Within days, Brian Shoemaker, Jay Fiondella, Hugh O'Neill and Heman McGuire Riley made an informal agreement under which each took responsibility for one quarter of the 'earnest payment' made to the Maritime Administration ($5,001), resulting in four individual cash payments of $1,250.25 cents into the group's 'pot'. In addition, each of the four agreed that they would make individual efforts to raise the outstanding amount of $45,009 within the next four weeks. As Brian Shoemaker relates, all now appeared to be plain sailing:

Once we had the title to the John Barry *we secured the finance we needed with amazing ease. In fact friends of each of us advanced the cash and we were able to make the final payment to the Maritime Administration well within the time limit. The next step was to organise ourselves formally into a registered corporation. This was promptly accomplished by the expedient of a straightforward contract, set down in basic terms, which made Fiondella, O'Neill, McGuire Riley and myself equal partners in the enterprise. The name of the partnership was a natural. The John Barry Group was born.*

The group's euphoria was to be short-lived. Within weeks of the transfer of rights in the wreck to the John Barry Group, Brian Shoemaker received a telephone call from the State Department's Arabian Peninsula Desk. He was both astonished and dismayed at what his caller had to say:

I was told that the government of the United States had made a mistake in selling the title rights of the John Barry *to our group and that the matter was being discussed at the highest levels with the Sultanate of Oman. I was soon to learn that this was indeed so, the principals in the discussions being none other than America's Secretary of State, James Baker, and Oman's Minister of State for Foreign Affairs, His Excellency Yousuf bin Alawi bin Abdullah. Such senior inter-governmental talks had become necessary because of Oman's declaration of 'rights of interest' in the wreck, given that it lay within the waters of the country's Exclusive Economic Zone.*

Given the effort Shoemaker had put into securing an Omani

involvement in the enterprise, his chagrin was understandable. He felt vindicated, however, by one aspect of the telephone call:

As the conversation drew to a close I was asked if I could make a contribution towards solving the problem. Human nature being what it is, I did take satisfaction in the State Department asking me for help, given that its officials had consistently refused to assist me in my early contacts with them on the John Barry*! My response was that Hugh O'Neill and I would negotiate directly with Oman's Foreign Minister, on behalf of the group. I simply was not prepared, on past performance, to permit the State Department to act on our behalf. But they refused, point-blank, to put me in touch with him.*

It was an impasse to which Shoemaker, Fiondella, O'Neill and McGuire Riley could see no early solution. Then, in October 1989, about six weeks after the State Department's telephone call, the Washington-based legal practice of Patton, Boggs and Blow contacted the group of behalf of the Sultanate of Oman and made what Shoemaker described as 'some offers'. O'Neill and Shoemaker began a round of telephone discussions with David Dunn, a senior partner in the practice, and initially progress towards a mutually acceptable solution appeared to be being made. But it was not to be. Without any prior warning Dunn broke off contact, offering the group no explanation for his decision.

A month later, however, there came to pass what Shoemaker describes as 'a congenial experience from which developed a rewarding partnership'. The arrival on the scene of Sheikh Ahmed Farid al Aulaqi, which was eventually to prove crucial to the whole operation, is best chronicled in Brian Shoemaker's own words:

In November 1989 Hugh O'Neill was contacted by Robert Hudson, a member of the Oman-based Ocean Group company. It was headed by Sheikh Ahmed who had, apparently, formed the company to represent and protect the Sultanate of Oman's interests in the wreck. The Ocean Group had a third member, Richard Simmons, an Englishman who had been living in the Sultanate for some years. Initial negotiations were between

O'Neill and Hudson, by telephone, although I quickly came to regard the process as painfully slow.

Brian Shoemaker decided that there was little to lose in telephoning the Sheikh direct.

My approach was that the John Barry Group held the American rights to the wreck, but that my colleagues and I granted that he, Sheikh Ahmed Farid, represented Oman's legitimate rights of interest in the vessel. We could argue for ever and a day over whose rights took primacy, as the diplomats and the lawyers had already done, or we could agree that there was enough in the ship for all to share and that the best way forward was to reach a mutually agreeable position and then get on with the salvage operation.

Shoemaker's initiative was immediately rewarded by an invitation from the Sheikh for the John Barry Group to meet him in London the following month. However, the meeting, held in December 1989 at a yacht club on the banks of the Thames outside London, proved unproductive.

Negotiations did not go well. The atmosphere was too formal. Frankly, there were too many of us sitting around the table trying to iron out an agreeable compromise. While individual members of both groups tendered proposals, and points of common interest were identified, the Thames-side meetings failed to bring us to an agreement. A bargaining position for both sides seemed elusive.

With Christmas approaching, it was agreed that the two sides should retire to consider their respective positions. The members of the John Barry Group flew home to America to be with their families for the holiday season. Once back in Oregon, Brian Shoemaker, remembering the strategy which had led to the two groups sitting around a table in the first place, decided to try it again. He reached for the telephone and dialled the Sheikh's number.

I opened the conversation by suggesting that perhaps he and I could arrive at a compromise acceptable to all our colleagues. He expressed willingness and there followed an hour of hard telephone bargaining, which brought us to the framework of a general agreement. It was one of the most important and enjoyable telephone calls of my life. Sheikh Ahmed understood our needs as well as his own and during our conversation allied both principles to the interests of the Sultanate of Oman. It was a masterly exercise in manoeuvrability.

The two men may well have reached verbal agreement in an amicable manner, but it still remained for their proposals (which included provision for generous settlements on members of the John Barry Group in exchange for a transfer of rights in the wreck to the Ocean Group; 'rights of personal observations' for the Americans at every stage of the salvage operation; and an upholding of the commitment to pay 10 per cent of the value of any silver recovered to Washington) to be endorsed by their respective partners and, most crucially of all, by the government of the United States. Shoemaker remembers:

Our partners were the easiest to convince and we were able to accomplish that exercise in short order. Persuading the American government to permit the John Barry Group to sell its title rights to the wreck to the Ocean Group was far more difficult. Sheikh Ahmed was obliged to hire the Washington law firm of McDermott, Will and Emery, in order that formal agreements could be drawn up between the two groups, an Assumption Agreement for the Maritime Administration and a Transfer Order by the Maritime Administration to the Ocean Group.

So it was that on 19 January 1990, Brian Shoemaker, Jay Fiondella, Hugh O'Neill and Heman McGuire Riley of the John Barry Group met in Washington's Madison Hotel with Sheikh Ahmed Farid al Aulaqi and Richard Simmons of the Ocean Group, an assembly of unlikely individuals who were, together, concluding another chapter in the story of the *John Barry*.

Just as Brian Shoemaker and Sheikh Ahmed were leaving the Madison for the signing ceremony at the law firm's office, Senator Robert Dole arrived in the hotel's foyer. Dole was an old family friend of the Shoemakers, so Brian promptly introduced him to the Sheikh, now the owner of America's most controversial ship. Shoemaker believes that this chance meeting between the Senator and the Sheikh represented a good sign for a venture that had been plagued by politics, and 'a particularly good omen for the goodwill that developed between the United States of America and the Sultanate of Oman through the negotiations over the *John Barry*'.

The next day, with only the details to be attended to by the lawyers, the six men departed to their respective homes. The documents were finalised the next month and, on 26 February 1990, 'all right title and interest' formally passed to the Ocean Group of the Sultanate of Oman. One chapter may have been at an end, but another, potentially the most exciting and the one which promised to answer the many questions which had puzzled two generations in so many lands, was about to begin.

'A joint adventure,' says Shoemaker, 'in pursuit of one of the most exciting treasure hunts in history, was now underway. Robert Louis Stevenson would have been proud of us all!'

Chapter Two

The Ocean Group

The Sultanate of Oman is an extraordinary land in an extraordinary region of the world, a highly distinctive part of the Arabian Peninsula and, for over half of the twentieth century, a very private place indeed. The maritime trade and diplomatic initiative which had led to Oman's becoming the first state in the Arab world to establish diplomatic relations with Washington waned in the opening years of this century, when sail-propelled ships gave way to steam. Oman's overseas trade suffered a drastic decline and the country turned its face away from the challenges and uncertainties of the new era. A seventy-year period of self-imposed isolation had begun.

The end of Oman's national slumber was heralded by the discovery of oil in 1964, with commercial production commencing in 1967. An event of even greater significance occurred just three years into the country's oil era, on 23 July 1970, when the current ruler, His Majesty Sultan Qaboos bin Said al Said, came to the throne. Faced with staggeringly poor levels of literacy, low standards of public health and virtual absence of systems of communication, Sultan Qaboos embarked upon an ambitious programme of national development, taking his people by the hand and leading them into the twentieth century. Schools, a university, hospitals and health centres were built nationwide, while the establishment of a communications network – roads across the deserts and through the mountain ranges, and a postal and telephone service – ended for ever the tyranny of isolation which so many communities in the country's vast rural areas had endured for so long.

A national development programme on such a scale obviously required a considerable amount of foreign expertise. Professionals from around the world were recruited to undertake a range of services. In addition to the chronic shortage of skilled personnel, which could well have hampered the country's development, there was the increasingly desperate situation in the south of the Sultanate, where a guerrilla war was being waged by insurgents from Marxist-inspired South Yemen, then styled the People's Democratic Republic of South Yemen, with which Oman had a common border. To aid the young Sultan and to support his nascent defence force in its effort to repel a determined foe came men with particular military skills, many with direct experience of counter-insurgency campaigns. Some served the Omani monarch on contract; others came for periods of secondment from their own country's defence forces. Some came from the service of the Sultan's fellow Arab sovereign, King Hussein of Jordan, some from the army of the late Shah of Iran and some from the military service of Queen Elizabeth II.

From this last category came Robert Hudson, a young Royal Marine who brought with him a range of skills associated with coastal operations; and Richard Simmons, a one-time trooper in the 11th Hussars and, like the Sultan he had come to serve, a graduate of Sandhurst's Military Academy. While neither would accept the assumption that they differed in any fundamental way from their comrades at arms, both Englishmen epitomised the qualities which were held in high esteem by generations of Britons and eulogised in the pages of *Boys' Own Paper* and the Henty adventure stories of England's Edwardian era. Such qualities, which encouraged the view that to look a little further, to go a little beyond one's immediate horizons, was no bad thing, bred a certain quality of confidence in the principle of service and, with it, an air of personal nobility.

To a seventeen-year-old fast approaching the end of his schooldays in the England of 1961, the future did not hold much promise for a life of foreign travel as a soldier of the Queen. The British Empire was being dismantled by the country's politicians and bureaucrats with what appeared to Richard Simmons unseemly haste; in the process, the far-flung places to which a British soldier could reliably expect to be posted were being wiped off the map. But the Simmons family had a tradition of military service, a tradition Richard's father urged his son to uphold. After a brief period of teenage rebellion young Simmons set off for Catterick Camp in Yorkshire, where he underwent training prior to becoming a trooper in the 11th Hussars. The personal qualities which were later to lead him to Arabia were quickly recognised by his senior officers, and the decision was taken to send Simmons on an officers' training course at Sandhurst Military Academy.

A commission in the Sherwood Foresters followed and, to the young officer's surprise and delight, a posting to the Far East came in double-quick time, proving that even in the sunset days of the British Empire it was still possible to join the army and see the world. For while Britain's route-march from empire was almost complete, a litany of global military commitments remained – commitments to defend the country's rapidly diminishing colonial possessions from external aggression as they approached their goal of becoming independent states.

Richard Simmons' appetite for a life of action and adventure was tested to its limits towards the end of the 1960s in another overseas posting, this time to the great port city of Aden, Britain's sole colonial toe-hold on the Arabian Peninsula, where a campaign for independence had turned particularly vicious. But it had at least brought him to the shores of Arabia, a region that had first begun to exert its spell when he had met fellow cadets at Sandhurst who were from the Gulf:

They were principally from privileged backgrounds, the sons of Sheikhs and Princes, but their innate sense of quiet confidence and personal freedom attracted me and from that time I harboured a desire to go to the Arab world.

Despite the fact that the conflict between the British and the various nationalist movements seeking to pick up her crown of authority in Aden was becoming bloodier by the day, Richard Simmons happily succumbed to the spell cast by the desert and mountains of Aden's hinterland, and by the spirit, warmth and often reckless courage of the people who inhabited the baking terrain. He had seen the stark splendour of the Arab's land, and was bound inevitably to return.

Back in Britain, in the wake of the chaotic collapse of British rule in Aden, in November 1967, Richard Simmons pondered his future. Having driven a tank in the 11th Hussars, he decided that one of the options on offer, to join a tank regiment, was not for him:

I had come to realise how vulnerable one was in such a vehicle of war. I considered that my best insurance for future survival was to be in a situation of self-reliance, even if it meant prosecuting a campaign primarily on foot.

It was a decision based on a well-balanced instinct for survival, and would, just three years later, make him an ideal candidate for a campaign which brought with it the much wished-for return to Arabia. In 1970 came the news of Sultan Qaboos' accession to the throne of Oman and an intensification of what became known as the Dhofar War, after the Sultanate's legendary southern region, from which the Queen of Sheba's emissaries collected precious frankincense to be sent as a tribute to King Solomon. Dhofar was now the scene of less romantic events, as armed insurgents laid siege to the new Sultan's realm. For Richard Simmons, now with the rank of major, there was not a moment's indecision. He applied to join the Omanis in their campaign to defend their new leader and the promise of better times that his accession had brought.

It was a hard-fought guerrilla war, much of it conducted on foot across deserts and through mountain ranges; Oman did not declare it won until the end of 1975. During one exercise, designed to ambush enemy patrols, Richard Simmons met Robert Hudson and a friendship was struck which, some twenty years later, was to see them joining forces as members of Sheikh Ahmed's Ocean Group.

With the end of the Dhofar War, many of those who had aided

the Omanis in their struggle to preserve their territorial integrity and maintain their cultural and spiritual independence sadly left the land they had come to love and turned their faces towards home. Among them were Robert Hudson and Richard Simmons. But Simmons had surrendered himself whole-heartedly to the charms of Arabia and took the first opportunity that presented itself to return to Oman. Turning his back for ever on the soldier's life, he became what he remains today, the General Manager of one of the Sultanate's largest trading houses.

His return brought him back into contact with many with whom he had shared the field of battle. One of those with whom he was reunited was Sheikh Ahmed Farid al Aulaqi who, like Simmons, had been turned towards Oman by the tide of conflict, in his case a conflict which had begun with revolution in his own native land, which lay to the west of Arabia, beyond the mountains of Dhofar.

The 1960s were a time of turbulence on the Arabian Peninsula, and, particularly for the young and politically aware, a period ripe with the promise of dramatic social change. In North Yemen, the royalist forces of the Imam were losing their battle against the forces of republicanism. On the eastern shores of the peninsula, in the Persian Gulf, the British-controlled Trucial States, now the United Arab Emirates, were on the threshold of untold riches as major discoveries of oil were being made in the sands of their Sheikhdoms, a development which was, in under a decade, to propel a deeply conservative, traditional people into the modern age, with all the political, social and economic consequences that would follow in its wake. And, in the south-west, the British, who had ruled the Aden Colony and Protectorate for well over a century, were clearly in retreat from the forces of nationalism and the anti-colonial culture which was gripping the imagination of so many.

For the traditional rulers of the principalities which lay to the east of Aden, across the deserts and mountains which formed natural boundaries between the tribes, the prospect of political change was, more often than not, a bewildering and not altogether welcome one. Many of the rulers in Abbyan, in the Lehaj, in Makulla, in the mountain settlements of the Hadhramaut, and in Shabwa, had worked for generations with the British; many had tried very hard to make London's concept of a 'South Arabian Federation' succeed. Now, among many of their own tribes, apostles of a new creed, Marxism, were challenging the principles of everything which had fashioned them as a spiritual people – the precepts of Islam which, together with their Arabic tongue, were the inspiration of their personal unity. Faced, therefore, with the prospect of a dual challenge – one to their past political allegiances, the other to the spiritual foundation of their lives – the unease of southern Arabia's traditional rulers in the mid-1960s is easy to understand. Change was now unstoppable, and the future a matter of urgent and increasingly alarmed discussion.

The al Aulaqis had ruled Shabwa since about 1700 BC, when the descendents from the Mainneen desert tribe of Al Jauf moved their capital there. Since the advent of British rule in 1839 they had treatied with the colonial government over the desert and the mountains in Aden, with several members of the family having taken senior roles in the administration. This being so, Ahmed Farid al Aulaqi's early years had been characterised by trips to the port city on the occasion of visits by members of the British Royal Family and Secretaries of State for the Colonies from Whitehall. He had, on important occasions, accompanied his father to Government House, above Steamer Point, the focal point of the British presence in southern Arabia, and paid visits to the palace of Aden's Sultan in the prosperous Crater District. In Shabwa, he also remembers calls being made to the family home by Ministers of the British Crown and Cabinet politicians out on 'fact-finding' missions from London; on these occasions picnic trips into the surrounding desert countryside would be organised for the entertainment of the VIPs. So, to Ahmed Farid, a teenager in the turbulent 1960s, the trappings of power and privilege were commonplace.

The prospect of the sun setting on British rule in his homeland did not alarm the adolescent Ahmed Farid, as he was of the opinion that the time had come for the people of South Yemen to take control of their own destiny.

I had heard on the wireless and read in the newspapers of people such as Kwame Nkrumah, who had led the people of Ghana to independence; of Jomo Kenyatta in Kenya, who had more recently achieved the same destination for his country; and, of course, the irresistible appeal that President Nasser of Egypt held for the young throughout the Arab world could not be denied.

But ominous clouds were gathering over the political landscape of South Yemen as the various nationalist movements campaigned for the allegiance of the various tribal communities. Many in the nationalist camps had taken up arms against the British – arms that, as London began to give signals that withdrawal was imminent, they often used against those of their people who held an opposing point of view about the country's future in the post-colonial era. In November 1967, the British, amid scenes of chaos in Aden, abdicated power to the National Liberation Front; many Britons left the city, which they and their colonial predecessors had built into one of the most prosperous ports in the world.

For the Al Aulaqis, in far-off Shabwa, the abrupt end of the British presence in what the new rulers proclaimed the 'People's Democratic Republic of South Yemen' proved to be a bitter-sweet time, as Sheikh Ahmed Farid remembers:

Even though we were unsure of our place in the new state it was, naturally enough, a moment of cautious pride that our own people were now in control of their own affairs. Our caution, of course, was set in historical precedent. Traditional rulers had not always fared well when change in their respective lands had been brought about principally by the revolutionary fervour of socialism. And my family, while having had members with anti-colonial attitudes, had for generations worked with the British in their governance of Aden Colony and Protectorate so, again, we were not sure just how our new leaders would regard us. It was very much a case of 'wait and see' and prepare ourselves to co-operate with any role in the national life of the country that might be asked of us.

In the event, the Al Aulaqi dynasty did not have long to wait to know what the new rulers had in mind:

The details are now consigned to the sands of time, very much in the past and best left there, as no useful purpose can be served by their resurrection, but it was not long after their assumption of power in Aden that the NLF government gave clear indication that no part was seen in the new order for the country's traditional rulers. This, in itself, was not that difficult for my family to accommodate, but what did quickly become hard to bear was the way people who for centuries had looked to us for guidance and protection began to be treated. It was an anxious time and when any member of any former ruling family attempted to intervene on the people's behalf, they laid themselves open to arbitrary arrest and confiscation of their own homes and lands. It was a time of profound sadness because we had hoped that we would all work together to make our new state a success.

It was not to be. Following the sudden arrest of some members of the family, including Ahmed's brother, Saleh (who spent five years as a political prisoner), the Al Aulaqis, their personal situation now untenable, decided to abdicate their age-old role as rulers of the province of Shabwa. The family crossed the desert into the Kingdom of Saudi Arabia. Their long period of exile had begun.

Adulthood now beckoned for Ahmed Farid al Aulaqi and, keen that his son should not only be better armed with academic qualifications, but possess a greater knowledge of the world and its ways beyond the lands of the Arabian Peninsula, his father made arrangements for him to go to London – as Sheikh Ahmed wryly remarks, 'I followed South Yemen's former rulers home!' He took avidly to London life, meeting Britons on their home ground and mingling easily with the administrative and military officer class to whom he had become accustomed back home in South Yemen. And, as a student at the London School of Economics, he learnt the skills of 'intellectual survival' in the clash of social and political ideas with which London was then awash.

My life was a far cry from the sheltered world of my early youth, but I quickly came to understand that the turmoil of ideologies which had swept South Yemen was equally on the boil in London. It was a time of challenging debate and much youthful excitement.

The times were indeed 'a-changing' and the life of Ahmed Farid al Aulaqi was not immune.

In 1971, with my studies at an end, it was decided that I should go to the Sultanate of Oman, about as close as I could get to home without actually being there. I had, naturally enough, followed events there with great interest since the accession of His Majesty Sultan Qaboos and had read of his call for all those Omanis living outside the country to return home and help him in the task of building a modern state. While I was, of course, not an Omani, I had a quiet confidence that there may well be a service I could render that would be of some small value.

That was not all that Ahmed Farid had read and heard of the new Oman being built out of the old. Indeed, he had learnt with mounting concern of the growing desperation of the Omanis' struggle in the south of their country with the agents of Marxism, which threatened so many of the new-found freedoms that their young Sultan was bringing into being. Ahmed Farid's concern was twofold, for he knew also that many of those now wreaking havoc on Omani villages and settlements were being sponsored in their guerrilla campaign by, and indeed operating from, his own homeland, the People's Democratic Republic of South Yemen.

While the tide of war in Dhofar was not always going the way of the insurgents, neither was it necessarily turning in Oman's favour. As a distinguished senior army officer in the service of the Sultan had earlier written, 'It is difficult to see the enemy winning, but they might. It is difficult to see us losing, but we might. The fear is of a long drawn-out war of attrition, during which the country would be bled white.'

It was becoming increasingly clear that every human resource would have to be tapped if Oman was to prevail over a well-armed, disciplined and seemingly fearless foe. A much-needed requirement was special knowledge of the tribes and the terrain over the mountains to the west of Dhofar. For Ahmed Farid al Aulaqi, the path of duty was clear, if difficult, in that it would mean working for a while against the land of his birth. But a balance had to be struck. The news filtering through from Aden, from Abbyan, the Lehaj, Shabwa and the Hadhramaut, was that the collectivist policies of the PDRY government were causing great distress to many and that the national economy had begun what appeared to be an inexorable slide. The Sultanate of Oman, on the other hand, had welcomed him in and given him a home, and he owed it and its ruler loyalty in return. Ahmed Farid al Aulaqi offered his services to Sultan Qaboos' military establishment.

Amid the clamour of battle came the inevitable human struggle for what the American military in Vietnam styled 'the hearts and minds' of men. The Sultan's armed forces had adopted strategies designed to win over the enemy, known collectively as the Adoo, to the Omani side, and by 1972 a considerable number had defected to the Sultanate. Once under the protection of Oman they were formed into brigades, known as the Firqat, who then turned their fire westwards, back over the mountains whence they had come.

Ferocious courage was not all that these new recruits had brought with them. They also brought knowledge of their former comrades' disposition, their methods of indoctrination, future plans for battle, details of military installations – in short, a welter of intelligence information. But once formed into brigades, the Firqat had to be motivated by men whose courage would match their own and who would inspire them to yet further exercises of valour. An obvious candidate to command such a brigade was Ahmed Farid al Aulaqi.

Even now, twenty years after the event, he declines to speak of his experiences in any detail, but there are many who served with him who are not so reticent. 'Ahmed Farid led his men as if without fear and they followed him far and wide,' remembers one of Oman's most senior establishment figures. It was sometimes wondered just what his private thoughts were, but his distress at what was being done to South Yemen was obvious and he saw quite clearly that if not stopped it would roll on into Oman, creating the same economic desert and human misery in his adopted land. 'He fought long and hard, served the Sultan well, and there are many here who recall the contribution he made to victory with much gratitude.'

But with peace came an opportunity for Ahmed Farid to turn his hand to business and by the early 1980s he had established one of the Gulf's most successful enterprises, Desert Line, which provides a range of support services to Oman's oil and gas industry. He later diversified into the construction industry and property, building up a considerable portfolio beyond the borders of the Sultanate, in other Gulf States and in France and Britain, demonstrating the same appetite for 'derring-do' in the marketplace that he had shown in the field of conflict.

Small wonder, then, that when, in 1989, concern was being expressed in Oman as to how best the country's rights of interest in the wreck of the SS *John Barry* could be exercised, Sheikh Ahmed Farid al Aulaqi promptly took decisive action to protect the prerogatives of his adopted home. He formed the Ocean Group with the express purpose of negotiating 'a just and amicable agreement which would bring honour to all concerned and, most crucially of all, solve once and for all the mystery surrounding the stricken vessel'. He recruited men he believed would make a positive contribution to what he saw as a particularly hazardous endeavour. It would require both diplomatic and technical skills, and would, almost certainly, be hugely expensive to develop.

Just as Ahmed Farid had seen himself, and been seen by others, as a 'natural' for the enterprise, so did Richard Simmons and Robert Hudson appear to be the ideal partners to join him in what the Sheikh describes as 'this great adventure'. Simmons, as we have seen, had long returned to the land he loved, while Hudson, following the conclusion of his military service in the Sultanate, had remained in Britain. In civilian life, he had turned to good account both his Royal Marine experience and that gained in Oman, by joining Britain's North Sea oil and gas industry as a deep-sea diver. His abilities would have a lot to contribute to the recovery of cargo from the *John Barry*.

But it was a human attribute beyond the proven skills of the three men which was to turn the enterprise into a success. Sheikh Ahmed Farid, Richard Simmons and Robert Hudson shared one unifying quality which, when combined with practical experience, proved to be the catalyst in setting the whole operation in train: it was the very human but sadly all too rare attitude of 'to hell with it'.

It was a small team, one that would have to call upon others for additional specialised skills. But, once the Ocean Group had been launched, with Sheikh Ahmed Farid, Richard Simmons and Robert Hudson squarely on the bridge, the battalions of intrigue and technical complexity guarding the *John Barry* seemed at long last to have met their match.

PART TWO

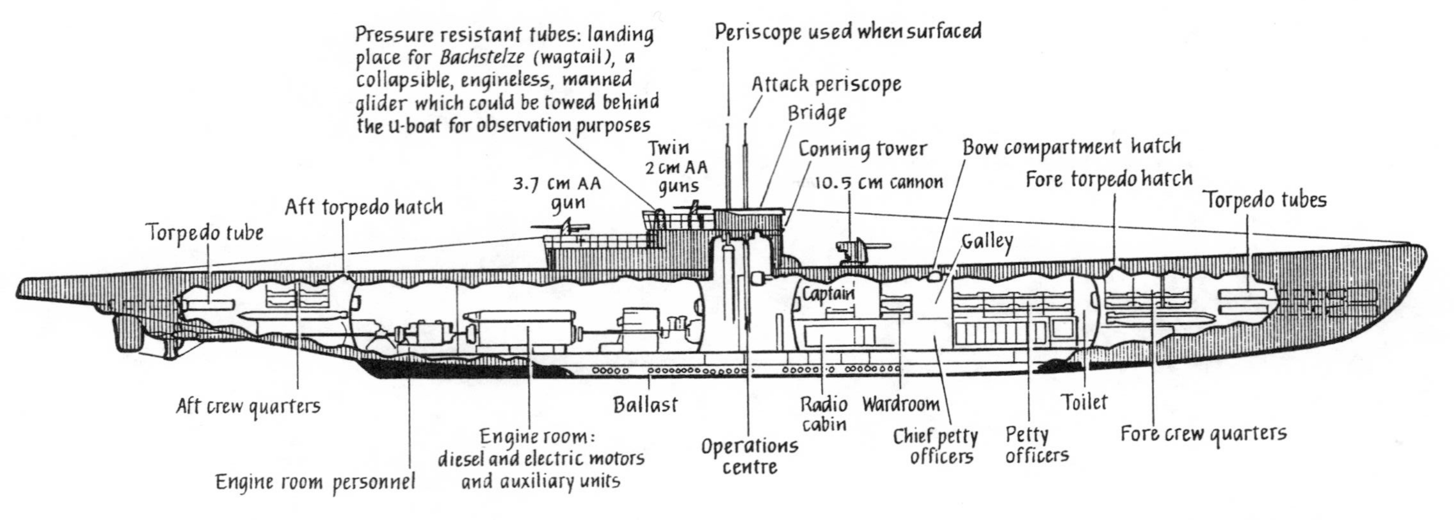

U 859
Pressure resistant tubes: landing place for *Bachstelze* (wagtail), a collapsible, engineless, manned glider which could be towed behind the U-boat for observation purposes
Periscope used when surfaced
Attack periscope
Bridge
Twin 2 cm AA guns
Conning tower
Bow compartment hatch
3.7 cm AA gun
10.5 cm cannon
Fore torpedo hatch
Torpedo tubes
Aft torpedo hatch
Torpedo tube
Galley
Captain
Aft crew quarters
Ballast
Radio cabin
Wardroom
Toilet
Fore crew quarters
Engine room: diesel and electric motors and auxiliary units
Operations centre
Chief petty officers
Petty officers
Engine room personnel
Overall length: 287 ft

Chapter Three

Buddy Can You Spare a Dime?

'First the Empire and then the sterling area were dismantled: this was called "lend-lease".' The historian Professor John Charmley, London Sunday Telegraph, *19 March 1995.*

Britain is a country in which memories of the past die hard. As they embarked reluctantly upon a course of war in September 1939, the nation's policy-makers were as worried about the government's ability to meet the costs of a prolonged conflict as they were about its ability to triumph militarily. Many in Whitehall had a keen memory of just how close the country had come to losing its economic independence and, therefore, its political sovereignty to Washington during the 1914–18 war, so inhibiting had been the vast American loans with which London had financed that awesome struggle with Kaiser Wilhelm's Germany. As it was, the British government was obliged by American pressure at the Washington Conference of 1922 to concede naval supremacy and to end its long-held alliance with Japan, which had been of such value during the four years of war, when the Japanese navy patrolled the Indian Ocean and the Mediterranean Sea on Britain's behalf.

At the start of the Second World War the British government

believed that its gold and convertible currency reserves would enable it to conduct the conflict for about three years without recourse to America for financial assistance, an estimation which took into account the vital need to place large orders for weapons with American arms manufacturers, orders that British industry was quite unable to meet. But with the fall of France in the summer of 1940, followed by the British retreat to the beaches of Dunkirk and the abandonment of military hardware which occurred during the evacuation, the levels of state spending on American arms and ammunition rose dramatically, with a consequent draining of British currency reserves. Earlier predictions that finances would hold out for three years had to be dramatically revised – during the summer of 1940 it was anticipated that the reserves would last barely another twelve months. (Ironically, these orders made a significant contribution to 'kick-starting' the American economy and lifting the USA out of the industrial recession that had plagued it for almost a decade.)

In July 1940, Sir Frederick Phillips, a senior Treasury official, journeyed to Washington, where he met President Roosevelt and his financial secretary, Henry Morgenthau. During the meetings Phillips outlined Britain's impending financial crisis, pointing out that, if current levels of arms expenditure continued, the country's dollar reserves would be exhausted within a year and that if London was to continue to stand alone in prosecuting the war against Nazi Germany, credit from the United States would be required. Phillips returned to Britain to report that Washington was not prepared to extend any major credit terms to His Majesty's Government until it had evidence that its finances were either 'exhausted or near exhaustion', and that this would entail meeting an American demand that Britain sell off its assets, securities and property holdings in the United States and South America, before any long-term credit strategy could be implemented.

By September 1940, when the war was just one year old, the value of British purchases from America totalled $10 billion. In July the country's gold and dollar reserves fell to £300 million (at 1940 exchange rates this was equivalent to approximately $1.2 billion), a situation which continued to deteriorate rapidly as the year wore on. By December the position was so grave that Winston Churchill wrote to Franklin Roosevelt, setting out the increasingly impossible situation Britain was facing. The letter, dated 8 December 1940, was frank on the question of the government's dwindling finances and consequently its inability to pay the United States for the supplies it was receiving, a looming debt that, in Churchill's own words, 'many times exceeds the total exchange reserve remaining at the disposal of Great Britain. The moment approaches when we shall no longer be able to pay cash.' Churchill argued that it would be immoral for America to demand that Britain disposes of her overseas assets before granting credit terms, at a time when she was fighting so desperately against a tyranny that threatened the whole of the Western world. The letter is both plaintive and self-righteous, and it left President Roosevelt unmoved – he never sent Churchill a reply.

A month earlier, the British Ambassador to Washington, Lord Lothian, had put Britain's plight in perspective when talking to a group of American journalists: 'Well, boys, Britain's broke. It's your money we want' – an honest remark for which he did not have to answer back in London, as he took to his bed in the British Embassy a month later and died. On 10 December, Sir Frederick Phillips was back in Washington for talks with Henry Morgenthau, with a brief from Churchill to resist demands that Britain sell her foreign-based assets as a condition for a further extension of credit terms. But the subordinate role Britain's impoverishment obliged her to adopt at the meeting quickly became apparent: Morgenthau dismissed Phillips' attempts to negotiate more favourable terms, demanding the fullest possible balance sheet to show which British assets American companies could purchase.

In fact, by the time the Morgenthau/Phillips meeting convened, President Roosevelt's administration had, without any reference to Churchill, already formulated a plan designed to deal with the problem. On 17 December, just a week after the first meeting between the American and British officials took place, Roosevelt addressed a Washington press conference. Introducing for the first time the concept of lend-lease, which he described in terms of a man lending his neighbour a hosepipe to extinguish a fire, but having it returned once the crisis had passed, he outlined the way in which the programme would work, seeking particularly to assure the American people of its cost-effectiveness and the fact that it was very much in their own interests. Indeed, the subsequent legislation that paved the way for the implementation of lend-lease was introduced to Congress with the title 'An Act to promote the defense of the United States'. Its Bill number was 1776, recalling the year in which America unilaterally declared its independence from Britain – a pointed snub to Winston Churchill that he can hardly have failed to notice. During the months intervening between Roosevelt's announcement and the spring of the following year, when the Bill passed into law on 11 March, American pressure on Britain to pay cash for the war supplies it was receiving was relentless.

Britain's rapidly diminishing dollar reserves were just one aspect of the financial crisis the country was facing. By late 1940, the government was obliged to consider the prospect that, if help was not forthcoming, its reserves of gold would be depleted too. In October help came from the government of Czechoslovakia (in exile in London) in the form of a loan of £7.5 million worth of gold. Canadian help followed, but it was not until February 1941 that disaster was avoided by a loan of £60 million worth of gold from the Belgians, granted by their London-based government-in-exile. A moment of painful truth had, however, come to pass in December, when Roosevelt sent an abrupt message to Churchill advising him that an American cruiser was on its way to South Africa to collect the £50 million worth of gold Britain was holding in reserve there. Churchill blustered, drafting a message to Roosevelt in which he compared America's conduct in the matter to 'a sheriff collecting the last assets of a helpless debtor'. In the event, this protest was never dispatched; instead, Churchill quietly backed down. He subsequently appealed to the Dutch and Norwegian governments, also in exile in London, for loans of gold, but both declined.

The Roosevelt administration was particularly anxious for Britain to sell its holdings in US, Canadian and South American companies, a process which would enable Americans to purchase shares at knock-down prices. It was a course which had only a limited run; as Roosevelt remarked to a colleague in early 1941, 'We have been milking the British financial cow which had plenty of milk at one time, but which has now about become dry.' But in the weeks leading up to lend-lease becoming operational, Henry Morgenthau continued to press Washington's demands on London. When Churchill dragged his feet, Morgenthau took the initiative and, in a unilateral announcement which left no one in any doubt as to Washington's determination to exercise its new-found power, told Congress in January 1941, 'Every dollar of property, real property or securities that any English citizen owns in the United States, they have agreed to sell during the next twelve months, in order to raise money to pay for the orders they have already placed; they are going to sell every dollar of it.'

Churchill was not consulted either before or after this statement. But British objections to such high-handed treatment remained and, on 10 March, the day before lend-lease passed into law, it became necessary for Henry Morgenthau to issue an ultimatum to the British Ambassador, Lord Halifax, who had replaced Lord Lothian. The demand was simple: sell a substantial British interest in America within seven days as an act of good faith. Britain had no choice but to comply and the Viscose Corporation, a subsidiary of the British company Courtaulds, was promptly disposed of. The nature and suddenness of its sale resulted in its being purchased by a group of American businessmen at just 50 per cent of its market value.

But on 11 March 1941, lend-lease became law and the $10 billion Britain owed America was placed under its umbrella, as indeed were all future orders until the end of the war. The cold facts of the events leading up to the implementation of lend-lease show that Washington was conducting its affairs on the principle of 'business as usual', despite the fact that if Britain had fallen America would itself eventually have faced the threat of attack (the Japanese assault of Pearl Harbor was still nine months away). But it cannot and should not be denied that, without lend-lease, Britain would have collapsed into financial chaos, and her ability to prosecute the war against Nazi Germany would have come to an abrupt end. America's outpouring of wealth saved Britain from the consequences of past economic mismanagement – in which Churchill had played a major role by insisting in 1925, when he was Chancellor of the Exchequer, that Britain restore Sterling to the gold standard at its pre-First World War rate.

While Churchill complained bitterly, in private, about Roosevelt's conduct, the American President, in his apparently unsympathetic attitude towards Britain during the first eighteen months of the war, was simply acting in the spirit of the American Republic, defending the economic interests of the people who had put him in the White House. It was also presumably this imperative which, in March 1941, the very month when lend-lease became operational, prompted Roosevelt to send another cruiser to Cape Town to collect more gold that had become available to Britain from South African mines. Again he advised Churchill of this only after the cruiser had set sail from America, even though it was well known in Washington that Britain urgently needed the gold to pay for supplies she was receiving from countries other than the United States.

When, at the end of the war, Britain's lend-lease account was drawn up, the country had received a staggering $27 billion worth of supplies under the terms of the Act. While, in common with other recipients of lend-lease goods, the British had not been required to pay for them in dollars at the time of delivery, they were far from being free of charge. An essential provision of the Act was the deferment of payment, with the terms of America's recompense being at presidential discretion. Indeed, within months of the Act passing into law, London and Washington embarked upon negotiations as to just how the British government would compensate America for the supplies it was receiving. While the introduction of lend-lease had ended American demands for immediate cash payments, British officials quickly learnt that there were other means at America's disposal to oblige His Majesty's government to pay, and pay dear, for services rendered. Mindful of Britain's role as a major trading nation and exporter of manufactured goods, Washington obliged London to accept that manufacturers produced from materials supplied under lend-lease could not be exported and that, furthermore, Britain should cease immediately exporting her goods to countries where products similar to those supplied under the Act would be in direct competition with American exports. Consequently, Britain was forced to make significant trading, and therefore economic, concessions to America, concessions that saw American suppliers supplanting their British counterparts in many parts of the world.

American negotiators also made it plain to the British that these concessions would have to prevail after the war. Foremost in this American strategy was the demand that Britain abandon the practice known as 'Imperial Preference', which grouped the trade of the Colonies, Dominions and Protectorates of the British Empire into the Sterling area of exchange controls and made it advantageous for these nations to trade with Britain. Following Britain's abject compliance, this huge and expanding market became open to American exports and investment.

Nor did American demands on the British government end there. With America's entry into the war in December 1941, it was only a matter of time before her troops began to arrive in large numbers on British soil. With them came dollars and a subsequent rise in Britain's reserves. Washington quickly realised that this would to a significant extent counteract the measures that had been taken to keep Britain in a state of financial compliance, and wasted no time in rectifying the situation. In another decision which spelt out the new relationship between London and Washington, President Roosevelt's administration issued an edict on 1 January 1943, to the effect that 'the United Kingdom's gold and dollar balances should not be permitted to be less than about six hundred million dollars, nor above one billion' – thus keeping Britain in a state of economic and political subservience while ensuring that the Sterling area remained operational. Churchill protested, and indeed continued to do so right up to the end of his wartime premiership in 1945, but to no avail.

Another initiative taken by Washington to curb London's garnishing of dollars through the presence of US troops was to remove tobacco from the list of goods that could be supplied under lend-lease, thus obliging Britain to pay for it in dollars. Yet another mechanism was known as reverse lend-lease, whereby Britain and her Dominions, most notably Australia and New Zealand, supplied goods and services to United States army and naval forces overseas, and America's merchant shipping fleet operating in foreign waters, free of charge. The cost of these same goods and services had to be met, of course, by the countries supplying them from their own Sterling reserves.

In his Sixteenth Report to Congress on Lend-Lease Operations (for the period up to 30 June 1944), delivered on 23 August 1944, President Roosevelt gave details of reverse lend-lease which make astonishing reading:

Expenditures for reverse lend-lease aid by the United Kingdom, Australia and New Zealand have been reported up to April 1st 1944. These expenditures for reverse lend-lease supplies and services provided to United States army and navy forces overseas and United States merchant shipping overseas in the three months between January 1st and April 1st 1944 amounted to $483,500,000. Reports on reverse lend-lease aid furnished to American forces in India have not yet been received for the full first quarter of 1944, but partial figures available indicate that more than $35 million have been expended in India for reverse lend-lease aid for our forces during this period. This would make the total of reverse lend-lease aid received from the British Commonwealth for the first quarter of 1944 well in excess of $500 million or an annual rate of more than $2 billion.

The cumulative cost of reverse lend-lease to Britain, Australia and New Zealand from 1 June 1942 to 1 April 1944 was $2,501,391,000 of which Britain had supplied goods and services to American forces and merchant shipping equivalent to $1,934,400,000, Australia $457,623,000 and New Zealand $109,368,000. Roosevelt continued:

These figures include only reverse lend-lease aid furnished to our forces and our shipping overseas. They do not include strategic raw materials, commodities and foodstuffs furnished by the British under reverse lend-lease without cost to us for shipment to the United States. Strategic raw materials and commodities governmentally procured in the United Kingdom and the British Colonial Empire are provided to us as reverse lend-lease. These supplies include crude rubber and tea from Ceylon, cocoa, palm kernels and palm oil, rope fibers, chrome and asbestos from British Africa, copra from the British islands of the Pacific and many other commodities needed for the United States war effort.

And, for the benefit of those in the Congress who may have believed that lend-lease and reverse lend-lease were giving America the worst end of the deal, President Roosevelt delivered encouragement of a particularly relevant kind:

In the first quarter of 1944 the expenditures reported by Australia and New Zealand for reverse lend-lease aid to our forces were more than the value of our lend-lease shipments to those two countries in the same period.

As for Britain's reverse lend-lease effort, the President gave Congress details that make fascinating reading:

Reverse lend-lease supplies and services from the British, like our lend-lease aid to the British, played a vital role in preparing for the operations for the liberation of Europe. One of the last-minute rush jobs done for us by the British was the waterproofing of many hundreds of wading tanks, as well as trucks and other mechanised equipment, so they would reach the invasion beaches in fighting condition after ploughing through the surf. The job was done for Allied mechanised equipment, United States and British alike, by British industry. In order to get it done in time the entire output of Britain's sheet steel rolling industry was taken for three months. To move the finished waterproofing sets from the factories to the hundreds of ordnance depots in the British Isles a great fleet of trucks was kept operating day and night. The waterproofing sets were assembled and installed by British engineers. General Eisenhower's headquarters have reported that the quantities of sheet steel used for this pre-invasion job would have been enough for a bridge 150 feet wide across the English Channel from Dover to Calais. The great majority of American wading tanks, as well as British tanks, armoured cars, supply trucks and scout vehicles used in the landings were fitted with this waterproofing equipment. The waterproofing equipment furnished under reverse lend-lease was only one of many thousands of other categories of supplies and services provided out of British stocks or by British facilities to the American forces taking part in the liberation of Europe.

These are a few examples of the scope of the aid. All rail transportation to the invasion ports, the cost of transporting many US troops on British ships, including the world's two largest liners, the Queen Elizabeth *and* Queen Mary; *1,100 Spitfires and other British-made planes; more than 100 airfields and other construction for our forces which cost the British $624,650,000 up to April 1st; fresh vegetables and other British-produced foodstuffs that took care of 20 per cent of our soldiers' rations; tens of thousands of easily jettisoned lightweight gas masks for our P-47 Thunderbolt fighters on long-range missions to the heart of Germany; more than 25,000 miles of steel landing mats; two million pairs of wool socks; thousands of parachutes; quantities of howitzers, anti-aircraft and anti-tank equipment; all heat, light and water bills at our bases and barracks. So wide is the scope of the reverse lend-lease aid we received from the British that a US naval base in Britain has been operated for a full twelve months without making a single cash payment.*

We have also benefited greatly from British engineering and research in new weapons. No money valuation is put on this type of aid, but it is made freely available to us. For example, rockets based on a British design are now being used by American forces against the Japanese in the Pacific; a British-developed radio set has been widely used in American tanks built for Britain and Russia; and the jet-propulsion plane uses an engine based on the Whittle design developed in Britain.

The President's statement was remarkable not only for the detail it delivered but for the candour with which it spelt out the essential purpose of lend-lease and the very considerable benefits accruing to Washington through reverse lend-lease, in the provision to the Americans of foodstuffs, raw materials, arms, manufactured goods, services such as the provision of utilities at US bases, transatlantic transport costs and, of particular significance, advanced technology, rockets, radios and the Whittle jet engine. Indeed, President Roosevelt, had he not been constrained by the necessity for secrecy in such matters, could have spoken to Congress with even greater candour. In the six months before lend-lease became operational,

Churchill had, in a 'bridge-building' exercise with Roosevelt, ordered that advanced technology at Bletchley Park, Britain's highly secret code-cracking centre and home to the deciphering of codes sent by Britain on the German Enigma machine, be made freely available to the United States. On a single visit to Washington, in the summer of 1940, the British scientist Sir Henry Tizard handed over details of the high-frequency direction-finding system known as Huff-Duff (of which we shall read more in Chapter Six) and other forms of radar technology, new explosives techniques, prototypes of magnetic mines and pioneering data on the development of the jet engine.

Even before that, 'Wild Bill' Donovan, a close confidant of Franklin Roosevelt, who established the Office of Strategic Service (the OSS, the precursor to the CIA) and who has a walk-on part in the *John Barry* story, had been allowed access to Bletchley Park. Whatever criticism may be levelled at lend-lease, the Roosevelt administration had, from the very moment of its inception, exercised commendable frankness on just what the legislation was designed to achieve. At the Washington press conference of 17 December 1940, Roosevelt himself had introduced the Act as one that would 'promote the Defense of the United States', and in his Congressional message of 23 August 1944, he commented, 'Everything that has been done under the Lend-Lease Act has been for the defense of the United States and for no other purpose.' It is pointless to complain that the principal motivation of lend-lease was American self-interest, for that is how the Americans themselves consistently portrayed it. Critics of the Act should vent their chagrin on their own national leaders, who for so long led their respective peoples to believe that lend-lease was the result of either a 'special relationship' with Washington or of a bilateral agreement that their own administrations had skilfully negotiated with the United States.

There is, of course, no refuting the fact that Roosevelt used lend-lease to extend his anti-imperial inclinations. He was antagonistic – in private and, when it was convenient, in public – towards the British Empire, but this was well known in London; the pained surprise which was expressed, and indeed continues to be expressed, that his administration and those that followed used lend-lease ruthlessly to weaken Britain's status as an imperial power, represents the belated lament of an establishment that artfully crafted the myth of a 'special relationship' between Great Britain and the United States. The British government created this myth entirely for their own, domestic ends – to demonstrate to the British public how skilful they were at what Churchill called 'statecraft' and to disguise the fact that British 'diplomacy' was entirely dependent on Washington – and then, sadly, came to believe it themselves. For all that, lend-lease, including the silver in the holds of the *John Barry*, was nothing more nor less than a political tool. In 'doing the job' of saving the world from what would undoubtedly have been a long and dark night of Fascism, it also 'did the job' of achieving for the United States at least some of its foreign policy objectives, none of which it attempted to conceal. Simply put, lend-lease marked the beginning of an American political and economic 'empire' in the world beyond the Americas.

Not that the Act did not have its critics at home, including some powerful members of Congress who, in common with some on the other side of the Atlantic, had failed to grasp lend-lease's wider implications for the post-war world. Indeed, President Roosevelt, in his message to Congress, spelt out in the most basic terms just how lend-lease worked, an exercise he obviously felt obliged to undertake in a bid to win over his own 'backwoods' men.

The accounting of lend-lease aid is kept in dollar figures. But no money is either loaned or given away to other nations under lend-lease . . . virtually all of the money is spent in the United States. This only goes into the pockets of American farmers and American war workers and American businessmen. Some of it comes back to the United States Treasury in the form of taxes. It is not money, but tanks, planes, guns and ships, war-production materials and food, that go abroad under lend-lease. And they go for one purpose only – to be used by our allies either directly or indirectly against our enemies, the Germans and the Japanese, whom our allies are able to kill or capture by using these supplies.

Take, for example, a lend-lease bomb. This particular bomb is turned over to the British and the dollar cost goes into the books as lend-lease aid to the United Kingdom. But the British don't keep the bomb. It is dropped by a British plane square on a German gun emplacement holding up our tanks in northern France. It is the German gun crew that ultimately gets the bomb and is wiped out in the process. We made that bomb for use against our enemies. The British used it against our enemies. Because the bomb was dropped by a British plane, its cost was charged up to lend-lease. If the bomb had been dropped by an American plane its cost would be included in the US Army Air Force's own procurement costs. In either case the ultimate destination of the bomb and the benefits of its use to the United States and to other United Nations are the same – the enemy is hurt, the lives of men in our own and allied forces are saved and victory is brought that much nearer. And the British workers who built the plane and the RAF crew that flew it against the Germans got enough to eat because lend-lease food was included in their rations. We gave lend-lease aid in order to aid ourselves. We have continued to provide lend-lease in order to aid ourselves. We should not permit any weakening of this system of combined war supply to delay victory a single day or to cost unnecessarily the life of one American boy.

Roosevelt's message to Congress was a straightforward declaration, in terms which no one could fail to understand, of national self-interest. It was brilliantly simplistic. It stated why lend-lease had been born. It was a message delivered by a republican for the people of a republic, a statement by the leading representative of the New World, a man who had a clear vision of how American power could be used to fashion the post-war world to his country's benefit. The fact that a new order emerged after the war – due at least in part to appalling financial mismanagement by the leaders of the Old World, and particularly the British – can be no valid excuse, then or now, to attack America for the terms extracted under the Lend-Lease Act. It could, of course, be reasonably levelled at Roosevelt that when, at the time of the introduction of the Act, he used the metaphor of one man loaning a hosepipe to another to put out a fire, he should have spelt out the premium rate of the water charge, but even such mild criticism was never dared in public, so subservient had Churchill become towards all that flowed from Washington's fountain-head.

How, in the second half of the twentieth century, Washington has used her global power is, of course, as much open to question in the

United States itself as it is beyond her own borders. But the steps that had to be taken, and were taken, in the 1940s to enable America to secure a world fashioned to her own advantage and in concert with her own scale of priorities took many curious routes. In one of them the *John Barry* was used to play what should have been a vital role.

Chapter Four

A Paw for the Bear

'Roosevelt spent the last two years of the war cultivating a special relationship with the Soviets.' Professor John Charmley, London Sunday Telegraph, *19 March 1995.*

When Roosevelt made his Second Lend-Lease Report to Congress on 11 September 1941, when the Act had been operative for just six months, he delivered a particularly evocative description of the magnitude the scheme would assume and, in the process, what it would achieve:

Planes, tanks, guns and ships have begun to flow from our factories and yards and the flow will accelerate from day to day, until the stream becomes a river, and the river a torrent, engulfing this totalitarian tyranny which seeks to dominate the world.

Since the Bolshevik Revolution that had engulfed Russia in 1917, successive American administrations had described the architects of the Union of Soviet Socialist Republics, Lenin, Trotsky and Stalin, in very much the same terms, as a 'totalitarian tyranny which seeks to dominate the world'. This was an official articulation of the fears then being expressed in Washington on 'the red menace' to home and hearth, and indeed to countries beyond. Yet it is an eternal truth that war makes for strange bedfellows and the concept that 'an enemy of my enemy is my friend' quickly took hold in Washington following Hitler's attack on the USSR in June 1941. Although this took place five and a half months before America's entry into the war, it signalled the introduction of war supplies to Moscow under lend-lease. As Roosevelt told Congress on 23 August 1944:

The program of lend-lease aid began on March 11th 1941, at a time when the security of the United States was already gravely threatened by the Axis aggressors who were seeking to dominate the world. We gave aid to Britain and the other nations resisting the aggressors because those nations held positions vital to our own defenses. If they had been defeated, the Western Hemisphere would have been left isolated and surrounded by overwhelmingly powerful forces that made no secret of their hostility to our continued existence as a free and independent people. We gave lend-lease aid in order to aid ourselves.

As ever, the President emphasised the self-interest inherent in the lend-lease programme; in its prosecution, the most baleful of enemies had quickly become 'friends'. Indeed, the heroic stand being made by the Soviet people against Nazi aggression, in what Moscow to this day describes as 'the great patriotic war', elicited much praise from Roosevelt:

The first American supplies reached Murmansk at a time when the Nazi armies were at the gates of Moscow. Now the forces of the Soviet Union, strengthened by lend-lease, have pushed the Nazis back 1,200 miles from the Caucasus to the gates of Warsaw. The Red Army is over half of the way to Berlin. In the three years from June 22nd 1941 to June 22nd 1944, the Soviet government has announced that the Soviet forces, while suffering the terrible number of 5,300,000 dead and missing soldiers themselves, have killed or captured 7,800,000 of the enemy. Hitler will not be able to use these men on the western front.

In one of the most rapid and overwhelming military campaigns in history, the Red Army has advanced to the borders of East Prussia and the gates of Warsaw. Fighting on an 800 mile front from the Gulf of Finland to the foothills of the Carpathian Mountains, the Soviet forces have broken through the German Baltic defenses, spanned the Vistula River in Poland, and covered more than half the distance to Berlin. The Soviet summer campaign began on June 23rd. In the first thirty-eight days the Red Army had driven the enemy out of 100,000 square miles of territory, an area larger than New York, Pennsylvania and Maryland combined.

With the assistance of more than $1.5 billion worth of industrial supplies and equipment that the United States has shipped to the USSR from October 1941 through June 30th 1944, the Soviet Union has strengthened its own industrial ability and capacity to meet the growing need of its armies. US government officials who have visited the Soviet Union have seen American steel, American machine tools and other industrial products in the Soviet Union factories, shipyards and repair shops that are providing the Soviet forces with the greater part of their equipment.

The rapid advance of the Red Army has meant increasingly long lines of transportation and communication to the rear, much of the way over lands that have been scorched by the retreating enemy. Lend-lease shipments of mobile equipment and large quantities of supplies for its transportation and communication systems have aided the Red Army materially as it advances farther and farther from its home bases. We have sent 300,000 trucks and other military motor vehicles to the Soviet Union. Half of all the supplies for the advancing Red Army that are sent by road are now being carried in American lend-lease trucks, according to estimates of US Army observers. Almost 84,000 military motor vehicles were shipped to Russia in the first six months of 1944 alone. Last year we began a program for shipments of railroad rolling stock to the Soviet Union. By June 30th 1944, we had sent to the Soviet Union 339 locomotives and 1,640 flat cars. We also increased our shipments of railroad rails and accessories. By June 30th we had shipped more than 455 thousand tons of railroad rails and accessories, car and locomotive wheels and axles to aid in the rebuilding and expansion of the Soviet railroads.

For the Soviet Army's communications system we have shipped 934 thousand miles of field telephone wire and 325 thousand field telephones. American supply officers attached to the US military mission have reported from the Soviet front that American transport and communications equipment have contributed immeasurably to success on the eastern front.

In the first six months of this year we sent more than 3,000 planes to the Soviet Union. From October 1st 1941, through June 30th 1944, more than 11,000 planes have been flown or shipped from the United States. Most of the planes sent to the Soviet Union have been Bell Airacobra P-39 and Curtiss P-40 fighters, Douglas A-20 attack bombers and North American B-25s. The ace of all Allied fighter pilots, Lieutenant-Colonel Alexander Pokryshkin of the Soviet Air Force, shot down forty-eight of his fifty-nine Nazi planes in a Bell Airacobra. Nine other Soviet aces have shot down between twenty and forty-four German planes each in lend-lease Airacobras. The German planes shot down by Russian airmen flying lend-lease planes cannot be used by Hitler against our men in France. American fighter pilots are now giving direct support to the Soviet offensive on the eastern front. From shuttle-bombing fields behind the Soviet front, American long-range pursuit ships have participated in operations in the Lwow area of Poland. American air forces stationed at these bases in Soviet territory are being provided with living quarters and other services and supplies by the USSR under reverse lend-lease.

Food shipments to the Soviet Union have totalled 3,079,000 short tons since October 1st 1941, and are valued at more than $900 million. These shipments include 588 thousand tons of wheat and flour, 510 thousand tons of canned meat, 356 thousand tons of vegetable oils and 62,000 tons of canned and dried milk. Our food shipments have made it possible for the Soviet Union to maintain the rations of the Red Army. To assist the Soviet people in the production of their own foods, particularly in the recently liberated Ukraine, and to relieve their dependence on outside sources, we have also shipped 17,000 tons of seeds since lend-lease aid to Russia began.

The reference to reverse lend-lease demonstrates that, besieged as the Soviets were, they, too, made provision for that aspect of the Act. Indeed, as Roosevelt went on to tell Congress:

The Soviet Union, which fought until this summer on her own soil, has needed virtually all she could produce for her own forces. Moreover, until this year, no United States forces were stationed on Soviet territory and the occasion for reverse lend-lease aid did not arise, except in connection with supplies, repairs and other services provided as reverse lend-lease for United States merchant ships in Soviet ports. With the establishment of the shuttle-bombing bases in Russia, the Soviet Union has provided our air force, as reverse lend-lease aid without cost to us, with much of the equipment, supplies and services needed for these bases. This aid has included many of the materials and most of the labor used in building the bases, part of the equipment, much of the food for our air force crews and mechanics, and many other operational supplies and services.

Roosevelt's statement on the nature and degree of the vital assistance Washington was giving to the Soviet people is as astonishing now as it must have been more than half a century ago. The commitment it represented to the survival and triumph of the Bolshevik state contrasted with the untold trillions of dollars the United States started to spend just four years after the end of World War II, at the onset of the Cold War in 1949, to bring the Soviets to destruction.

American lend-lease aid to the Soviets was governed by a series of protocols which spelled out the goods which would be supplied and the terms of payment. At the time of President Roosevelt's sixteenth Lend-Lease Report to Congress (23 August 1944), which we have just reviewed, the Third Protocol still had some time to run and the Fourth (and final) Protocol was the subject of negotiations between Washington and Moscow. In his report, the President told Congress, 'The schedules of the Third Protocol have been extended with necessary modifications to meet special circumstances.'

Although Roosevelt did not elaborate on *what* the 'necessary modifications to meet special circumstances' entailed, he could not be accused of unconstitutionally concealing facts from Congress, or indeed of misleading it. For Section 5, subsection b of the 'Act to Promote the Defense of the United States' (the Lend-Lease Act), reads, 'The President from time to time, but not less frequently than once every ninety days, shall transmit to the Congress a report of operations under this Act except such information as he deems incompatible with the public interest to disclose.' All available evidence suggests the President felt it necessary to avail himself of these discretionary powers concerning an extension to the schedule of the Third Protocol.

The first protocol dated from 1 October 1941, and between then and 30 June 1944 (the period covered by Roosevelt's Congressional report) the Soviets received lend-lease aid from the Americans of goods valued in excess of $5.9 billion, a figure that includes the supply of industrial goods, food, weapons and military hardware. It was an aspect of lend-lease in which Roosevelt took a particularly close interest, regarding aid of this nature as a crucial part of his administration's plans for the post-war world; he asked to be kept personally advised of the monthly progress Washington was making in sending assistance to the Soviets.

On 10 July 1944, the Under Secretary of the US Treasury, D. W. Bell, wrote a letter to the President at the White House:

My dear Mr President, there is attached a report of lend-lease purchases made by the Treasury Procurement Division for the Soviet government, indicating the availability of cargo for July. The inventory of material in storage as of July 1st 1944 was 290,521 tons, or 30,486 tons less than the June 1st inventory. Production scheduled for July shows a decrease of 33,100 tons as compared with June.

The attached report lists a cornucopia of industrial materials awaiting shipment to the Soviets: aluminium, auto parts, brass, bronze, bearings, chemicals, construction machinery, copper, cutting tools, lead, nickel, paper, plastics, rubber, steel, tin plate and zinc, to name but a few. The list also contains 420 tons of 'non-ferrous metals', a consignment designated as having 'priority' for shipment during the month of July. The total weight of 'priority' cargo for shipment in July is recorded in Bell's report as 96,684 tons. The 'total available' for the month, however, is given as 359,245 tons – a cargo that would have to be carried on a considerable number of vessels.

On 24 June, Nick Larsen at the New York office of the War Shipping Administration had written a letter designated 'secret' to Mr A. I. Vassiliev, Chief of Transport at the Soviet government's

Purchasing Commission on Madison Avenue, which, having dealt with the shipment of 'P-47 unboxed planes', concluded:

We expect to have . . . 'a steamer' (to be named) on berth Philadelphia about July 5th for Ras Tanurah and Bahrain, on which we have indicated to you we are in a position to book about 1,500 tons of close-stowing bottom cargo and we await with interest your advice as to whether or not you will be in a position to furnish our requirements.

Although this wording reads slightly oddly, it merely reflects the arrangements for the supply of goods to the USSR. Not all of these were covered by lend-lease – the Soviet Purchasing Commission obtained large quantities of supplies from sources other than the US government and liaised with the WSA over shipping. Any space not required by the Soviet Purchasing Commission could be used for shipping lend-lease goods, and this the WSA would arrange.

Larsen copied this letter to his senior colleague, John Hutchins at WSA headquarters in Washington, where it was received the next day and duly endorsed with the 'Russian Area' stamp.

So, there were significant tonnages of materials available for shipment to the Soviet Union during the month of July, and the WSA had 'a steamer' destined for the Gulf which would have space for up to 1,500 tons of 'close-stowing bottom cargo'. It is intriguing that Bell's report declined to identify, even to the President, the exact nature of the 'non-ferrous metals' when, in the same report, other non-ferrous metals such as brass, bronze, copper, tin and zinc had been clearly listed. Ally this curious reticence with President Roosevelt's remarks about the modification of the Third Protocol, and it becomes possible to theorise intelligently about the secret role of the *John Barry*.

Several questions beg to be answered. What was the nature of the extension to the Third Protocol? If it included the supply of non-ferrous metals, what exactly were they? Why should the transaction be shrouded in secrecy when other arrangements of a similar nature were being clearly documented? What were the 'special conditions' that wartime had forged between Washington and

Moscow, and why, fifty years after the end of the Second World War and five years after the collapse of the Bolshevik state, is Washington still reluctant, to use its own inimitable parlance, to either 'confirm or deny' the existence of silver bullion in the holds of the *John Barry*, and, if it is there, to declare for whom it was intended?

In order to answer these questions, it is now necessary to go back to the events of summer 1944, which led to the fateful encounter in the Arabian Sea between the American liberty ship SS *John Barry* and the German U-boat *U859*.

Chapter Five

For Freedom and Liberty

America's wartime production of a merchant fleet which ran the gauntlet of German submarines and aircraft across the Atlantic, through the Mediterranean, the Indian Ocean and up into the Persian Gulf carrying vital supplies to her allies, is one of the Second World War's largely unsung songs of tragedy and achievement. The cost, in terms of lives lost and ships sunk, was very high. The precise number of liberty ships lost on the Persian Gulf run is difficult to establish, as Washington recorded casualties on a geographical basis, deeming all the ships sunk east of Suez as having been lost in the Indian Ocean. However, in 1942, the year in which the merchant vessels came into service on the sea lanes of the Gulf, a total of 205 American ships were sunk worldwide; in all, 385 were lost in the Indian Ocean during the war, many of them the valiant little liberty ships. Of the 200 liberty ships lost, fifty were sunk on their maiden voyages.

In 1942 President Roosevelt described the vessels as these 'dreadful-looking objects' and, at the end of the war, John Gorley Bunker was to refer to them in the title of his book as 'the Ugly Ducklings of World War II'. The imagination of the American people was not immediately captured by them either. The vessels' inelegant lines were, it was recorded at the time, principally responsible for the concept failing to win early public support. This negative attitude was rectified only when a clever wordsmith in Washington penned the term 'Liberty Fleet', and, hence, liberty ships, which encouraged the American people to think of their country upholding in wartime one of its founding principles.

But whatever anybody thought of them, these squat little vessels made a huge contribution to the eventual outcome of the war. It is a contribution that, to the present day, many Americans feel has gone largely unchronicled and, therefore, unappreciated both at home and abroad. In his 1982 work, *A Careless Word . . . A Needless Sinking*, Captain Arthur Moore attempted to draw the world's attention anew to what he described as 'the staggering losses suffered by the United States Merchant Marine, both in ships and personnel, during World War II'.

The book, which contains an account of the sinking of the *John Barry*, has a foreword by Frank Braynard of the American Merchant Marine Museum, in which, following a lament for America's merchant fleet, which he describes as being 'virtually dead', he writes, 'By highlighting the great risks run by the Merchant Marine in the Second World War, Captain Moore's fine new work can do much to show leaders throughout the country that shipping is indeed our fourth arm of defence.'

This line of thought was not lost on the decision makers in Washington following America's entry into the war in December 1941, in the wake of the Japanese attack on Pearl Harbor. Indeed, within five months the first liberty ships were being launched. By the end of the conflict in 1945, a total of 2,710 had gone down the slipway. It was an awesome achievement, a brilliant combination of those two canons of American faith, 'know how' and 'can do'. In order to speed essential supplies to the Allies and, later, to her own forces in Britain, the European continent and the Far East, Washington's instructions to the country's shipbuilding industry were sharp and explicit – replacements for the heavy shipping losses being inflicted upon the Allies by German submarines had to be made available, and fast. Shipbuilders responded to the call with an outpouring of cash, ingenuity and sheer physical effort which was truly remarkable.

The design of the liberty ship was based upon a blueprint drawn up by a British company, J. L. Thompson and Sons of Sunderland, an area with a proud shipbuilding heritage of its own. In the great American industrial tradition of 'adopt, adapt, improve', Thompson's design, which was for a cargo vessel of simple proportions, saw the addition of diesel engines, an innovation that considerably enhanced the liberty ships' capability. The basic design having been adapted and improved, the 7,176-ton, 12-knot vessels were built all over the country, coming out of the yards as if on an unstoppable conveyor belt. In one superhuman effort in November 1942, a yard at Richmond, California, built the liberty ship *Robert E. Peary* in four days, fifteen hours and thirty minutes. This impressive mass production was achieved by the introduction of practices that constituted a revolutionary departure from traditional shipbuilding methods. The yards which produced the vessels were, in fact, assembly plants, where the 30,000 prefabricated parts which made up a liberty ship were welded together. Welding the sheets of steel, as opposed to the traditional way of riveting them with nuts and bolts, speeded up production to an astonishing degree.

There were, however, very real penalties to be paid for using these revolutionary methods, especially in the formative years. More than a few of the early liberty ships sank when their welded plates came apart in running seas. Indeed, an early official estimation of their durability gave them only a five-year operating span.

The concept of a 'Liberty Fleet' keeping open lines of supply to a world beleaguered by war had by now caught the imagination of the American people. A reflection of this enthusiasm was that many American industrialists, with no previous experience of shipbuilding, took up the challenge and went smartly into business. One of the most celebrated exponents of this 'up and at 'em' school was a civil engineer, Henry Kaiser. Kaiser's zeal for his new-found cause was so strong that he did not permit his manifest absence of experience in the art of shipbuilding to inhibit his sense of urgency to get on with the job. In 1942, in a single press notice in the 'Help

Wanted' columns of American newspapers, he appealed for '20,000 shipbuilding workers' and, in enthusiastic conversation on his new enterprise, took to referring to the 'front' and the 'back' of the liberty ships he was building.

The Liberty Fleet was now clutched enduringly to the American breast. A quarter of a century after the end of the Second World War, John Gorley Bunker wrote of the *John Barry* in romantic terms, proving that the concept conjured up in the minds of wartime Americans had not waned with the passing of the years:

As prosaic merchant ships plodded up the trade routes where a 'quinquereme of Nineveh' once carried 'ivory, apes and peacocks', it would have been only fitting that one of them carried something more exotic than jeeps, mules and C-rations. Such a ship was the John Barry, *a most unlikely looking treasure ship as she steamed across the Arabian Sea in August of 1944. But securely crated and locked in her holds was a fortune more fabulous than Ali Baba and his forty thieves could have hoped for – 26 million dollars in silver bullion.*

Bunker continued his narrative by describing the sinking of the liberty ship by *U859* and then, in a far-sighted commentary on what has come to pass twenty-five years later, added:

Somewhere in the Arabian Sea one of the richest treasures of all time waits, well protected by a mile of saltwater, for the future technique that may enable salvage crews to bring it up.

He went on:

Even more intriguing than the treasure in the John Barry *was the mystery about her. Why was such a fortune shipped in an unescorted, 12-knot liberty ship? The answers will probably remain hidden among her unexplained mysteries of World War II.*

The vessel recorded in 1944 official American documentation as 'the Steamship *John Barry* no. 241375, a freighter' had been built by the

Oregon Shipbuilding Corporation at Portland, Oregon, in February 1942 and was one of the first liberty ships to be launched. Her gross weight was 7,176 tons, her length 441 feet 6 inches and her width 57 feet. She was owned by the American government's War Shipping Administration, but operated by the New Orleans shipping company Lykes Brothers. She made her first appearance in official documents on 30 May 1944.

That morning Colonel Moore in the Mediterranean Section of Washington's War Shipping Administration sent a 'teletype' message to his colleague Nick Larsen in the WSA's New York Office on Broadway: '*John Barry* assigned to lead New York to Red Sea Account British Lend-Lease.' That same day Moore wrote a letter to Lykes Brothers, addressed to its New York office at 17 Battery Place, in which he gave brief, formal notice of the vessel's new assignment and advised that the berthing agents in New York would be the Isthmian Steamship Company. The letter bore the WSA's 'Secret' stamp.

On 10 June Vice-President Devoy of Lykes Brothers wrote to the WSA in Washington confirming receipt of its letter of 6 June advising the company that the *John Barry* had been diverted to Portland, Maine, to offload her cargo before proceeding to New York. Devoy gave the anticipated date of the liberty ship's arrival at Portland as between 15 and 18 July. He obviously understood that Washington was attaching a sense of urgency and confidentiality to the vessel arriving in New York and being cargo-free just as soon as this could be arranged. His letter, which upon arrival in Washington was also stamped 'Secret', concluded with the assurance that 'We will exert every effort to give this vessel a good turn-around at Portland.' The *John Barry* had been on a voyage to Mombasa, Bahrain and Durban, ports on Africa's eastern and southern shores, and was returning to America with a cargo rather less romantic than John Gorley Bunker's lyrical 'ivory, apes and peacocks' – hides and skins, gum, bark and sisal.

We come now to the first oddity in the story of the liberty ship. Devoy's letter establishes that the WSA claimed to have sent diversion orders to the *John Barry* on or before 6 June – which seems probable, as on 30 May she had been assigned to load again in New York.

Yet her secret log book records that her diversion orders were not received until 13 June, a whole week later. From Durban, the *John Barry* had sailed up through the Atlantic and into the Caribbean, to Port of Spain, Trinidad. On 13 June she was eleven days out of Port of Spain, in convoy, but her original destination, before she was ordered to make for Portland to discharge her cargo, has never been established – which suggests that Washington already had her lined up for a special assignment. From now on, nothing to do with the liberty ship would be free of obfuscation.

The log does record, however, that upon receiving the diversion order the *John Barry* left her convoy on 13 June and made her way independently to Maine via the Cape Cod Canal. Devoy was as good as his word, for nineteen days after he had assured the WSA that the *John Barry* would not be delayed, the vessel had arrived at Portland, Maine (on 15 June, just as Devoy had predicted), offloaded her 9,040 tons of cargo and put in to Fletchers Dry Dock, Hoboken, New Jersey, just across the Hudson River from Manhattan. Here her entire crew, including her then Master, were paid their dues and discharged from the ship's service. Four days later, on 3 July, Master Mariner Joseph Ellerwald, whose German parents had emigrated to the United States with their baby son in 1919, arrived in New York from his home in New Orleans and took command.

The matter of the ship's log assumes further mystery when it is known that the last entry is that recording her arrival at Hoboken on 29 June. With the discharge of the Master and crew on that date, the log, although far from full, was impounded and placed in the archives; only in recent years has it become declassified under America's Freedom of Information Act. Obviously the new voyage of the *John Barry* was considered so special that it had to have a log all of its own. The one issued to Joseph Ellerwald is presumed to have been lost when the *John Barry* was sunk, although that is one of the few documents he should have taken with him when he abandoned ship. If he did, it has long since been pulled from the archives by the long and secret hand of Washington.

While the *John Barry* was making her way to Portland and thence to

Hoboken, plans for her next voyage were being laid in Washington and New York. On 13 June John Hutchins of WSA Washington sent a 'secret' teletype message to Nick Larsen in New York. The vague, esoteric nature of this communication gives the first direct indication that the government of the United States was making arrangements for the movement of cargo to which it was not only attaching particular significance, but about which it was also unusually sensitive. Hutchins' message opens in terms obviously designed to reveal little to unauthorised eyes: 'Proposed plan for July for friends is as follows.' The subsequent text details a skilful grouping, rescheduling and cancellation of vessels that would have been loading cargo at the New York docks during the first week of July. Once this exercise in marine snakes and ladders has been completed, the message closes with the cryptic remark, 'This would leave New York clear during the month for your special.'

On what is believed to be 25 June, four days before the *John Barry* arrived at Hoboken, Nick Larsen wrote to the vessel's berthing agent, the Isthmian Steamship Company, with a copy to John Hutchins in Washington where, upon arrival, it was stamped 'secret'.

The opening remarks of Larsen's letter contain evidence that an official exercise of camouflaging the movements of the *John Barry*, by sowing the seeds of confusion, was now almost certainly underway: 'With reference to previous correspondence regarding "A Steamer" at Philadelphia July 5th/8th for Ras Tanurah and Bahrain, we beg to inform you the SS *John Barry*, now at New York, has been allocated for this operation with expected readiness to load at Philadelphia about July 6th/7th.'

But the secret log of the liberty ship records that on the day Larsen is supposed to have written the letter, 25 June, the *John Barry* was at anchor in Portland, Maine, offloading her African cargo and, as we have already seen, she did not arrive on the Hudson River and dock at Hoboken until the 29th. Either Larsen was promoting an officially inspired untruth when he wrote that the liberty ship was 'at New York' on 25 June or the then Master of the vessel lied to his log-book. Either way this prompts the question why? Larsen's letter to Isthmian could, for reasons known only to those involved, have been written on 30 June, but backdated to the 25th. Many of the dates given on correspondence in Washington archives have been partially obliterated, including the date on this letter of Larsen's. All supporting documents point to its having been written of the 25th, yet the copy to John Hutchins in Washington is stamped as having been received on 1 July. As correspondence between the WSA's offices in the capital and in New York was conveyed by the organisation's own couriers, copies arrived the day the letters were written or, at the latest, the day after, as many examples clearly establish. It is just not credible that such an important letter would have taken a week to arrive on John Hutchins' desk.

Larsen went on to request the *John Barry*'s berthing agents be kept 'fully posted' as to the tonnages that the Arabian American Oil Company (ARAMCO) and the Bahrain Petroleum Company planned to load aboard the *John Barry*, evidence that his 'special' was to be of considerable dimension and weight. The letter continues:

Vessel has a 30-ton boom at No. 2 [hold] and a 15 ton boom at No. 4 [hold]. However, in accordance with our conversation, arrangements have been made to have a 30 ton boom installed at No. 4 while the vessel is at New York.

A new 30 ton boom was indeed installed at hold No. 4, as witnessed by a certificate issued on 3 July by the American Bureau of Shipping, which confirmed that the new heavy-lift equipment had been satisfactorily tested. This approving certificate, bearing the emblem of the American bald eagle with its mighty wings spread out affording protection to a man o' war and a three-masted schooner, constitutes a particularly crucial piece of the *John Barry* jigsaw, proving, as it does, that Washington planned to load the liberty ship's holds with cargo of 'special' weight, cargo that was regarded as so confidential that even in secret official correspondence it could not be identified.

The American Bureau of Shipping certificate also affords one more important clue. It clearly states that when the Bureau's surveyor proof-tested the new boom on 3 July, the *John Barry* was lying at Pier 39, on the New York side of the Hudson; she must have crossed the river from Fletcher Dry Dock, Hoboken, some time after 29 June. This repositioning is a crucial factor in any attempt to draw conclusions about when any bullion was loaded into her holds.

Two days after Joseph Ellerwald joined the ship, on 5 July, the *John Barry* sailed out of New York harbour bound for Philadelphia, where, as the Master himself was later to record, the last Articles were opened on 7 July. According to statements made by her crew on their return to America in late 1944, she left New York without cargo, but 'in level ballast' – a clear indication that the vessel was carring a load of considerable weight. It might have been water or sand, used purely for ballast, but this seems unlikely given the constant demand for storage space on board the liberty ships.

A 'Cargo Allocation Sheet' dated 5 July with the handwritten annotation 'John Barry', lists 'Russian Cargo Allocated not On Hand' and 'On Hand', amongst which are tractors, telegraph wire, canned meat, dry eggs, Studebaker trucks, machine tools, cotton cloth and radio equipment – supplies for the Russian war effort amounting to 3,468 tons. At the bottom of the list are details of what is to constitute the ship's 'Bottom Cargo'. This includes 175 tons of steel sheets, 42 tons of steel billets and 819 tons of rails. The final item is given as 'Metals to Arrive – 464 tons', a total of 1,500 tons, exactly what Nick Larsen had offered Mr Vassiliev of the Soviet Government Purchasing Commission. As the amount of 464 tons is in excess of the 420 tons of 'non-ferrous metals' listed as 'priority cargo' for loading in July (in Bell's report of 10 July to President Roosevelt), it would appear that the shipment of metals was subject to fluctuation (governed by the immediate availability of the commodity at the ports and the availability of vessels and cargo space) and, therefore, represented an arrangement between the two governments that involved more than one consignment.

What is perfectly clear, however, is that the officially generated air of ambiguity surrounding the *John Barry* extended to the 'Vessel Performance and Cargo Report', a document similar to a manifest which was submitted to port authorities on completion of loading and prior to sailing. For under the 'Russian' section of the report, made out in Philadelphia on 19 July 1944, no 'non-ferrous metals' are listed as being contained in the lend-lease cargo destined for the Soviet Union.

The report contains many handwritten deletions, the most curious occurring on the last page, on which is recorded a breakdown of the vessel's supposed total cargo weight of 8,233 tons. The original typed text lists two ports of destination, Bahrain and Ras Tanurah, and two recipients of cargo stored aboard the *John Barry*, 'US Army' and 'Russian'. The two ports, together with their tonnage allocations, are left unaltered. The two recipients and their tonnage allocations, on the other hand, have been deleted. Alongside the designations of 'US Army' and 'Russian', carried in the port of destination section, is the handwritten annotation 'unk', presumably an abbreviation for 'unknown'. In the 'Country' section is written the vague 'Persian Gulf'. On page one of the report the total tonnages given for the 'US Army' and 'Russian' designations are '246' and '1,093' respectively, the latter being classified as 'Lend-Lease Cargo' comprising steel sheets and rails. On page four, however, both tonnages are deleted and, by hand, combined to '1,339', suggesting that both consignments were destined for the same unidentified port in the Persian Gulf. As cargo allocations often varied between the time of initial calculation and actual loading, the discrepancy between the weight of steel sheets and rails given on the cargo allocation sheet of 5 July, 1,036 tons, and the actual weight loaded, given on the cargo report of 19 July, 1,093 tons, is not that remarkable. What is remarkable is the apparent absence on board the *John Barry* of the 'non-ferrous metals' destined for the Soviet state, irrespective of whether the consignment amounted to the calculated 420 tons given in Bell's report of 10 July, or the 464 tons given on the cargo allocation sheet on 5 July. And while either consignment would have exceeded the 1,500 tons of 'close-stowing bottom cargo' space allocated to the Soviets by the WSA, this would not have been an impossibility in relation to the actual tonnages loaded – shipping analysts who have studied the cargo report indicate that the total carrying capacity of the *John Barry* was 11,200 tons. Of this 2,037 tons would have been taken up with bunker supplies and water, leaving 9,163 tons available for cargo. So the figure of a total cargo weight of 8,233 tons given on all official documentation indicates quite clearly that the *John Barry* sailed either with some 800 tons of cargo unaccounted for, or with space in her holds. The latter is highly improbable, given official pressure for ships to sail to war-supply ports loaded to capacity. Add to this the fact that the *John Barry* was reported as being overloaded – the final report (1 August) from WSA's District Manager in Philadelphia records that the liberty ship steamed out of the port with '51,841 cubic feet' of cargo 'stowed on deck' – and the possibility that she sailed light becomes even more unlikely.

On 19 July the *John Barry* sailed from Philadelphia for Norfolk, Virginia, to join an Atlantic and Mediterranean-bound convoy. It was her sixth officially recorded voyage, and was to be her last. On leaving Philadelphia Joseph Ellerwald recorded that his cargo consisted of '8,233 tons of general' and that his crew comprised 'forty-four men, including myself' – a curious discrepancy in view of the fact that the crew of the *John Barry* numbered forty-two, including the Master. We shall come back to this point later.

The following day, 20 July, Archibald King, Vice-President of the Isthmian Steamship Company, wrote to John Hutchins at the War Shipping Administration in Washington. Beneath the notepaper's mast-head the letter bore the typed legend 'Secret – Registered'. Under the heading '*SS John Barry*', King reported, 'The subject-named vessel recently departed from the port of Philadelphia having loaded cargo under our berth agency, destined for the ports of Ras Tanurah, Bahrain and a port in the Persian Gulf.' This letter yields a further crucial clue – beyond, that is, the air of secrecy conveyed by the cryptic third 'port in the Persian Gulf'. The WSA official 'received' stamp carries within its circle the legend 'Russian Area'. That particular endorsement had first made an appearance on a document naming the *John Barry* on the copy letter written on either 25 or 30 June by Nick Larsen to Isthmian, which had been copied to John Hutchins in Washington and to J. F. Doyle, the WSA's District Manager in Philadelphia.

Indeed, it was left to Doyle to write a final WSA report on the liberty ship's time at Pier 98 South, Philadelphia. In a letter dated 1 August marked for Nick Larsen's attention in New York and copied to John Hutchins in Washington, Doyle reported that the *John Barry* had 'completed loading cargo at 11 p.m. July 18th', with the 'lashing, securing and spraying of deck cargo' having been completed 'at 1.30 p.m. July 19th'. Doyle continued, 'The vessel sailed from Philadelphia 1.45 p.m. July 19th, passing out of the Breakwater at 12.52 a.m. July 20th. Total cargo loaded was 8,233 tons, 471,697 cubic feet, of which 461 tons, 51,841 cubic feet were stowed on deck. Draft sailing from Philadelphia – Forward 28′6″ – Aft 29′0″ – Mean 28′9″. Fuel oil on board, sailing – 8,692 barrels. Fresh water on board – 480 tons.'

With this report the *John Barry* sailed out of the pre-sinking records kept on the vessel by the War Shipping Administration. She passed out of Philadelphia Breakwater under the cover of darkness in the early hours of 20 July 1944, on the last leg of the journey to her final home port, Norfolk, Virginia.

The convoy escorted the *John Barry* across the dangerous waters of the Atlantic, beneath which German submarines stalked Allied ships, through the Mediterranean as far as that great junction of the seas, beloved of mariners across the centuries and now gateway to the Suez Canal, Egypt's Port Said. The *John Barry* arrived there on 19 August. From then on she was on her own, with the convoy returning to home ports in America.

Having been guided through the Suez Canal and sailed down through the Red Sea, the liberty ship arrived at Aden on 26 August. As Ellerwald was later to record, she was there only 'for a few hours to receive naval instructions', before sailing out alone into the Arabian Sea on the last leg of her journey to her first port of call, the Gulf port of Ras Tanurah, where some of her cargo would be unloaded. She was now totally without protection, other than that which she carried on board.

All liberty ships carried heavy swivel guns, mounted at the prow and the stern, and on board the *John Barry* were twenty-seven American naval personnel who manned them at times of attack. Known collectively as the Armed Guard, they were commanded by what were referred to disparagingly as 'ninety-day wonders', US naval ensigns, a junior rank in the officer corps, whose average period of service on any one vessel was three months. Both the Armed Guard and the ensigns were unpopular with the merchant crews, many of whom had been sent to sea after only four months of training at what were known as boot camps – America's answer to the manpower demand prompted by the huge wartime increase of its merchant fleet. The crews of the liberty ships were, more often than not, scathing in their criticism of those sent to protect them. A 1944 report records that a crew member of one vessel described the Armed Guard as 'mainly young farmboys with unbelievable appetites who ate continuously throughout the day'. Another report describes the ensigns as 'pompous, arrogant and secretive as a result of their navy training'.

However uneasy the social alliance born of this professional friction aboard the *John Barry* may have been, as she sailed through the warm waters of the Arabian Sea in the summer of 1944, her sole protection from any enemy offensive was the presence on board of the Armed Guard. Her encounter with the German submarine *U859* just three days out of Aden was to prove that this protection was far from sufficient to ensure her survival.

Chapter Six

The Maiden Voyage of No Return

When Prime Minister Neville Chamberlain broadcast to the British people on the morning of Sunday 3 September 1939, telling them that a state of war now existed between Britain and Germany, it has long been an article of faith that by comparison with the military strength of the Third Reich the British forces were ill-prepared for war. In many respects this is, of course, correct, but German war records demonstrate just how badly equipped the German navy was at the outbreak of hostilities.

The First World War had been formally closed with the signing in 1919 of the Treaty of Versailles, the principal burden of which were measures designed to inhibit Germany's ability to wage war in the future. Measures had most effectively shackled the German navy. Under the terms of the treaty Germany had been expressly forbidden to equip herself with a submarine fleet. While a small number of submarines had secretly been built on the country's behalf in Dutch yards, it was only in 1935, following the repudiation on 16 March of the Treaty of Versailles by Hitler's National Socialist government, that a German-based submarine construction programme was launched. By then, of course, Hitler was in a hurry and in September of the same year the country's first post-First World

War submarine flotilla was commissioned; six new U-boats, the Weddigen Flottille, at Kiel, the same port from which nine years later *U859* was to begin its maiden voyage. On 18 June 1935, only three months after Hitler's repudiation of the Versailles Treaty, London and Berlin signed a naval agreement, the terms of which permitted Germany to equip herself with a fleet of submarines equal in number to Britain's. However, it was not until 1938 that large-scale production commenced.

But even then German U-boats were limited in both number and range. The early models were classified as types II and VII, both of which were suitable for operations only in the waters off the British Isles. They were followed by type VIIC, whose range restricted it to patrolling the sea lanes into Britain's ports and harbours, and a very limited number of type IXC, which could only travel as far as the mouth of the Mediterranean Sea. IXC was the forerunner to the considerably more effective type IXD2, the class to which Korvettenkapitan Jan Jebsen's *U859* belonged. While type IXC had a range of 11,000 miles and carried a crew of forty-eight, class IXD2 had a range of 30,000 miles and a complement of sixty-nine, proof of the advance that German naval architects and engineers were capable of achieving.

The year 1940, however, saw a slackening of the pace of submarine construction in Germany. Hitler, seeking an early end to the war through his army and air force, devoted disproportionate resources to the Wehrmacht and the Luftwaffe, at the expense of his navy. During 1940 only thirty-seven new U-boats came into service, a short-fall of over sixty in what had originally been planned. In 1941, with the prospect of a quick victory rapidly receding, Hitler turned his attention once again to the necessity of increasing the strength of his navy. But a whole year's submarine production had been lost and the German fleet, while achieving much for the Axis cause through skill, courage and human endurance, remained stretched to the limits for the remainder of the war.

Yet, under pressure as the German navy undoubtedly was, its submarines went just that bit further in the early months of 1943; they commenced operations in the Indian Ocean, a theatre of war opened up by the technical advance Germany's naval engineers had by then achieved, as represented by the long-range capabilities of class IXD2. Essentially, submarines of that type were long-range, ocean-going craft, designed for offensive operations on the Allies' far-flung trade routes. They were, in fact, the very last conventional submarines commissioned into Hitler's navy.

Dispatching the country's U-boats halfway round the world from the Fatherland was a courageous endeavour designed not only to sink Allied shipping east of the Suez, but to carry urgently needed war supplies to the Japanese in the ports they were occupying in South-East Asia, such as Surabaya, Batavia, Singapore and Penang. According to at least one contemporary report these Japanese-occupied ports were more often than not ill-equipped and manned by naval personnel who were 'less than capable'. To what can only be considered a very bad bargain for Germany, was added Japanese ingratitude. Shortly after German naval architects and engineers had developed the type IXC submarine, with its increased range and speed, one of the craft was presented to the Imperial Japanese navy, only to have this advanced vessel described by Admiral Fukutome, Chief of Staff of the Imperial Japanese navy's combined fleet, as 'small and therefore of little value to Japan'.

The Japanese, with some justification given the speed of their military success throughout South-East Asia, and having occupied virtually all of the territory of the Dutch and British Colonial Empires in the region, considered the Indian Ocean their own sphere of influence and therefore operations. This attitude was endorsed by the fact that the Japanese navy had at the time a fleet of the largest sea-going submarines in existence. Their type I boats, for example, had a surface speed of 20 knots, a range of 16,000 miles and carried operational crews some ninety strong. Japanese 'invincibility' was, however, showing signs of vulnerability as early as the first half of 1942, nine months before German U-boats arrived in the Indian Ocean. In January of that year the celebrated Japanese Admiral Yamomoto had predicted total military success within six months for Emperor Hirohito's forces. Yet on 14 April US General Doolittle's air-crews bombed Tokyo and in June, in the waters of the Pacific, Vice-Admiral Nagumo lost four irreplaceable aircraft carriers at the Battle of Midway. An early 1942 advocate of pressing German U-boats into Indian Ocean service was the Third Reich's Naval Attaché in Tokyo, Admiral Wenneker. Back in Berlin the brilliant naval strategist Grossadmiral Karl Doenitz was initially unimpressed, having other priorities than stretching the limited number of submarines at his disposal still further by dispatching them to the distant Indian Ocean. Indeed, on 12 January of that year, Doenitz launched Operation Paukenschlag, or Drumbeat, in the Atlantic, a submarine campaign which inflicted heavy losses on the Allies. In 1942 alone German submarines sank five and a half million tons of Allied shipping, bringing Doenitz's strategy of sinking ships faster than the Allies could build them ever closer to success. An additional, crucial factor was that with Hitler, albeit belatedly, giving the German navy the resources Doenitz desperately needed, submarines were now coming into service at a quicker pace than the Allies could destroy them. As Doenitz recorded in his diary on 15 April 1942, in a commentary on Operation Drumbeat:

What counts in the long run is the preponderance of sinkings over new construction. Shipbuilding and arms production are centred in the American zone. By attacking the supply traffic – particularly the oil – in the American zone, I am striking at the root of the evil, for here the sinking of each ship is not only a loss to the enemy, but also deals a blow at the source of his shipbuilding and war production.

As 1942 wore on, Doenitz, emboldened by his success in the Atlantic, did eventually turn his attention to more distant seas. No Allied convoys sailed through the Mediterranean in 1942 – this route to the Far East was not used again until May of the following year. During that sixteen-month period the Allies sent both troops and supplies round the Cape of Good Hope, resulting in a concentration of shipping that the German navy could no longer ignore. Indeed, with the new submarine type IXD2 with its 30,000-mile range now fully operational, Doenitz was able, at last, to consider extending his strategy to the Indian Ocean. German war records show that by

October 1942 five U-boats lay off the Cape; during that month they sank twenty-four Allied ships, representing 'kills' of 161,000 tons. Not that the month went entirely Doenitz's way. *U170*, a type IXD2 submarine, having sunk an Allied ship, was, within days of arriving in the new area of operations, herself sunk whilst on the surface, in a surprise attack by HMS *Active*, a destroyer out of South Africa's Simonstown naval base, west of Cape Town.

In November, in an operation codenamed Drumroll, after Operation Drumbeat in the Atlantic, five more U-boats arrived in the area and rounded the Cape; entering waters south of the Mozambique Channel, they sank a further twenty-four Allied vessels, totalling 127,000 tons. This was Doenitz's first venture into waters adjacent to the Indian Ocean proper, but with the Allies now alerted to Berlin's new initiative, pressure on the U-boats quickly mounted, with the result that that first sortie to operate east of the Cape was the only one to return in its entirety to ports in German-occupied Europe. In December 1942, total Allied shipping sunk by Operation Drumroll fell to 23,000 tons. In the event the Allies took a heavy toll from this strategy; nevertheless it continued right up to the closing stages of the Second World War. Writing after the end of the conflict, Fregattenkapitan Gunter Hessler, Grossadmiral Karl Doenitz's son-in-law, who had himself been a U-boat commander and Staff Officer (Operations) to Flag Officer U-boats, observed:

Five days after the commencement of the Normandy invasion, the few boats still operating in remote areas were instructed to start for home with sufficient fuel to take them, if necessary, to Norway. Operations in the Indian Ocean, however, continued satisfactorily, using about three Penang-based boats at a time. In August U198, U859 *and* U862 *encountered considerable traffic around the Mozambique Channel and to the north of Madagascar, where they sank eight ships.*

Hessler went on to record the high fatality rate suffered by Germany's U-boats on the Indian Ocean run, a commentary in which he included the *John Barry*'s bête noire *U859*: '*U859* was torpedoed and sunk by an Allied submarine while entering Penang after an operational cruise lasting nearly six months.'

Principal in the story of Allied success in sinking submarines in the Indian Ocean was a system of submarine detection with a codename which made it sound like a character from a children's story – Huff-Duff. Despite its name, it was a deadly opponent of German naval strategy. Huff-Duff was a ship-borne 'high-frequency direction-finding' system, whereby a U-boat's contact signals could be detected and its precise bearing displayed on a cathode-ray tube. Once the submarine was detected, the measures required for its destruction were set in motion. Huff-Duff was an Allied weapon the German navy was never able to counter effectively and, as we shall see, led to *U859's* destruction after she had sunk the *John Barry*.

The use of Huff-Duff in the Indian Ocean relates in no small way to the significant contribution made by the Ultra system of submarine detection to the Atlantic campaign against German U-boats attacking the great Allied convoys. (Ultra was, of course, the system used to gather what the British Admiralty described at the time as 'Special Intelligence', gleaned from deciphering enemy signals encrypted on the German Enigma ciphering machine, one of which British Intelligence had obtained before the war.)

In his introduction to Volume One of *The U-boat War in the Atlantic* (1989), the Royal Naval historian Lieutenant Commander Andrew Withers urges caution on any assumption that such systems of intelligence gathering were 'the decisive instrument' in the Allied campaign against German U-boats:

Its value depended upon the success of the cryptanalysts in breaking the ciphers, upon the time taken to do so, whether the correct deductions were made from the decrypts and, not least, upon operational considerations such as the availability of ships or the presence of bad weather.

Withers continues his caution by recording that until March 1941, when the German Naval Command's 'Home Waters' key, Hydra, was broken by the British, an operation which they codenamed Dolphin, Ultra was 'largely blind to naval traffic'. Until that time, the British government's Code and Cypher School at Bletchley Park, outside London, apparently had little to contribute beyond traffic analysis. In an important addition to any realistic evaluation of the contribution made by electronic intelligence-gathering systems in the Allies' anti-U boat campaign, Withers comments that it has to be borne in mind that from February 1942 until the early months of the following year the German navy's Triton code, which the British styled Shark, remained for all practical purposes unbroken. Consequently, Allied losses at sea continued to be high, reaching such 'alarming proportions' that consideration was given to abandoning the transatlantic convoy system altogether. Withers concludes, 'Given these difficulties, it will be recognised that Ultra was dependent for its success upon a complex and dedicated organisation, and upon an element of good fortune.'

The fact remains, however, that the Allies' success against the U-boats was crucial to the victory which was finally won. Not even the German Naval Command was fully aware of the devastation wrought on its submarines until the very end of the war. As Fregattenkapitan Gunter Hessler wrote, 'When, after the capitulation, the Allies ordered all boats to report their positions, many failed to respond and it was only then that the magnitude of our losses in the last months of the war became apparent.' And as Lieutenant Commander Withers himself observes, 'It is worth recording that almost three-quarters of the men who went to sea in U-boats lost their lives.'

While, of course, the majority of Germany's submarines were lost in the North Sea and the Atlantic Ocean, those that made passage for tropical seas fared little better. Out of the total of forty-five U-boats that set sail for the Indian Ocean and the Far East from home ports and German-occupied ports in Europe, only four made the return journey. A staggering thirty-four were sunk either on their way to the Indian Ocean or in it. Following Germany's capitulation, four were interned by the Japanese in ports they were occupying in the Far East, and three surrendered in May 1945, two of them upon arrival in European ports from the Far East, and the third putting in to a port in New Hampshire upon hearing of the end of the war while outward bound for Tokyo.

The most significant statistic in all this is that while only twenty German U-boats took part in offensive operations in the Indian Ocean, between them they sank 170 merchant ships – among them the *John Barry* – having a combined weight of over one million tons, a remarkable success when offset against the high fatality rate of their sister submarines.

Nonetheless, the overall endeavour of dispatching German submarines into the Indian Ocean came to be seen by the Allies as a courageous but ultimately futile strategy, one which gave insufficient return. During the American Naval Institute's proceedings of August 1961 the policy was described as 'misconceived, misdirected and tragically wasteful in spite of the devotion to duty, the valiant efforts, sacrifices and successes of the Far Eastern U-boat cadre'.

By the spring of 1944 the prospect of victory for the Third Reich was growing ever bleaker. Italy had surrendered in the previous September, the Anzio landings had taken place in January and, while the liberation of Paris and Brussels was still five months away, the eventual outcome of the conflict was becoming increasingly obvious for all to see. The year was to end with General von Runstedt's Ardennes offensive, which rekindled hope in Berlin, but in April, German successes on the battle fronts were becoming a rarity. The crew of *U859* prepared for their long and perilous voyage to the Indian Ocean against a mood of national pessimism. But, with that quality of camaraderie unique to submarine crews of all nationalities, the men of the newly commissioned U-boat, under the command of Korvettenkapitan Jan Jebsen, a twenty-seven-year-old professional navy officer with a record of distinguished service, were in a mood of quiet determination as they gathered in the port city of Kiel in the closing days of March 1944 to prepare their new craft for its maiden patrol.

Jebsen, a graduate of the German navy's training ship, the *Gorch Foch*, which is still in commission today, was very recently married, and two of the submarine's officers, Oberleutenant Kiehn and Dr Hans von Gehlen, *U859*'s medical officer, took brides only days before they set sail from Kiel. Unusually, von Gehlen had no previous maritime experience, but joined Jebsen's command at his special request, the two men having long been close friends.

Morale among the men of *U859* was good; the attraction of undertaking the maiden voyage of the latest class IXD2 submarine, with its increased operational range of 30,000 miles and its twenty-four torpedo tubes, and being commanded by an experienced naval officer held in esteem and affection, resulted in any anxieties the men may have had about the perilous patrol ahead being well concealed. Jan Jebsen's wife, on the other hand, was full of foreboding and openly expressed her fears. During Jebsen's last home leave he had told his wife that *U859*'s departure was scheduled for 4 April. On the last day of March Frau Jebsen telephoned her husband in a distraught state, begging him to set sail the very next day. She had a strong interest in astrology and the prospect of her husband putting to sea at a time of war on a date which was a combination of four fours – 4.4.44 – held, for her, very bad omens indeed. Of course, Jebsen could not comply with his young wife's wishes, but he was disturbed enough by her plea to speak of it to at least one other member of his officer corps.

One of the Korvettenkapitan's youngest officers was Horst Klatt, who had joined the German navy in October 1940, at the age of seventeen. He had long planned a naval career and his rise through the ranks had been rapid, with the result that when he joined Jebsen's command in the spring of 1944, he did so with the rank of Oberleutnant and the duties of First Engineer.

As the great submarine, with due naval ceremony, slowly moved out of the waters of Port Kiel on the morning of 4 April 1944 under a cloud-scudded spring sky, young Oberleutnant Klatt, now twenty-one years of age, did have certain misgivings about 'the ordeal of marching to war'. While he kept such thoughts to himself he had been surprised, as had other senior members of the crew, at the amount of cargo the submarine was carrying. *U859*, Klatt recalls, 'was, quite frankly, overloaded'. In every available space were crammed boxes and chests for the Japanese-occupied ports in the Far East – Penang, codenamed Poula, and Singapore, codenamed Siegfried. The crew of the submarine paid an immediate price for the absence of space.

'Even in their quarters the men could only move about on all fours, with food having to be eaten lying down. It was only towards the end of the long, difficult journey, when the supplies for the crew stored in their quarters, which would usually have been kept elsewhere in the U-boat, were exhausted, that they were able to stand upright again,' Horst Klatt remembers.

U859 was carrying a complement of sixty-three ratings, plus Jebsen and five other officers. Their craft was equipped with the latest technology, including the means of maintaining radio contact with their home base and the very best devices with which to locate enemy shipping.

The opening days of the long voyage were 'bearable', as the submarine made its way northwards to the German-occupied Norwegian port of Kristiansund, where the German navy had a supply base. The 'ordeal' aspect of the patrol started on 8 April, when *U859* was obliged to remain submerged in the cold waters of the northern Atlantic for twenty-three hours a day, surfacing at eleven o'clock each night for just one hour.

'For fourteen consecutive days the temperature never rose above four degrees Celsius,' Klatt remembers. 'As we had been issued only khaki shorts and vests as a "second uniform", many of us spent as long as we could manage in the engine room, where the temperature was about 30 degrees Celsius.' Another hazard for the men of *U859* was that when the device which located enemy vessels, which had initially so impressed them, was working, it created noise levels within the submarine that were 'difficult to bear for long periods and in some cases impaired the hearing of crew members'.

Consequently, many of the men developed a terror of the locating device. To minimise their own noise levels, they were obliged to move about the submarine either in bare feet or wearing only socks, with the result that many suffered cuts and abrasions. A further irritant was that they were ordered to converse with each other only in whispers. In addition, as *U859* moved further into the central Atlantic, with its greater frequency of Allied patrols searching out German submarines, the time that Jebsen could safely send his craft to the surface was reduced to fifteen minutes a day. Very soon the men's health began to deteriorate as a result of spending so many hours every day submerged. Diesel fumes led to sickness and sore eyes, while the frequent sudden drops in pressure produced an atmosphere inside the submarine equivalent to the thin air experienced at 13,000 feet, exacerbating hearing difficulties and frequently causing nausea. Former Oberleutnant Klatt recalls, 'The very air we had to breathe was heavily polluted, poisoned, in fact, with carbon monoxide.'

But there were compensations. On the twentieth day of *U859*'s patrol, she made her first 'kill', with the sinking of a Panamanian tanker, the *Coliu*, north of the Equator. But with the submarine having moved into warmer waters, the bitter cold experienced during the opening days of the patrol was replaced by uncomfortably high temperatures, up to 40 degrees Celsius in the crew's quarters and 70 in the engine room, with 95 per cent humidity. To add to the discomfort the tropical seas were generating storms to match. Horst Klatt remembers his craft's rounding of the Cape of Good Hope with particular clarity:

A Force Eleven gale blew which tossed U859 *through the water like a toy. The storm rapidly increased to Force Fifteen, causing in its wake damage to* U859's *emergency generator and one of the guns mounted on the fuselage. It was a truly terrifying experience.*

When the mountainous seas subsided, the craft had to surface (under cover of darkness) so that damage caused by the storm could be repaired. Korvettenkapitan Jan Jebsen allowed his ratings to emerge from the fetid atmosphere of *U859* to witness the lights of Cape Town, which were bright enough to illuminate the night sky. Horst Klatt remembers:

The younger among the crew were visibly moved by the sight, for they had lived for almost ninety days either in the artificial light of their quarters, or restricted to only brief intervals on deck, in the open air but under cover of darkness. It was a rare moment of wonder and pleasure for many of them. And for the majority the very last such human experience they were to have.

Within days this pleasant experience was replaced by one of a very different nature. On 5 July, shortly before dawn, Korvettenkapitan Jebsen ordered his submarine to the surface for her usual ventilation, dumping of refuse and the brief surface run during which her batteries were recharged. The vessel was now in the waters of the eastern Cape, east-south-east of the port of Durban, capital of the South African province of Natal. Just as the first light of dawn was dissolving the covering of darkness and as *U859* was making ready to return to the safety of the sea's depths, a Catalina aircraft appeared out of the early morning sky. The swiftness and ferocity of its attack made submerging impossible. It was a time of alarm clearly recalled by Oberleutnant Klatt:

The Catalina made long, low runs over U859, *dropping a total of five depth charges, one of which ruptured a fuel tank. It was only the outstanding skill and control of his craft exercised by Korvettenkapitan Jebsen, his ability to manoeuvre* U859 *repeatedly across the surface of the sea, which saved us from total disaster.*

The force of the exploding depth charges produced horrifying conditions. *U859* had a displacement of over 1,800 tons and was 295 feet in length, yet so violent were the Catalina's depth charges that at one terrifying moment, the submarine was lifted clean out of the water, to a height of about three feet above the surface of the sea. But the crew, encouraged by Jan Jebsen's courage and leadership, fought back. As Horst Klatt recalls:

Our men were at gun positions and as the Catalina made yet another turn over U859, *we opened fire, scoring two hits on its engines. With that it flew away, smoke streaming in its wake. The arrival of silence, as abruptly as it had departed with the arrival of the Catalina in the skies above us, had its own drama.*

But there was no time to rehabilitate shattered nerves in the still morning air; Jebsen quickly gave the order for the submarine to return to the relative safety of the deep, leaving on the surface a dark stain of oil, streaming from the ruptured fuel tank, as witness to the incident which had just taken place.

The Catalina, although it had not succeeded in destroying *U859*, had dealt the craft and its crew bitter blows. On one of its final runs over the submarine the aircraft had raked *U859*'s defending crew with cannon fire, hitting two men, a young rating and an officer. Even before *U859* had completed her diving manoeuvre, Dr Hans von Gehlen had prepared an operating table in the officers' wardroom and immediately the craft was on a steady course began to give the two men the urgent medical attention they needed. Within minutes, however, Rating Bolt had died, while Lieutenant Lask was diagnosed as having sustained serious head injuries. After an operation lasting four hours, von Gehlen told Jebsen that he had done as much as he could for the young lieutenant who, for the remainder of the voyage, was in a very poor way indeed, drifting in and out of consciousness and losing his memory completely.

U859 herself had also sustained serious damage. When Jebsen gave the order for the submarine to submerge, the rupture of the fuel tank quickly became apparent. The Korvettenkapitan had to trust to fortune that his craft would carry himself and his men to safer seas where, once again on the surface, repairs could be carried out. But Jebsen's first priority had to be to make good his vessel's escape, which placed renewed strain upon an already exhausted and nervous crew. It was necessary, in the Korvettenkapitan's judgement, for *U859* to spend at least thirty-six hours submerged, during which as much distance as possible would be put between her and the area in which the Catalina had made its attack. But after thirty hours beneath the waves, a professional disagreement arose between Jebsen and his old friend Dr von Gehlen. The day of the Catalina's attack had been the ninety-third day of *U859*'s patrol and the strain on the men was now very much in evidence. This was causing Dr von Gehlen considerable concern. Klatt recalls:

His principal worry was the high level of carbon monoxide in the submarine's atmosphere. After the Catalina attack von Gehlen's carbon count rose to 0.28 per cent, which alarmed him considerably, and understandably, when it is known that 0.37 per cent is fatal if inhaled for a period of just in excess of two hours.

Yet it was at this very time that Jan Jebsen decided that the submarine should stay submerged, to protect herself from further attack, for a day and a half. Conditions became so bad that von Gehlen told Jebsen that he could no longer take professional responsibility for the health of the men.

'Yet,' as Horst Klatt remembers, 'atrocious as conditions had become inside *U859*, Korvettenkapitan Jebsen really had little option but to continue with his chosen course of getting as far away from the area where we had been attacked as possible, without running the risk of taking the submarine back up to the surface.'

A slow poisoning by carbon monoxide fumes was not the only difficulty being experienced by the submarine's crew. Many were now disorientated by an absence of the natural rhythm of night and day. Many had to share bunks, sleeping in shifts around the clock, which often led to friction between individual ratings. There was a constant shortage of fresh drinking water, with the result that many of the men were drinking coffee far stronger than was good for them. Showers had to be taken in the engine room, using sea water, with the inevitable result that men could not keep themselves clean, and because of this, developed skin rashes. Smoking was strictly forbidden, which, for many, was a considerable burden. Indeed, in addition to stomach and kidney ailments, many were now suffering from stress. And, had Jebsen and his brother officers known it, the fast-deteriorating conditions of the men of their command were not the only factors working against them.

Following the surrender of Italy in the previous September, many of Benito Mussolini's officer corps had been volunteering to the Allies information they had gained during Combined Service Operations with Germany, information that the Allied powers had put to effective use. One such informant was a Captain Jannucci, who had co-operated with British military intelligence by giving them a code the German navy used to maintain contact with its submarine fleet.

Grossadmiral Karl Doenitz had earlier given an order to allied

U-boat commanders in the waters of Africa to report the passage of any Allied vessels round the Cape of Good Hope and to transmit such information on a special coded frequency. It was this code which Captain Jannucci gave to the British. Consequently, wherever any German submarine transmitted coded signals on the frequency, the British could 'eavesdrop' with impunity and, in the process, ascertain the number and general location of the craft sending the signal. At the time, of course, Korvettenkapitan Jebsen and his men were unaware of this.

The seven weeks after the where sprint away from the waters the Catalina had launched its attack were uneventful, despite the atrocious conditions within the submarine. Indeed, during this relatively calm period, there was even time for two small celebrations. Jan Jebsen turned twenty-eight and, on 1 August, Horst Klatt celebrated his twenty-second birthday in the officers' quarters, with canned fruit, milk and one bottle of beer. The crew continued to be encouraged by news from home, particularly when they heard that the people of Germany, despite increasing privation, were bearing up well and were cheering their sons towards future victories. As Horst Klatt remembers:

Men used to gather round the receivers at special hours to listen to broadcasts from home on a light-wave frequency. The broadcaster was codenamed 'Goliath' and his words came to us via what was then the highest radio station mast in the world, 100 metres from top to bottom.

Not that the news was always encouraging, although that depended very much on the private thoughts and political inclinations of individual members of the crew. The report, on 20 July, of the attempt to assassinate Hitler was by any yardstick a sensational development, and was received accordingly by the crew of the submarine. But, as with their comrades in the wider German fleet, only a minuscule number of ratings or officers in the U-Bootwaffe were members of the Nazi Party; the majority had simply sought to serve their country by joining its navy.

As July gave way to August, it had become apparent to Jebsen and his small officer corps that their craft was under surveillance. *U859*'s sophisticated locating equipment began to identify not only enemy aircraft in the skies above but enemy ships shadowing the submarine on the waves below. The capitulation of the Italians had led to the reopening of the Suez Canal, allowing greater Allied warship formations to reach the Indian Ocean without having to make the long and hazardous voyage down through the Atlantic and round the Cape of Good Hope. Consequently, German shipping and submarines operating in the Arabian Sea and the Indian Ocean were often obliged to run the gauntlet of the Allied ships which came in search of them in ever increasing numbers. However, Jebsen was a skilled seaman; as he took his craft onwards into the Arabian Sea, he identified and subsequently evaded the hostile attention of two British men-o-war, the *Barth* and the *Tay*. Indeed, despite recent reversals in Jebsen's fighting fortunes and the realisation that he was now being hunted down by the British (or, perhaps, because of these circumstances), he decided to fight back – although he was aware that he was running a risk of giving away his approximate position and, in the process, having increased pressure put upon him by the British.

So it came about that on 27 August, the 146th day of his craft's patrol, Jebsen sighted and torpedoed an unidentified British tanker. Just twenty-four hours before her date with the SS *John Barry*, *U859* was back in business.

Chapter Seven

Voyage to the Deep

The first draft of history invariably comes best from those most closely involved in it, even if the confusion of war often leads to contradictory accounts being given. Let us, therefore, allow the words of Master Joseph Ellerwald tell us about the event aboard his vessel on the night of 28 August 1944, as sworn by him in front of a 'Notary Public, Kings County, No. 424' in the 'County of New York, the State of New York' on 17 October 1944.

I, Joseph Ellerwald, being duly sworn, depose and state: I have held a Master's licence, unlimited, since 1942 and I joined the SS John Barry *as Master on July 3rd 1944 at New York. The last Articles were opened on this vessel on July 7th 1944 at Philadelphia. We sailed from Philadelphia on July 19th to join a convoy in Norfolk. On leaving Philadelphia our cargo consisted of 8,233 tons of general; the crew on leaving Philadelphia comprised forty-four men, including myself; in addition there were twenty-seven navy gunners aboard.*

We left Norfolk in convoy on July 24th, bound for Ras Tanurah, Arabia, via Suez; upon reaching Port Said, we proceeded on alone. We stopped at Aden on August 26th for a few hours to receive naval instructions. There were no changes in our crew from the time we left Philadelphia.

At 10 a.m. ship's time, August 29th 1944, the SS John Barry *was struck by two torpedoes. The first torpedo hit in the after part of No. 3 hatch, starboard side and one half-hour later a second torpedo struck the vessel in the way of the engine room, starboard side.*

When the first torpedo hit us, I was in my office and the concussion threw me from the chair. I immediately went out on the bridge; the general alarm had been given by the Mate on watch and I know that the Radio Operator sent off an SOS call. The engines were ordered stopped. At the time the torpedo struck us, our position was 15° 10'N, 55° 18'E. There was a west-north-west wind at the time, about force 6; the sea was rough and the visibility poor.

As the vessel was going down by the head rapidly, I ordered the crew to abandon ship. The John Barry *was equipped with four lifeboats and four square rafts. All of the rafts were tripped, but two of the lifeboats were rendered useless; No. 3 lifeboat had been blown on the after deck by the concussion and the forward starboard lifeboat had been blown off the ship. About 10.10 p.m. the crew started to leave the vessel; at 10.20 p.m. I went over the side into No. 2 lifeboat, and the Chief Engineer and the Radio Operator followed soon after. In lowering No. 2 lifeboat, it was capsized, and some of the men who were in her swam either to a raft or to the remaining lifeboat which had already been launched. The Chief Engineer and the Radio Operator jumped over the ship's side soon after I had gotten into the swamped lifeboat and joined me there with other members of the crew.*

About 10.30 p.m. August 28th, while No. 2 lifeboat was standing off the vessel at about 300 feet, the second torpedo struck the John Barry *in the way of the engine room, starboard side. The ship immediately broke in two and sank, her bow and stern being the last to sink beneath the surface of the water. We stayed in the swamped lifeboat that night and at dawn it was bailed out.*

Because of the direction of the current, I knew that we were in a sea lane and would probably be picked up shortly by some vessel appearing in the vicinity, so both the lifeboats that had got clear of the ship put out sea anchors. At 10 a.m. August 29th, a vessel was sighted on the horizon and we signalled her by a radio which we had saved. At 1 p.m. August 29th, the men in No. 2 lifeboat were picked up by the SS Benjamin Bourn*;*

there were twenty-eight in all, including myself. I later learned that a Dutch tanker, whose name I do not know, had picked up the remaining members of the crew from the remaining lifeboat and the two rafts about 1/2 hour before we were picked up. These men were taken to Aden and when the Santa Barbara, *the vessel on which I was repatriated, arrived at Aden on September 16th, I learned these crew members had been taken aboard the Dutch tanker and landed there.*

As a result of the torpedoing and sinking of the John Barry, *two of the crew are missing. They are:*

1. Gordon W. Lyons, Chief Officer. I believe this man was in his quarters at the time we were torpedoed. I had not seen him since 8.30 that night. I questioned members of the crew and two of them, the Chief Cook and the Bosn., said that they thought this man was on the boat deck shortly before the vessel sank. When questioned further, both the Chief Cook and Bosn. admitted they were not sure that it was the Chief Officer they saw on deck.

2. Tan See Jee, Messman. I questioned members of the crew and none of them had seen this man after the vessel was torpedoed.

We arrived at Khorramshahr on the Benjamin Bourn *on September 5th; twenty-nine of the crew, including myself, were repatriated on the* Santa Barbara, *leaving Khorramshahr on September 9th and arriving in New York on October 15th. The two following men were injured:*

1. George Wilgas, A.B. This man was standing on the boat deck at the time No. 2 lifeboat was swamped. The forward davit broke off and the end hit him on the head and he was left in hospital at Khorramshahr.

2. William Watler, Ch. Eng. This man suffered a leg injury.

One man, Rucker, Messman, suffered an injury to his side when he fell on the dock at Khorramshahr.

As a result of the torpedoing and sinking of the John Barry, *the crew lost all of their personal effects. As to the disposition of the lifeboats, two were lost by the torpedoing and the remaining two were abandoned when the men were taken aboard the rescue vessels.*

The Master's tale, with its air of bureaucratic understatement, cannot be dissimilar to many delivered by men of both Axis and Allied powers during the Second World War, reports which describe in almost droning terms the circumstances attending the destruction of their ships upon the high seas by one or other party to the conflict. All drama drained, all human emotion exhausted from the text in order to meet the demands of authority for precise detail, Master Joseph Ellerwald's statement does not disguise, however, the confusion of the hour, nor the chaos that understandably occurred when the torpedoes struck home. War is a human activity characterised by organised confusion, as anyone who has been on a field of battle will confirm.

This being so, it is inevitable that accounts of the same events often vary, depending upon the powers of recall of the principal players, or upon their vantage points. The account given by *U859*'s only survivor, Horst Klatt, differs from that of Joseph Ellerwald in tone and emphasis, while recording substantially the same facts:

August the 28th 1944 was the 147th day of our patrol. We had submerged for over twenty-four hours and our batteries were all but exhausted. Consequently, as twilight fell, we began to make ready for surfacing. Jan Jebsen gave the order for the submarine to sail at periscope level, so that we could check that it was safe to go to the surface. The seas were clear of enemy craft, the visibility was good, although there was a strong sea running under a full moon. A Petty Officer took our position and with that done our four diesel engines of more than 3,200 horsepower each were started and we accelerated through the waves at 15 knots, an exercise which recharged all our four batteries simultaneously. This also served to ventilate the U-boat, a necessity after having cruised for so many hours beneath the waves. In the conning tower, six young ratings were on look-out, scanning the horizon with night binoculars for enemy ships and aircraft. Each rating had orders constantly to sweep a 60-degree range and to keep a special watch for mast-tops, smoke stacks or superstructures and, of course, for any approaching planes.

When our surface exercises had been completed, we pitched U859 *in an easterly direction, along the fifteenth northern latitude. Shortly before 8 p.m., the port look-out sighted mast-tops and stacks of a ship without any visible escort. The vessel appeared to be sailing in conditions of total black-out and at high speed, an estimated 12–13 knots. Upon receiving this information, Korvettenkapitan Jebsen ordered the whole crew to action stations. The look-out reported that he was occasionally losing sight of the vessel, due to its abrupt and frequent changes in course. In* U859*'s Central Station we registered this erratic behaviour on our charts in an attempt to see if there was a consistency to the swiftly changing course, which was quickly established by the submarine's First Officer. At 8.30 p.m. Jebsen gave the order to the engine room for maximum speed, so that we could secure an optimum firing position, in effect to be in front of the target, after having submerged, with the four torpedo doors open at the bow, and we would then wait at periscope level for the ship to make its approach towards us until it was at the best firing position.*

At 9.30 p.m. the Korvettenkapitan gave the order 'alarm diving' and the crew went to their respective 'torpedo attack' positions. Within minutes U859*'s sound-detector operator told Jebsen that the target was continuing a steady approach towards us and now without changing its course or its speed. And then at 10 p.m., with the ship continuing its approach towards us, at an estimated speed of 12 knots and at about 850 metres distance, Jebsen gave the order for three torpedo tubes to be made ready for a 'fan-shaped' shot from a depth of about 4 metres. He had earlier told his officers that he estimated the target to be a merchant ship of about 8,000 tons displacement, with a single stack amidships, a surrounding superstructure and heavy guns mounted at both the prow and the stern. Seconds later he gave the firing order – 'Torpedo No. 1, No. 2, No. 3, go!'*

We waited in silence, Jebsen at the periscope, for the fifty-five seconds of the torpedoes' running time to pass. Immediately following there was an explosion and Jebsen reported that one of the three torpedoes had struck the target, amidships, on the starboard side. The ship stopped at once, its engines cut dead. U859*'s wireless operator reported that the target was not transmitting any SOS signal on its international emergency frequency, although Jebsen, still at the periscope, observed that while the target was not showing any signs of sinking, its crew were already abandoning ship,* *taking to both the lifeboats and the rafts. Jebsen was anxious to surface, but with the surrounding sea well illuminated by a bright moon and the target well armed, he decided to wait, a delay that would also give the crew time to make good their escape from the ship before we fired another torpedo.*

At 10.20 p.m., with the crew having continued to abandon their ship, Jebsen decided that it was safe enough for U859 *to surface. He gave the order that sent us slowly up out of the waters of the Arabian Sea and into bright moonlight. We were about 500 metres from the ship, which was still not showing any signs of sinking, so Jebsen gave an order for torpedo tube No. 5, at the submarine's stern, to be made ready for firing. It was at this point that our wireless operator reported that he was picking up a weak SOS distress call, which he thought was probably being transmitted from one of the lifeboats. The Korvettenkapitan waited a little while longer to be as sure as he possibly could that all the crew were well away from the ship and then, at 10.30, he gave the order for the firing of No. 5 torpedo. It hit the target, as had the first, squarely amidships, but this time on the port side. Within minutes the target started its long descent to the seabed, sinking slowly beneath the waves in a slightly sloping condition over the stern.*

Realising that the end was near, Jan Jebsen invited his officer corps to leave the Central Station in the submarine, its operations room, and join him in the conning tower in order to witness the last moments of the now rapidly sinking ship at the position later recorded in the submarine's log as 15° 10′ N, 55° 18′ E. So, in the company of my Korvettenkapitan and four of my brother officers, I witnessed the last moments of the American liberty ship that the world now knows was the SS John Barry, *as, under a summer moon, its bulkhead disappeared from sight in an eruption of bubbles and it commenced its final voyage towards a dark and deep grave in the Arabian Sea.*

It is strange that Horst Klatt should remember the night sea as being illuminated by moonlight, so much so that Jan Jebsen was initially reluctant to order his submarine to the surface for fear that the heavy guns on the liberty ship's prow and stern would open fire, when Master Joseph Ellerwald recalls visibility being poor. As we shall see, Ellerwald's view was not shared by members of his crew when they gave their own version of events to American officials in Aden and Khorramshahr.

Joseph Ellerwald died in November 1975, having never spoken publicly about the nature of the cargo in the holds of the *John Barry*, although he was well aware of the speculation surrounding it. In a garrulous age, the confidentiality in respect of information gleaned in the service of his country, which Joseph Ellerwald exercised to the end of his days, has to be respected. Nonetheless, statements sworn by other survivors of the liberty ship differ in a number of points from those given by her Master.

As Ellerwald's statement says, he and twenty-eight other survivors of the attack were picked up by the SS *Benjamin Bourn* – which, incidentally, was a sister liberty ship of the *John Barry* – and taken to the northern Gulf port of Khorramshahr, on the eastern side of the Shati al Arab waterway in Iran. They arrived there on 5 September. Exactly a month later, on October 1944, Lieutenant Barbara Conrad, a staff member in the Washington-based office of the Chief of Naval Operations, completed a 'summary of statements' taken from the survivors by a US official from the American Legation in Basra, in neighbouring Iraq, who had travelled to Khorramshahr to conduct interviews with Ellerwald and his men. The Lieutenant records the collected memories of the survivors in terms a touch more illuminating then those of the *John Barry*'s Master.

Ship was on base course 72; had been zigzagging continuously since leaving Aden and was swinging from port to starboard leg of pattern; wheel was just put over to change course from 17 to 64; course at time of explosion 44; speed 12 knots; blacked out; 'radio silence'; seven look-outs – two forward, three amidships, two aft. The weather was clear with a low haze; sea rough; wind WSW Force 6; bright moonlight; visibility good. No other ships in sight.

At 22.00 hours torpedo struck ship starboard side in the bulkhead between Number 2 and Number 3 hatch. One crew member on watch thought he saw a deep torpedo track several hundred yards distance at 55° angle just before ship was struck. Extent of damage undetermined owing to presence of deck cargo. There was no fire, but immediately after torpedo struck, the entire forward section of the ship was immersed with water. Flooding was through the hatches – only one was battened down. Engines were secured within ten minutes. One group of survivors stated that at 22.15 a second torpedo struck ship; other survivors make no mention of this. At 22.45, after ship had been abandoned, a torpedo struck port side amidships and ship broke in half and sank. Distress signal sent seven times, no reply received. No time for counter-offensive. Master's confidential codes thrown overboard in weighted canvas bag, radio codes sank with the ship in overboard box in the radio room.

Third Mate turned in general alarm and crew almost immediately took to lifeboats and rafts. Number 1 lifeboat had been blown away by explosion; Number 2, Number 3 and Number 4 were loaded and in the water by 22.15, at which time the 'Abandon Ship' whistle was sounded. Number 2 lifeboat swamped, throwing its crew into the water. The last boat was away from the ship at 22.25. The Chief Engineer and Radio Operator, the last to leave the ship, jumped over the side at 22.30 and were picked up by Number 2 lifeboat. Approximately 22.15, 28 August, thirty-one survivors were picked up by the SS Sunetta *and landed at Aden. At 10.00, 29th August, thirty-five survivors in two lifeboats were picked up by the SS* Benjamin Bourn *and landed at Khorramshahr, Iran, 5 September. Total ship's complement sixty-eight, including forty-one merchant crew and twenty-seven armed guard. There are sixty-six survivors – two merchant crews missing, presumed lost.*

The attacking sub was not sighted.

Interviewing officer at Basra, Iraq, stated that whilst the Master described the crew as behaving in an orderly manner, this statement is doubtful since the ship was quickly abandoned without orders and while there was reason to think it was not in a sinking position. Ship was then left an easy target for the second torpedo.

While this version of events is not substantially at variance with that recorded later by Master Ellerwald in New York nor that remembered by Oberleutnant Klatt, there are several curious discrepancies in the reports. The question which most urgently demands an answer, however, is why no record exists of an official statement taken in Khorramshahr from Ellerwald himself as Master of the stricken vessel. We know that he was among the survivors landed there by the *Benjamin Bourn*. If an official statement was taken from him at the time, it must have been removed from the documents deposited in Washington's archives that chronicle the sinking of the *John Barry*. Why should this be? After all, documents of far greater sensitivity concerning the Second World War have been released for public scrutiny.

The only rational explanation is that Joseph Ellerwald, as Master of the *John Barry*, was a principal player in an exercise that the government of the United States regarded as politically sensitive. It was certainly too delicate for any detailed statement taken from Ellerwald which would have contained information on the 'special' nature of his vessel's cargo, to be seen, either then or now, by those not immediately involved.

Then there is the curious decision by Joseph Ellerwald to make his own sworn statement before a Notary Public, at his own effort and expense, two days after his return to New York from the Gulf. This could have been an attempt to counter the implied criticism of his command contained in the Conrad summary; in any event, the statement was subsequently made available to the authorities, who placed it in the archives. The statement is significant, of course, in what it does *not* record, which is presumably why it has been allowed to see the light of day. While, as we shall see, later official statements contained reference to silver bullion in the holds of the *John Barry*, Ellerwald says nothing of this, merely observing that his cargo consisted of '8,233 tons of general'. There is a school of thought which suggests he may have been unaware of exactly what his ship was carrying, but that seems highly improbable, particularly as, as we have read in the Conrad summary, 'the Master's confidential codes [were] thrown overboard in [a] weighted canvas bag'. These codes would have carried details of a cargo amongst which was silver bullion, together with arrangements for its discharge at its port of destination.

It is also relevant that when Ellerwald's New York statement was declassified – after his death in 1975 – his residential address, which appeared at the top of the statement, had been deleted by the declassification authorities, which strongly suggests that, post war, he was no longer living at 1344 Camp Street, New Orleans, the address given on the official crew list of the *John Barry*, and that Washington did not want any unauthorised contact to be made with him. Another curious anomaly is that Ellerwald himself makes no reference to his confidential codes being thrown overboard in a weighted canvas bag, an astonishing omission if taken at face value, given that it would have been a crucial measure for him to adopt to prevent the possibility of the codes falling into enemy hands. It is almost as if, in his statement, he was seeking to distract attention from the fact that the *John Barry* had been on a 'special' mission.

Yet another discrepancy is that while all the reports taken from other survivors and from Oberleutnant Klatt clearly state that at the time of the sinking there was 'bright moonlight', with consequent good visibility, Ellerwald stated under oath that visibility was 'poor'. Why he should have made this apparently false assertion is unclear, unless it was an attempt to protect the men of his command from the officially implied criticism that they panicked following *U859*'s attack, something they would have been more likely to do in poor visibility.

Even less easy to explain away is that part of Ellerwald's statement in which he confirmed that his crew numbered forty-three men excluding himself (the Naval Armed Guard were, of course, commanded by their own ensign). Yet the US Coastguard count identified forty-one crew members, as does the Conrad summary and a report written by a US Naval Observer in Aden. It is virtually inconceivable that Ellerwald would have made an error in such an important statement as to the exact number of men aboard his ship for whom he had direct responsibility. For not only did he remove any possibility of doubt as to the number of men on board when the *John Barry* finally sailed from Norfolk, Virginia, by stipulating that 'there were no changes in our crew from the time we left Philadelphia', but in an exercise obviously designed to verify his version of events, he had his statement authenticated, under oath, by his Chief Engineer, William Watler. Indeed, the only conclusion that can be drawn from this is that when the *John Barry* sailed from Philadelphia there were indeed two more 'crew' members on board than appeared in the Coastguard's headcount – two individuals whom Washington presumably did not wish to be recorded or identified.

That there should have been two people on board who could not be officially listed is not, in itself, very remarkable. During times of peace and of conflict state personnel are routinely transported from one place to another in secret. But in the case of the *John Barry*, what exactly was their function? What made their presence necessary? Where were they going and what were their intended duties upon arrival? And, at the very heart of the matter, why did their presence on board have to be concealed? In the light of the vessel having assumed, over the years, the status of 'one of the most controversial treasure-ships of all time', it is unlikely that these two unnamed people had nothing to do with her cargo; the mystery which has grown up around the *John Barry* is based solely on speculation as to what that cargo was and where it was going. Indeed, this internationally based speculation was initially generated by America's apparently disproportionate fury at the sinking of the *John Barry*, the wave of accusation and counter-accusation which arose as a result of her loss. This hostility may well have prompted Ellerwald to take the unusual step of preparing his own, independent statement – particularly when it is borne in mind that implicit in all official statements is criticism of his command.

Although any statement made by Ellerwald in Khorramshahr immediately after he arrived there has long since disappeared from the archives, his sworn statement before a notary public is not the only first-hand report from the Master to survive. Six months later, on 23 March 1944, he made a statement to the officials of the US Coastguard. This handwritten document differs in one intriguing particular from Ellerwald's previous evidence: in response to the question 'Cargo on board – Nature' he has written 'General + $26,000,000 in silver bullion'.

This clear indication from the pen of Joseph Ellerwald of the existence of bullion, 'non-ferrous metals' or however one chooses to describe what can now legitimately be regarded as concealed cargo in the holds of the *John Barry* is without doubt the most crucial piece of evidence yet to surface in the case.

However, it is only when the US Naval Observer's report, written at Aden on 7 September 1944 and based on an 'Interrogation of

Survivors' – those who arrived aboard the *Sunetta* on 2 September – is taken into account, that many of the most persistent questions regarding the *John Barry* begin to be answered. The opening remarks of the Aden report are little short of sensational. Following a brief introductory paragraph that recites the liberty ship's pedigree, the report continues:

The facts surrounding the sinking are as follows. The ship put out of Aden on 26 August 1944 bound for Abadan. She was carrying a general cargo, including $26,000,000 worth of silver.

These three short, astonishing sentences strike down long-held theories on the *John Barry* with as much force as the German torpedoes slammed into her sides half a century ago. For this was the first official document to disclose that silver bullion had been loaded into her holds in either New York, Philadelphia or Norfolk, Virginia, and, of crucial significance, that one of her ports of destination was Abadan, Iran, at the northern end of the Gulf. For Abadan was one of the ports regularly used to offload American supplies which would then be forwarded by road or rail to the USSR.

The Naval Intelligence report continues:

Under its routing instructions it proceeded singly on a zigzag course to 57° 30'E, thence to GAC, thence to PGW. These last two points are code points under British routing instructions. The night of 28 August was clear. The sea was running heavy swells. There was a south-westerly wind of 56 force and three-quarters moon. Visibility was good. The track of the first torpedo, which struck the ship a few degrees forward of the starboard beam, was seen, but at such a distance as to preclude any evasive action on the part of the ship. This was at 21.55. The second torpedo came fifteen minutes later, at which time the ship was abandoned and the crew, using life-lines over the sides, took to their life rafts. The bow of the ship at this time was under water. Approximately thirty minutes after the first torpedo struck, a third torpedo hit the Barry, *at which impact the ship is thought to have broken in half and is known to have sunk.*

The thirty-one survivors were brought into this port aboard the SS

Sunetta, *a Dutch merchantman, owned by La Corona, the Anglo-Saxon Petroleum Company Limited, St Helen's Port, Great St Helen's, London EC3, whose Master is A.W. Mayboom. All the survivors saw the* John Barry *sink and know that she was not boarded by the enemy. Further, they all feel that any confidential papers and codes which were aboard the* Barry *went down with her. The Armed Guard Officer, who was not among this group of survivors, was seen by four or five of these men with a steel box in which he kept his confidential papers and is thought by them to have thrown the box over the side. The coxswain of the Armed Guard crew was the senior rating brought into this port and the Assistant First Engineer and Purser and Chief Steward were the only officers in the merchant crew amongst this group.*

While it could be said, dismissively, that the survivors' comments on the presence of the silver bullion, upon which the Aden report was based, were born of nothing more than shipboard rumour, it would be far less easy to dismiss the men's belief that one of their ports of call was to be Abadan. Furthermore, it is not without relevance that at no point in the text does the American Naval Observer who wrote it use standard, official terminology to describe an unproven fact, such as 'The crew alleged that the holds of the vessel contained $26,000,000 worth of silver.'

In any event, it is an assertion that appears more than once in official American documents. Indeed, in the spring of 1995, as this book was being written, proof of a particularly incontrovertible kind came to the hand of its author in the form of an American Naval Intelligence report, filed in Aden on 3 September 1944, four days before the report based on the interrogation of the survivors. Titled 'Enemy Attack on Merchant Ships', the report carries in brief, official terms details of the *John Barry*; it goes on to confirm that she was indeed sailing for Abadan when she was sunk and that she was carrying 'general cargo $26,000,000 in silver'.

Nor is that all. Two secret reports from British Naval Attachés in Aden and Khorramshahr written in September 1944, based on their own independent intelligence sources, throw yet more light on the *John Barry*'s cargo and her ports of destination. On 5

September 1944, Lieutenant Commander John Oldney, a Royal Naval Intelligence Officer, based in Khorramshahr, wrote in an official report to London that the liberty ship's cargo consisted of 'mixed aid to Russia and oil refinery materials for ARAMCO', the Arabian American Oil Company, which had begun operations in the Saudi Kingdom in the 1930s. ARAMCO's lines of supply from home during the Second World War were principally through the Saudi port of Ras Tanurah, where the silver coins abroad the *John Barry* were to have been offloaded.

On the actual sinking of the vessel, Oldney reported:

Immediately the ship was struck the engines were stopped and the crew proceeded to abandon ship, apparently without any direct order. The ship stopped, but continued to swing to starboard and thus presented a sitting target. All available boats and rafts were clear by 23.30. The survivors saw the second torpedo strike the port side at about 22.45. The Master was in his cabin at the time of the attack. The door jammed and he had to break out, thus not being on deck for some minutes.

This British version of events is in sympathy with the American summary by Lieutenant Conrad containing an implied criticism of the Master and crew and recording that one torpedo from *U859* struck the port side of the vessel, while the other hit the starboard side. Ellerwald maintained, both in his New York statement and in one he made on 23 March 1945 to officials from the US Coastguard, that both strikes were on the starboard side. Oldney's only departure from previous versions of the sequence of events is his assertion about Ellerwald being in his cabin at the time of the attack and not appearing on deck 'for some minutes'. Ellerwald's sworn statement, of course, contradicts this: 'When the first torpedo hit us, I was in my office and the concussion threw me from the chair. I immediately went out on the bridge.'

In a second British secret intelligence report, filed to the British Admiralty in London on 4 September 1944, Lieutenant Commander Woods of the Royal New Zealand Naval Reserve, who was based in Aden, makes two important contributions. He records that the *John*

Barry was struck by three torpedoes, the first and second hitting the starboard side of the vessel, the third port side: '1st hit scored starboard side, No. 3 hold. 2nd hit scored starboard side, Fuel tank. 3rd hit scored port side, Engine room.' But as we have already seen, Ellerwald stated that his ship received only two hits, both to starboard, while both the Conrad summary and the Aden report written by the US Naval Observer make inconclusive judgements as to whether or not the second torpedo hit the ship and, if it did, which side it struck. Oberleutnant Klatt recalls three torpedoes being fired from *U859* but only two striking the *John Barry*, the first starboard, the second port side.

The sources upon which Lieutenant Commander Woods based his report are not given, but the preciseness with which he compiled it suggests they were authoritative. Just one example serves to support this assumption – Abadan being one of the *John Barry*'s destinations. The Woods report is the only British-inspired document which carries the name of the Iranian port and which records that the vessel was carrying 'General cargo, including $26,000,000 in silver. Government (Lease Lend)'.

News of the loss of the liberty ship which, it should not be forgotten, was also carrying the three million silver Saudi riyal coins minted in Philadelphia and destined for King Abdul Aziz ibn Saud's Treasury, was received by American officials with predictable dismay. On 27 July 1944, three days after the *John Barry* had sailed out of Norfolk, Virginia, Livingston Short, the Acting Director of the American Middle East Economic Mission in Cairo, wrote to 'the Honourable James Moose, American Minister, American Legation, Jeddah, Saudi Arabia'. The letter, whilst classified 'Secret', is in marked contrast to other official correspondence and documentation on the ship's cargo, being precise, detailed and without ambiguity of any kind.

Short begins by agreeing with Moose's earlier suggestion that delivery of the silver riyals to the government of Saudi Arabia should be undertaken by the new American Consul, Parker Hart, in Dhahran, on the Kingdom's eastern shores, close to Ras Tanurah. Following a request that Moose make sure Hart obtain 'a formal receipt from Saudia Arabian officials' for the coins, Short continues:

The Foreign Economic Administration have telegraphed that the riyals were shipped in mid-July on the SS John Barry *from Philadelphia, with Ras Tanurah as the port of discharge. The material is stowed in hold No. 2 and is contained in 750 boxes, numbered 1 to 750, and consists of a total of three million riyals. The boxes are marked 'AB,SZ505(AB)DA-TPS62922' and the word Dhahran is stencilled on the bottom of each one. FEA will telegraph further details as to the time of arrival.*

The silver coins were destined for Abdul Aziz's Treasury under lend-lease. Washington knew that Saudi Arabia would assume a special significance in its post-war political and economic strategy and, as the letter from Short to Moose suggests, there was little or no confidentiality about America having Saudi Arabia on its lend-lease books. Indeed, in President Roosevelt's 'Sixteenth Report to Congress on Lend-Lease Operations', read in both the Senate and the House of Representatives on 23 August 1944 and covering the programme up to 30 June of that year, Saudi Arabia featured openly as a lend-lease client.

So another question arises. While no one would deny that for reasons of security in time of war the movements of a state-sponsored supply vessel might have to be kept secret, what made it essential, even in inter-governmental communications and correspondence, for one part of her cargo to be regarded as so secret that it was surrounded by a web of intrigue, while another part of it was treated as an 'open' secret, as the Short/Moose correspondence about the coins proves?

News of the *John Barry*'s sinking set Parker Hart, the recently installed American Consul in Dhahran, into a fury of activity. In a secret airgram to the Secretary of State in Washington on 3 September he wrote:

This currency shipped on the SS John Barry, *which cleared Suez for Ras Tanurah August 20th 1944 and sank off the southern Arabian coast near the end of that month. The Department may already have seen details from the Consulate at Aden concerning the sinking of the vessel, which was reported to me today by the Commanding Officer of the British Naval Forces on the Bahrain Islands. Apparently the* Barry *went down off the coast of the Hadhramaut or Aden near the end of the month. Thirty-one survivors, picked up by another ship from one lifeboat, were landed at Aden September 1st 1944. As this is the exact quota for ordinary lifeboats of liberty ships, it is hoped that there may be other survivors.*

Parker Hart then launched abruptly into an attack on the British for what he obviously believed was their failure to protect the liberty ship:

This is just another instance, so frequently reported here, of the complete lack of protection by the British Naval Forces given to any and all Allied vessels proceeding from Suez to the Persian Gulf. The Commanding Officer above mentioned admitted that no regular protection is given, but the patrols are usually sent out only after the presence of a submarine in these waters has been reported. The SS Sidney Sherman, *another liberty ship which recently arrived at Ras Tanurah, also reported insufficient and utterly incompetent British escort from Bizerte to Egypt. It underwent a bombing attack during this passage but suffered no known damage.*

Two days earlier, on 1 September, Hart had received instructions from the US Legation in Jeddah advising him that the authorised representative of the Saudi government who would sign the receipt for the coins in Ras Tanurah was one Sayid Sami Huthi and that he had been given the task by one of the King's confidants, Sheikh Abdulla Suleiman. Consequently, on 2 September, Hart sent a 'Personal and Confidential' telegram to Colonel William Eddy, who had replaced Moose as the resident American Minister in Jeddah:

SS John Barry *with three million riyals for Ras Tanurah lost off South Arabian coast. Thirty-one survivors landed Aden September 1st. As Sheikh Abdulla Suleiman had requested that one million of these riyals be furnished to Saudi government, Lebkicher suggests you inform him of disaster. Thereafter, if desired, I can inform Sayid Sami here. British Naval Authorities anxious matter by kept as secret as possible for security reasons.*

There are three curious aspects to this telegram, the first being that, although it was addressed to the American Minister of State, it was routed through the Jeddah offices of ARAMCO. The second is that the telegram clearly suggests that only one third of the silver coins, one million riyals, were to be handed over to the Saudi authorities, while previous official documentation states that the full consignment, three million, was destined for King Abdul Aziz's Treasury. It is now believed, however, that ARAMCO itself was to receive the remaining two million coins, further evidence of how inextricably linked the company's affairs in the Kingdom had become with those of the US government. The third and final curiosity is the identity of 'Lebkicher'. Contemporary sources in Washington now suggest that it was almost certainly a coded nom-de-plume, although why this should have been deemed necessary in a communication that clearly named both Eddy and Hart is not immediately obvious. Hart's comment on British sensitivity over the destruction of the *John Barry*, and their wish for secrecy, is less mysterious: London was by now well aware of Washington's dismay over the liberty ship's loss and of the blame which the Americans were attaching to the British for its sinking.

In fact, as recently declassified British Admiralty U-boat Operations charts show, London had been aware of the existence of *U859* since 27 May 1944, when she crossed the Equator. The British had tracked the U-boat's movements through the South Atlantic for over a week, sending the Catalina to attack her as soon as she was within range of their shore base in South Africa. It is true, of course, that they subsequently lost track of her, although the charts show that she was known to be in the Arabian Sea or the Indian Ocean; it was presumably this temporary 'loss' which prompted the Bahrain-based commanding officer of British Naval Forces operating in the region to ask Hart to keep the whole affair 'as secret as possible'. The British got their revenge less than a month after the sinking of the *John Barry*, when, on 23 September, in the Straits of Malacca, HMS *Trenchant*, a T class submarine, destroyed *U859*. This did not, however, stop the Anglo-American row from rumbling on.

The British were unaware of the consignment of silver riyals destined for the Saudis, as the secret reports from their naval attachés in both Aden and Khorramshahr show. When they later learned of the coins' existence, they believed them to be a gift to the Saudi monarch from the government in Washington ever anxious to obtain yet further oil concessions in the Kingdom and, in the process, undermine British authority in the Gulf. In this, London was quite mistaken. Contemporary (1944) records in Washington show that at the end of the war, King Abdul Aziz's government would have been expected to reimburse the United States for the silver contained in the coins on an 'ounce for ounce' basis. However, President Roosevelt was known to be hostile to Britain's imperial inclinations, which he regarded as a threat to Washington's long-term view of the post-war world – he was on record as saying that the British could not use Washington's lend-lease arrangements with London to strengthen their hold on Empire once the war was over. Bluntly put, Roosevelt believed that the British Empire's time had passed, an opinion which became a cornerstone of American foreign policy in the post-war years, long after President Roosevelt had died.

The British in Arabia in August 1944 were, then, very much on the diplomatic and political defensive as they saw the power of the New World challenging the imperial prerogatives of the Old and the possibility of a 'new order' on the Arabian Peninsula coming ever closer. This situation led to increasing rivalry between the British and American resident Ministers in Jeddah. Indeed, one of James Moose's last acts as Washington's representative was to protest so strongly to his government about his counterpart, British Minister Stanley Jordan, and his 'anti-American activities' in the Kingdom, that Washington sent an official note of objection to London with the demand that Jordan's actions be curtailed.

The Foreign Office remained unruffled, adopting in an internal memorandum the air of a parent dealing with an over-enthusiastic child:

American impulsiveness and inexperience with the Arabs may sometimes lead them to act injudiciously, but we must endeavour to persuade and guide them on the right lines and be patient with their many mistakes.

Jordan himself was more direct on the subject of Washington's lavish gifts to Abdul Aziz (these ranged from a wheelchair to a DC-3 aircraft) and reported to London, 'The Americans wish to sink millions of dollars in the desert sands of Saudi Arabia because they will be taking billions out of the same sands in the form of oil.'

It was in this petulant diplomatic and political atmosphere that Anglo-American recriminations increased as a direct result of *U859*'s sinking of the *John Barry*. Diplomats representing both London and Washington sought to undermine each other's Arabian ambitions and, in the American case, used the loss of the liberty ship as further ammunition in the campaign.

German IXD2 class U-boat, the class to which *U859* belonged.

Oberleutnant Horst Klatt, First Engineer of *U859* and the only officer to survive its sinking.

Oberleutnant Klatt (circled) and fellow officers and men of *U859*.

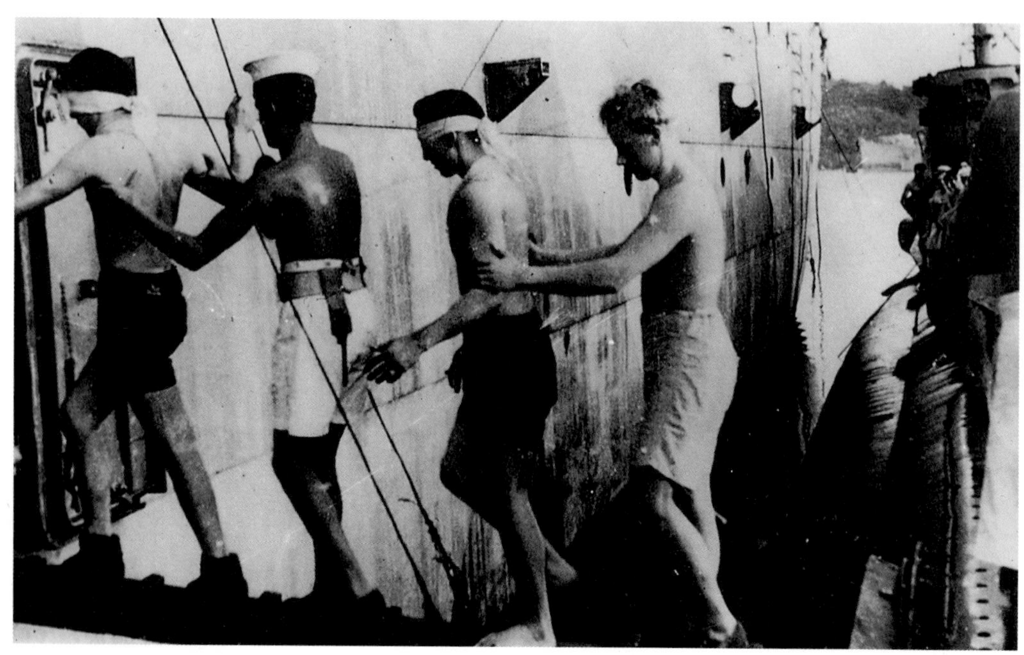

Survivors of *U859* being transferred from *HMS Trenchant* to the depot ship *Adamant*, at Trincomalee, Ceylon.

His Highness Sheikh Ahmed Farid al Aulaqi, Prince of the Yemen (foreground), with kinsmen, June 1994.

Left, and below, second from left: Sheikh Ahmed waits on the dockside at Salalah for the arrival of the *Flex LD* on 20 October 1994. He was accompanied by (from left) Jay Fiondella, his brother-in-law, Adel al Bakry, and Brian Shoemaker.

The *Flex LD* in dock in Salalah.

The cartoon of Sheikh Ahmed that appeared in *Asharq Al Awsat* depicting him as a modern-day pirate.

Brian Shoemaker beside the moon pool aboard the *Flex LD*.

Jay Fiondella with the 'grab', aboard the *Flex LD*.

Horst Klatt at the dockside in Dubai.

From left: Brian Shoemaker, Jay Fiondella and Robert Hudson.

Jean Roux, mastermind of the exploration of the wreck of the *Titanic* and a director of the French International Maritime Institute, aboard the *Flex* LD.

Aboard the *Flex LD* showing the adapted drilling rig above the moon pool.

Above and right: The 'grab' emerges from the moon pool.

Above and right: The 'grab' fixed in position above the moon pool.

Overleaf: Work continued on the *Flex LD* night and day.

Below decks aboard the salvage ship.

Stores are transferred to the *Flex LD* from an Omani warship.

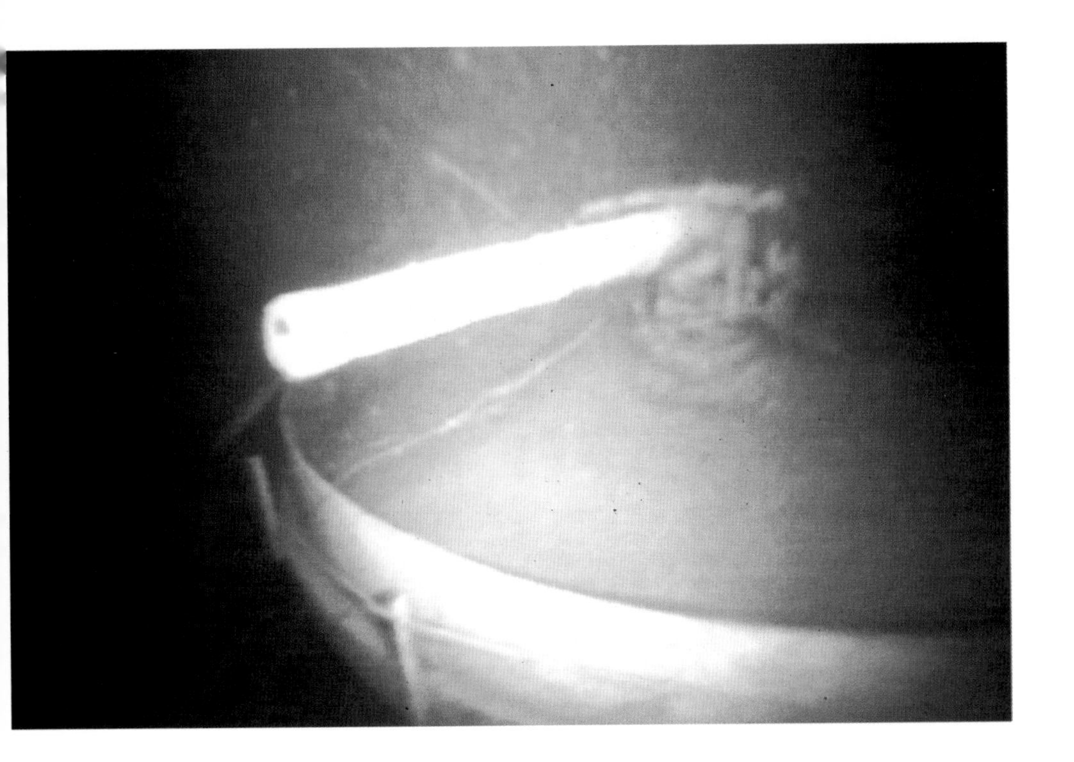

This page and overleaf: Some of the first pictures of the wreck of the *John Barry* transmitted by the remote-operated vehicle hired by the Ocean Group in March 1991.

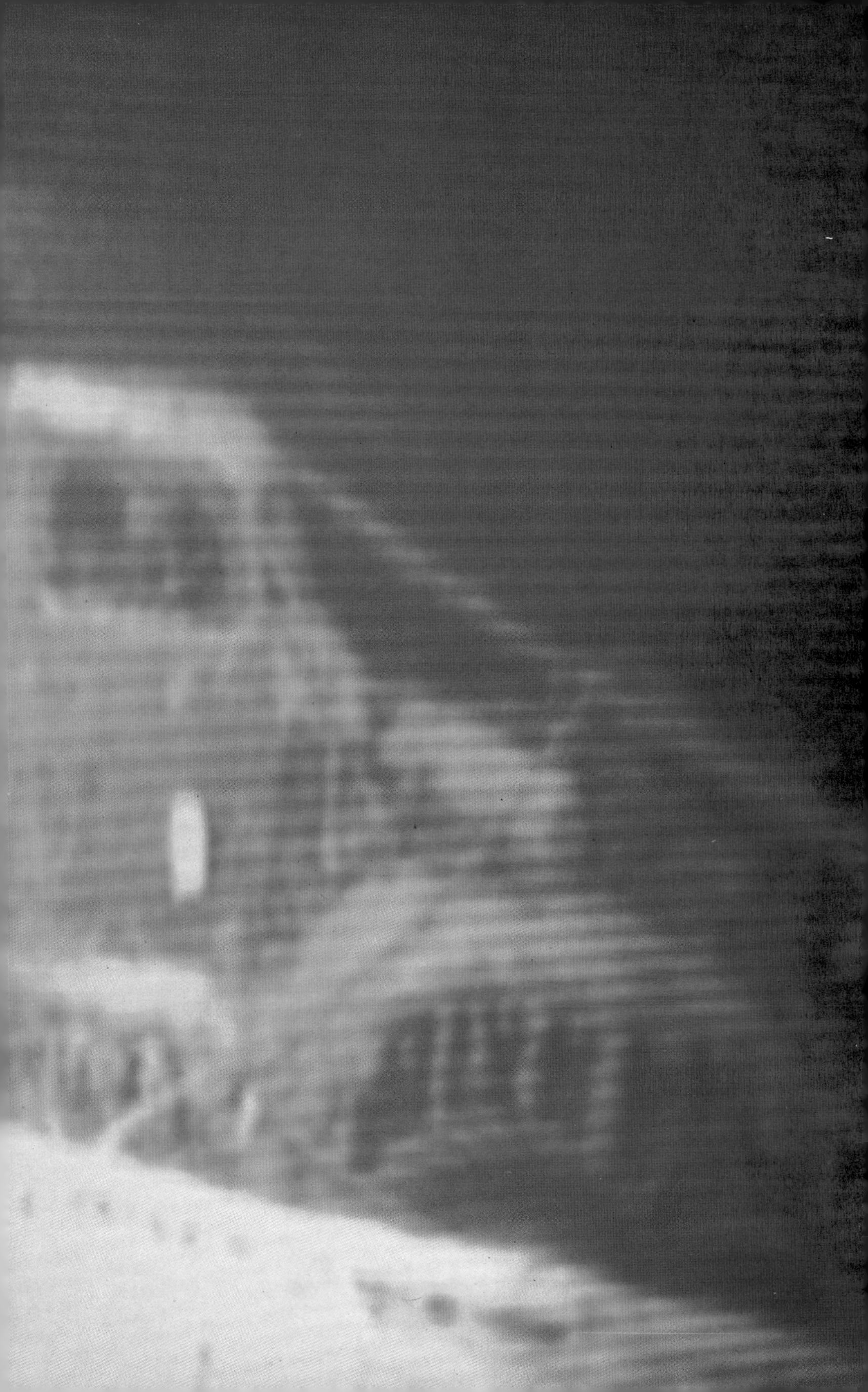

Scale model showing the two halves of the *John Barry* lying on the bed of the Arabian Sea.

One of the first glimpses of the silver riyals scooped up by the 'grab'.

Silver cascades from the 'grab'.

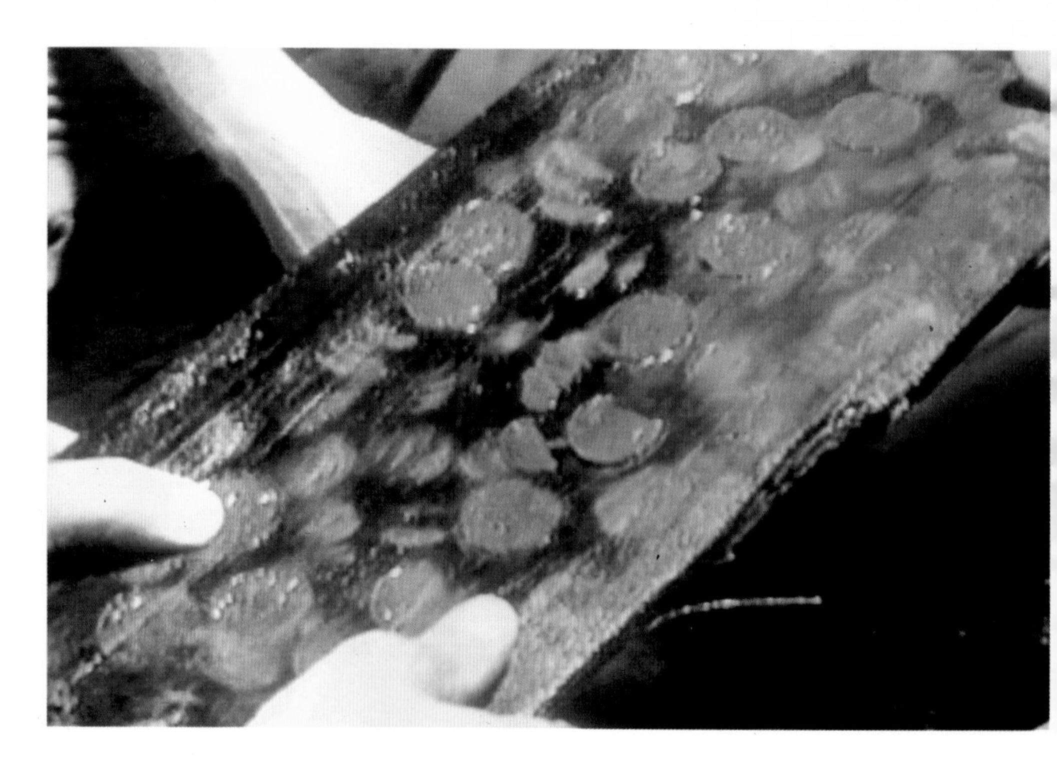

After fifty years it becomes clear how the silver coins were bagged and crated.

Sorting and boxing 1.4 million coins.

More than fifty years on: Horst Klatt at the press conference at Dubai on 27 November 1994.

Chapter Eight

In the Straits of Malacca

Korvettenkapitan Jan Jebsen wasted no time in compounding his victory over the liberty ship, which, naturally enough, raised the spirits of his men, if only temporarily. Just three days after the sinking of the *John Barry*, during the early hours of 1 September, *U859* fired three torpedoes into the sides of a Blue Funnel liner, all of which struck home with devastating effect. The MV *Troilus* was carrying a cargo of tea, copra and coconut oil, the latter consignment causing the ship, as Horst Klatt remembers, to 'burn furiously'. The *Troilus* had a crew of eighty-six, mostly Chinese, and eighteen passengers. Six of the crew lost their lives when the burning vessel sank in the Arabian Sea. The survivors took to the open waters in five lifeboats and, after five harrowing days, were rescued by Royal Navy frigates.

This event has a significant place in the story of the *John Barry*. As we have already seen, when the American Consul in Dhahran, Parker Hart, reported the sinking of the liberty ship to his Secretary of State in Washington on 3 September, he complained vigorously of 'a complete lack of protection' being given to American ships in the Arabian Sea and the Indian Ocean by 'British naval forces'. Yet those same British naval forces had been tracking *U859* since 27 May, and on 5 July had sent a Catalina aircraft to destroy her. It is true, of course, that the British navy temporarily lost track of the enemy U-boat, and, as we are about to see, made a decision that its vessels should not pursue her in what was assumed to be an easterly direction. But recently declassified reports demonstrate that other efforts to hunt down and destroy the submarine continued. Indeed, there is ample evidence to support Horst Klatt's belief (at the time) that the British were taking a special interest in *U859*.

The secret war diary of the 'Persian Gulf and Red Sea Naval Reports' for September 1944 establishes that on the first day of the month concern was mounting in British naval circles about the continuing failure to locate the U-boat. The entry for 1 September reads:

Force 65 in position 10° 11'N, 56° 16'E was moving to eastwards at 16 knots in an endeavour to cut off the U-boat located by D/F on 30th August. Force 65 in position 06° N, 52° 27'E was also closing the position and as her squadron were inexperienced in night deck landings, night cover by land-based aircraft was requested.

The diary then records the sinking of the liberty ships in a 'basic fact' form that ignores the high drama of the event:

Thirty-one survivors, including the Chief Engineer of SS John Barry, *arrived in Aden on SS* Sunetta *and it was learnt that the ship had been torpedoed on 29th August at 22.00 (ship's time) in 015° 10'N 055° 18'E. (A further thirty-five survivors including the Master were picked up by SS* Benjamin Bourn *and landed at Khorramshahr on 6 September.)*

The next day's entry provides yet more evidence of British attempts to locate the submarine:

September the 2nd. Wellington aircraft on patrol reported an ADV [Anti-submarine vector] contact at 22.15 in position 13° 21'N 56° 52'E.

The following day the tempo increased still further.

September the 3rd. Force 66 investigated the ASV contact from first light, until the escorts were withdrawn shortly before midnight (local time). Operational of Force 65 was taken over by Commander-in-Chief, Easter Fleet, who ordered Whelp *and* Wager *to join that Force.*

On 4 September the hunt was still in progress, but it was also on that day that evidence surfaced in the war diary that *U859* had struck again.

HMS Awe *reported sighting of a possible periscope at 05.30 in position 04° 49'N 65° 57'E. Force 66 reported at 16.00 hours that one of her aircraft had sighted a large oil patch, wreckage and a raft in position 014° 13'N 061° 2'E at 11.55. This position was taken as datum point for a search by Force 66 from daylight next day.*

And the next day's search does indeed record the rescue of the survivors from the *Troilus,* sunk by U859 five days before:

September 5th at 16.42 a Catalina aircraft sighted five lifeboats with survivors in position 16° 22'N, 62° 02'E. By 17.30 Force 66 was approaching the boats, which contained the Master and ninety-eight survivors (mostly Chinese) of MV Troilus, *sunk by a U-boat in estimated position 14° 00'N 60° 00'E at 22.30 on 31st August (six of the crew were missing).*

The *Troilus* had, in fact, been sunk during the early hours of 1 September, but the survivors were traumatised by the attack and the ordeal of having been on the open seas in lifeboats for five days, so the discrepancy in their report, in which they claim to have been attacked about three hours earlier than was the case, is understandable. On 6 September the diary continued:

As it was now fairly obvious that the U-boat had left the area and gone south-east, Force 66 turned towards Aden, searching west along the latitudes of 15°N from first light.

It would presumably have infuriated Parker Hart still further to read that Force 66 had turned westwards when it was 'fairly obvious that the U-boat had left the area and gone south-east'. However, the decision for Force 66 to abandon its hunt for the German submarine spoke more of just how stretched the British navy continued to be in the Gulf and the Indian Ocean even as late in the war as the summer of 1944, than, as Hart saw it, of its 'complete lack of protection' of Washington's warships. In any event, as the diary records, the presence of the U-boat in the area was not forgotten. For in its last reference to the craft we now know to have been *U859*, an entry confirms that the search did indeed continue:

September 14th. Wellington aircraft from Socotra commenced cross-over patrols at 01.30 on latitude 12°N between 57° and 59° 30′E, in response to a signal received from Commander-in-Chief, Eastern Fleet, at 01.30 on 13th reporting a German U-boat to have been D/Fd within 200 miles of 04°N, 50° 30′E at 20.40 on 12th September.

But *U859* sailed on, having evaded all attempts by the British navy to locate her in the waters of the Arabian Sea. While the crew had taken heart from their successes in sinking the *John Barry* and the *Troilus*, their health continued to deteriorate, with the inevitable result that the lifting of their morale was only temporary. Horst Klatt well remembers the sad state of his comrades at arms:

The men's failing heath had, of course, a negative effect on their mood and, consequently, their spirits. Conditions within the submarine became increasingly intolerable, which only added to the depressed state we were all in. Indeed, on 16 September, the day we received our orders from Berlin to proceed to Base Poula [Penang] it would not be an exaggeration to describe the crew as being at the end. 16 September also marked the 166th day of our patrol, during which we had covered 22,000 nautical miles, equivalent to some 40,744 kilometres, and had done so, for the greater part of the time, in extremely difficult conditions. So it is small wonder that we were all in. And of that distance, 18,000 of the 22,000 nautical miles had been covered when the submarine had been submerged.

U859 herself was also beginning now to show signs of strain. At one point during those early days of September her engines became so overheated that they had to be cooled by covering them with the crew's blankets, soaked in sea water, and, on the very day that the order was received to make for the Malacca Straits and Penang, Klatt, as First Engineer, discovered that one of the submarine's torpedoes had become stuck fast in its tube. But, as ever in wartime, orders are given to be complied with, and although her crew was now, in Horst Klatt's own words, 'in a terrible state', *U859* headed for 'Base Poula'.

It was during his routine work aboard the submarine that Oberleutnant Klatt made a surprising discovery:

By sheer coincidence I came to know that in place of the usual cast-iron weights in the keel of the submarine which were normally placed there as ballast, there were a large number of metal flasks containing mercury, which we had to hand over to the Japanese upon our arrival in Penang and which, apparently, they had urgent need of. I discovered what the flasks contained by the weight of the contents, 35 kilogrammes. Each flask had a 2.5 litre capacity and the specific weight of mercury equates to 14 kilogrammes per litre.

Although Klatt was astonished at his discovery, for the moment the mercury was not his principal concern as he went about the task of ensuring that the submarine, which was by now 'in bad need of repair', was as safe as he could make her for the final leg of her outward journey.

Five days after receiving the order to proceed to Base Poula, on 21 September 1944, *U859*'s 171st day at sea, Korvettenkapitan Jan Jebsen took his submarine to the surface and transmitted a radio message to Penang, reporting his position, which, Klatt recalls, was approximately 150 nautical miles, 227 kilometres, off the western tip of southern Sumatra. The order came back for Jebsen to make a rendezvous on the following day at the same time with *U861*, which would escort *U859* into Penang harbour.

German war records show that *U861* had arrived off Penang that very day, following a patrol that had, like *U859*'s, begun from Kiel in April. She was commanded by Korvettenkapitan Oesten, and was one of the very few U-boats to return safely to a German-occupied port from an Indian Ocean patrol, arriving at Trondheim in Norway exactly a year after having departed from her home base in the Fatherland. Korvettenkapitan Oesten had not only a safe return, but a most successful one as well. On 20 August; some 400 miles east-south-east of Durban, *U861* sank HMS *Berwickshire* (7,464 tons) and torpedoed, but failed to sink, the tanker *Daronia*. Then, on 5 September (the very day after the British navy Force 66 had turned westward, in *U861*'s direction) she sank the *Fafalios* (5,760 tons) off the island of Zanzibar.

Having received his order of rendezvous, Jebsen took *U859* back to the depths, surfacing the following day, the 22nd, and again making radio contact with Penang, only to be told that his appointment with *U861* had been postponed for twenty-four hours. The next day, the 23rd, he should surface at dawn, midway between the islands of Lanskavi and Botong, twenty miles north-west of Base Poula; he would then receive his final docking instructions.

At dawn on 23 September, *U859* rose up out of the milk-warm waters of the Indian Ocean. It was five months, two weeks and five days since she had set sail from Kiel. Korvettenkapitan Jan Jebsen, his five-man officer corps and sixty-three ratings had endured conditions of extreme cold and heat, had been subjected to a tropical storm and a ferocious airborne attack, during which one crew member had been killed and another seriously wounded. All the men aboard had suffered the most appalling privations, which had broken the health of many of them. Indeed, the men of *U859* had good cause to take pride in their achievement. They had just completed one of the longest and most dangerous voyages of any submarine in the German navy and had sunk some 30,000 tons of Allied shipping. It was, by fair measure of human skill and devotion to duty, no small feat.

Jan Jebsen gave the order that those ratings who were in a particularly poor way should be brought up to the conning tower, where they could get fresh air, see and feel the sun, and, on the horizon, see the mantle of greenery that cloaked the islands between which *U859* had surfaced. As a special treat, group of young men standing in the conning tower, staring out at a world which had for so long been lost to them, were permitted to smoke.

Young Lieutenant Lask, who had lain in his bunk drifting in and out of consciousness since the Catalina's attack on 5 July, was told that the journey would very soon be over; he laughed with relief and happiness as other ratings embraced him. But up in the conning tower, Jan Jebsen scanned the horizon and became increasingly apprehensive as the morning wore on without any sign of the escort he had been promised to provide cover on the surface run to Base Poula.

At 8 a.m., with an early morning fog advancing across the tropical waters, Jan Jebsen became visibly uneasy. He moved nervously about *U859*, testing his craft's instruments, only to discover that many were malfunctioning. At 10.20 a.m. he made radio contact once more with Penang and put in an urgent request for the promised air and sea escort into the harbour. The response was not encouraging. Anxiety and disappointment were clearly written on Jebsen's face as he turned from the radio and told his officers, 'Because of the deteriorating weather conditions, we have to try for the harbour on our own.' But that was not all. 'We have,' he continued, 'to increase our look-out strength from the conning tower. The Japanese believe there are British submarines in the area. I have been told that we are in imminent danger from the enemy. They say that they will expect us in three or four hours and wish us good luck.'

Oberleutnant Klatt remembers saying to himself, 'Well, I will keep my fingers crossed.' Bleak as the message from the Japanese had been, Jan Jebsen was left with little choice but to begin the sprint to Base Poula and safety, unescorted and, therefore, unprotected. The guard in the conning tower was strengthened and shortly afterwards, in increasingly confident spirits as the surface run continued without mishap, the crew tried on their khaki shorts, the 'second uniform' with which they had been issued in Kiel for use in the tropical conditions of the Far East. But as Klatt watched the crew's exuberance, his sense of unease increased to one of foreboding.

'We have come so far and we are so close to our destination, but we are not yet safe,' he recalls thinking as *U859* cut swiftly through the water, drawing ever closer to Swettenham Pier, Penang, and safety. Klatt was also haunted by other thoughts. Since the early days of August it had become apparent that the British navy was aware of *U859*'s presence and had taken measures to have her 'shadowed'. Klatt's anxiety had increased since his discovery of the secret flasks of mercury for the Japanese in *U859*'s keel, for if the Allies had, through intelligence sources, come to know of the consignment, then surely their efforts to prevent the U-boat reaching her destination would be all the greater. While they had managed to evade hostile attention, Horst Klatt was well aware that *U859*'s sinking of the *John Barry* and the *Troilus* would not only have added to Allied determination to destroy the offending submarine, but would have given details of her approximate location and direction.

Klatt's anxiety continued to dominate his thoughts when he was summoned to an officers' meeting in the Central Station, the submarine's Operations Room. The time was now 10.45.

At Swettenham Pier, the Japanese began to prepare for *U859*'s arrival, together with *U861*'s Korvettenkapitan Oesten, his crew and a small group of German naval engineers who were garrisoned there to undertake repairs and maintenance of the Third Reich's U-boats. Garlands of flowers had been prepared for *U859*'s crew and a Japanese naval brass band was tuning up. The atmosphere was one of excited anticipation, the flowers and the band, with its instruments shining in the tropical sun, giving the group of Germans and Japanese standing on the pier a carnival air.

Back on *U859*, Korvettenkapitan Jebsen was conducting a briefing of his small officer corps on the procedures to be followed upon arrival at Base Poula, identifying the many repairs that would need to be carried out on the craft and the arrangements that would have to be made for the care of the ill and exhausted men once they were ashore. Just as this briefing was drawing to a close, Oberleutnant Klatt asked to be excused and made his way to the bulkhead lavatory. Up on the conning tower, the double-strength look-out crew continued to scan the waters around the submarine and the skies above, watching anxiously for land to appear on the far horizon. *U859* was now approximately 20 nautical miles north-west of Penang, in the Straits of Malacca.

Beneath the royal blue waters of the Malacca Straits, HMS *Trenchant* moved ever closer to her quarry. A T, class submarine *Trenchant* had a displacement of over 1,500 tons, speeds of 9 knots when submerged and 15 knots when on the surface, an operational range of 10,000 miles and ten torpedo tubes. She was operating out of the port of Trincomalee, on Ceylon's eastern seaboard, and her complement of fifty-two ratings and officers was commanded by Arthur Hezlet, a graduate of the Royal Navy College at Dartmouth, in the west of England, who, at thirty years of age, represented a winning combination of youth and experience. For the past few hours, Commander Hezlet had shadowed *U859* as she made her way towards Penang. The German submarine's signals to the Japanese had all been detected by Huff-Duff. Indeed, Commander Hezlet had been in possession of *U859*'s anticipated time of arrival off Penang for a day and a half. And, as Oberleutnant Klatt had feared, the British had long been taking a particular interest in Germany's IXD2 submarines in the Indian Ocean.

HMS *Trenchant* closed in on *U859*. On the U-boat, the young look-outs failed to detect the approach of the enemy. They were exhausted and the submarine's once sophisticated locating device, which had been so instrumental in sending the *John Barry* to the bottom of the Arabian Sea, was now malfunctioning. At 300 yards distance, with his quarry now well within his sights, Commander Hezlet knew the time was right and fired a torpedo at *U859*. It struck the U-boat astern of its conning tower, smacking into its side at 15 knots, 14 feet below the water line.

At the moment of impact, Oberleutnant Klatt was on the point of leaving the lavatory.

There was a terrible bang. All the lights went out and an impenetrable darkness descended. U859 *made a noise which filled me with a dreadful terror as it broke, almost immediately, into two halves. There were explosions from within the submarine, which competed with the cries of the men. Water was pouring in and I had this terrible sensation of bursting pressure all around me. I was chest high in water, in total darkness, and all around me the desperate cries of men trapped and drowning assaulted my ears. All hell had been let loose. As the raging water crossed over my head I began to swim back down the corridor along which, only moments before, I had walked.*

U859's end came within seconds. One young rating, a radio operator, who was thrown high in the air when *U859* broke in two, saw half of the submarine disappear beneath the surface of the sea before he hit the water. Other survivors, seven of whom made an astonishing escape from the sunken bulkhead, swam to the surface and clung to wreckage. One of them was Horst Klatt.

Commander Hezlet made the immediate decision to bring his submarine to the surface and rescue as many of *U859*'s survivors as he could. Once there, his crew began the task of plucking the German sailors from the water. Only minutes into the exercise, however, Japanese vessels appeared on the horizon and, seconds before Hezlet gave an order for *Trenchant* to submerge as the enemy drew closer, a Japanese fighter plane appeared overhead. Consequently, of the nineteen survivors from *U859* seen in the water, Hezlet had time to rescue only eleven, including Horst Klatt. The young Oberleutnant was the only officer from the U-boat to survive the attack. The Japanese attacked *Trenchant* from both sea and air, but without success. They did, however, rescue the remaining eight survivors and took them to safety in Penang. As for *U859*, the two halves sank, taking Korvettenkapitan Jan Jebsen and forty-nine men of his command down to a depth of over 150 feet, where their remains and the remains of the submarine that took them so far from home bear witness to their valour in the face of so much adversity.

On board *Trenchant*, Klatt and his comrades were given food, water and fresh clothes as Commander Hezlet turned his craft westwards towards her base at Trincomalee. There, on 2 October, the survivors were put ashore to begin a period of captivity – first in Ceylon and later in a prisoner-of-war camp in Egypt – which was to last until 1948. Commander Hezlet returned to the enemy-infested waters of South-East Asia and to further success. Indeed, one of his operations sits with particular distinction in the annals of British naval triumphs of the Second World War. Using what was at the time the highly secret method of 'Chariot' attack – a torpedo-shaped underwater craft manned by two frogmen sitting astride it which set out on its mission of limpet mine destruction from a submarine – *Trenchant* sank two 5,000-ton Japanese warships anchored in the Siamese port of Phuket, today a celebrated tourist resort in Thailand.

It was as research for this book was nearing its end that the opportunity arose to hear Commander Hezlet's tale from his own lips. Now a retired Vice Admiral, he is living in a land that has only in recent times seen a peace of sorts. I met Vice Admiral Sir Arthur Hezlet, KBE, CB, DSO & Bar, DSC and holder of the US Legion of Merit, in Portrush, Ulster, on 1 May 1995; we drove to the Headland and sat in the car while he spoke of his experiences aboard HMS *Trenchant.*

When we attacked U859 *we were nearing the end of our second patrol of operations off the eastern seaboard of Africa and in the Indian Ocean.* Trenchant, *interestingly enough, sailed out of the Clyde within a week of* U859 *leaving its home port of Kiel, in April 1944. It was the longest of hauls, but since May of 1943 we had had the use of bases in the Azores. This made passage for German ships en route for the southern Atlantic and beyond difficult, if not impossible, so submarines became their only relatively safe means of passage. Britain had greatly feared that, with the fall of France in the summer of 1940, Spain's General Franco would seize Portugal and with it, of course, the Azores. I suppose it's all right to tell you this now, fifty-two years on, but we did, in fact, send two of our submarines to the Azores, in 1943, before London had reached formal agreement with Lisbon. I also believe that contingency plans existed to seize the islands, if Franco had acted.*

The signal that sent *Trenchant* Commander Arthur Hezlet in pursuit of Korvettenkapitan Jan Jebsen's *U859* was received on the evening of 21 September 1944, as the British submarine was off Sumatra:

We had surfaced just before seven in the evening, following a patrol south of the Brothers Islands. At 8.15 we received a signal from 'Senior Officer Submarines' ordering us to patrol off Penang's north channel. Within twenty minutes we had set our new course and were on our way. We went flat out, arriving at the position we had been ordered to patrol shortly after half-past two in the morning of the 23rd. The night was very dark. It was raining and there were heavy swells.

In reply to a question, Sir Arthur was able to confirm that intelligence methods, based on interceptions of *U859*'s radio signals, had enabled his Senior Officer Submarines to obtain information as to the precise location of the enemy submarine. The British had been able to 'break' *U859*'s coded radio signals and, consequently, keep track of her movements.

Submarine commanders weren't in possession of the exact means by which such crucial detail for each offensive was being obtained. We weren't, in fact, meant to know, in case we were subsequently captured by the enemy. But the methods represented a remarkable intelligence coup.

The Vice Admiral went on to reveal, however, that he did have with him aboard *Trenchant* intelligence documents on the IXD2-type submarine, one of which, of course, was *U859* – a clear indication of the special interest held by the British navy in these submarines. Orders had been given that as many of them as possible were to be destroyed, particularly those on offensive operations on distant routes, such as in the Indian Ocean. But of any special use to which they were being put by Berlin to aid their Axis partners, the Japanese, Sir Arthur Hezlet had no knowledge.

Our orders were to destroy them, as many as we could, with no special reasons being given to us during the patrols designed to hunt them down. I do recall hearing in about 1944 that the Japanese were desperately short of supplies with which to manufacture certain munitions, but of what nature I never knew.

He does, however, remember the first sighting of his quarry.

The reason why we had been ordered to patrol off Penang, to a certain position, became clear at precisely 10.55, when a vessel was sighted, at a bearing of 296 degrees. It was immediately identified as a large German U-boat and we were exactly in its path, at the precise point we had been told it would probably make a rendezvous with a Japanese escort. The heavy swells were continuing and the officer of the watch was having difficulty; we were maintaining our depth only in parallel with the swells. I decided to put the periscope up over the swell, and there she was, about 2,700 yards distant, about 20 degrees on the port bow and without an escort. We were running on a 90-degree track and were much too close, making any torpedo shot unlikely to succeed; they could, from our position, just run under her.

I had to take immediate action, and decided to run fast across the German submarine's bow and fire my torpedoes from the stern. I ordered the helm to be put hard to port and that our speed be increased to seven knots, to turn 180 degrees, away from the enemy. While this manoeuvre was being carried out the torpedoes were being prepared for firing. When we had slowed down I put the periscope up again and saw the U-boat dead astern. It was clear that we now only had time in which to turn, and fire the stern tubes. The time was 11.05 precisely, and I ordered a stern salvo of three torpedoes, firing them individually, by eye, as the bow of the German submarine passed. I pulled the periscope down and waited for thirty seconds. I knew that the torpedoes would have run into the swell, and was anxious. I then put the periscope up, in time to see one of the torpedoes make a direct hit, just before the U-boat's conning tower, between the gun and the bridge. At the moment of impact, the U-boat jumped clear out of the water, an awesome sight, and sank immediately on what appeared to be an even keel. I came to learn later that she was blown apart by the impact of the middle of the three torpedoes, which struck her at about 14 feet below the water line, just as I had set them, but I didn't see her break in two. She was travelling at 14 surface knots at the time of our attack upon her.

Following the attack, Commander Hezlet ordered that *Trenchant* be turned round, in readiness to proceed to the position of the U-boat's sinking.

I was cautious, wary in fact, as I had been warned that there were German submarines in the area.

Indeed there were, for *U861*, under the command of Korvettenkapitan Oesten, was meant to have escorted *U859* into Penang for her tying up at Swettenham Pier. However, at 11.19 Commander Hezlet gave the order for *Trenchant* to surface.

The sea was black with oil, amidst which heads and yellow life jackets were bobbing about. Members of my crew began pulling the Germans out of the water and, at one moment, there were about six of them standing on the casing. They had made their escape from the U-boat's fore and aft compartments, at a depth of about 15 fathoms, one, the First Engineer and the only officer among the survivors, having made an astonishing exit through a hatch. He had been in the forward lavatory at the moment of impact. His name was Horst Klatt.

The rescue operation, however, was not to last.

My look-out, who minutes after surfacing had warned of imminent tropical rainstorms, saw on the far northern horizon what he thought was a Japanese vessel, a sub-chaser. Being on the surface our situation was precarious in the extreme. I didn't wait for any verification. I immediately blew my whistle, ordering Trenchant *to dive. At that point we had managed to take aboard ten of the U-boat's crew, who had gone below, but even as we began to submerge, there were people still running along the casing. One of the Germans who, at the moment I blew my whistle, was being hauled aboard by one of my crew, lost his grip and fell back into the water. He somehow, quite remarkably, managed to regain a hold and climb on to the casing. I was in the hatch, just seconds before ordering its closure, when this earnest face appeared above me, shouting, 'Wait for me, please!' He was the last one to be rescued; the rest we had to leave in the water for their Japanese allies to take care of.*

As *Trenchant* disappeared beneath the waters of the Malacca Straits it was 11.45. She had been on the surface for a dangerous twenty-six minutes. Commander Hezlet, having taken his craft to a safe depth and distance, and curious to see what sort of reception the Japanese would have given him, went to his periscope.

I got a distant view of what I thought to be a sub-chaser. Shortly afterwards a hydrophone effect was heard to pass down our starboard side at some distance, but it quickly faded. Shortly after one o'clock in the afternoon, some two hours after our attack, heavy explosions were heard, followed by silence. We turned Trenchant *away from the area of attack and proceeded ahead at full submerged speed.*

Military archives show, according to statements made by German personnel in Penang, that Japanese aircraft also took to the air in an attempt to attack *Trenchant*, but Sir Arthur says he was unaware of this at the time. That evening, at 19.02 precisely, *Trenchant* surfaced in safety: her position was 05° 48.5′ North 100°01′ East. Her mission to sink *U859* was at an end, yet Commander Hezlet had no time to contemplate any possible place in wartime history that *Trenchant* might take on account of her destruction of the U-boat.

We were now very full, and with eleven prisoners of war on board, I was obliged to take extra security measures. I had a sixty-six-man crew, plus a team of underwater commandoes, so conditions were somewhat cramped. My main concern was to get to the Ceylonese port of Trincomalee as quickly as I could and deposit the POWs there. The men from the U-boat were no trouble. Given Horst Klatt's rank of Oberleutnant, we accommodated him in the ward room and he ate his meals with us. He actually slept on the ward room table, so he was with us for much of the time, and, on occasions, we had to be careful what we said in front of him. His English was really quite good. The other POWs were billeted with the crew. As a routine security measure I did issue my Petty Officers with pistols and kept one in my desk.

To keep the German sailors occupied for at least some of the time, they were given duties, one of which was to assist with the dumping of refuse over the side, during surface runs when *Trenchant* was ventilated. It led to an amusing sight:

I had a Petty Officer of the Watch who used to wear his pistol on his waist, like a cowboy. On one refuse dump he was casually sauntering along, with two of the POWs directly behind him carrying buckets of refuse. They could so easily have disarmed him.

One of the POWs was, however, put to service in a very useful way, as Sir Arthur remembers:

We had a water distiller on board, which was of German origin, but which we were having difficulty in getting to work efficiently. It was using an awful lot of electricity and produced only minimal amounts of tepid water. It was eventually discovered that one of the POWs had been responsible on U859 *for operating their distiller, so we pressed him into service to make ours produce better results.*

On 2 October *Trenchant* put into Trincomalee and the German survivors from *U859* were transferred to the depot ship *Adamant*. During the eight-day journey, Commander Hezlet had got to know Oberleutnant Horst Klatt rather well and went to say goodbye to him aboard *Adamant*.

He was in a cabin that was terribly hot because the porthole had been closed for security reasons. He was, on account of this, rather uncomfortable, but there was little I could do. He was with a fellow survivor, who came from Aachen and who had just heard that the British Army had overrun his home town. They were sad and dejected and I did feel really rather sorry for them.

And of the young Oberleutnant, the former British Naval Commander has a particular memory:

Shortly after he was taken aboard Trenchant *I asked him to tell me the number of his U-boat. He, of course, declined, giving me only the name of his commanding officer, Korvettenkapitan Jebsen. Having earlier studied the intelligence file I had on the IXD2-type submarines, I had calculated that it had to be one of three, so I decided to guess. Staring at Klatt, I said, 'You are from* U859.*' The look of total astonishment which crossed his face told me that I had guessed correctly. I don't know what he would have thought had he known that it was pure guesswork on my part.*

But although Oberleutnant Klatt did not know it at the time, he was in possession of information of even greater value to the Allies than the number of his own submarine. For it was he who, by pure chance, had discovered the flasks of mercury in the bowels of *U859*, a consignment, one of many as it has now been established, of which the Japanese were in urgent need as they tried with increasing desperation to turn the tide of war in their favour.

And, in an extraordinary epitaph to this episode, Horst Klatt was himself to return to the waters of his wartime experience, though not until twenty-nine years had passed. In 1970 a report in the London-based *Sunday Times* chronicled the activities of a group of Englishmen trying to salvage a consignment of 30 tons of mercury from the wreck of a German submarine sunk off Penang Island during the Second World War. The paper claimed that the mercury was worth half a million pounds. The publication of this report alerted the West German government to the fact that information about *U859* had surfaced into the public domain. Bonn's concern was two-fold. Given that the salvage expedition to which the report referred had ended in fiasco off the coast of West Africa (the ship being used by the English adventurers had been barely seaworthy and had all but capsized with less than a quarter of its outward-bound voyage completed), it was feared that a 'free for all' would ensue, a scramble for the prize the mercury was now reported to be, and that *U859*, described today by Horst Klatt as 'a metal coffin', would be desecrated. Indeed, the wreck of *U859*, containing as it does the bodies of some fifty German sailors, had, years before, been officially designated a burial site by the German War Graves Commission.

Then there was the additional concern, paramount in the priorities of the late twentieth century, of pollution. It was feared that the metal flasks in which the mercury was contained, may, over the years, have become corroded, with the possibility that the material would contaminate the waters off Penang and, in the process, poison the seafood chain which plays such an important part in the island's economy. Consequently Bonn made diplomatic contact with the Malaysian government and, at home, attempted to trace any survivors from the stricken submarine.

It was not long before Horst Klatt received a letter from the German War Graves Commission enquiring how many men had died in the sinking of *U859*. This was followed just two weeks later by a letter from the government itself, asking if Herr Klatt could provide details of how much mercury had been on board, how many torpedoes had been in *U859*'s tubes when it was sunk and if it was at all possible that the wreck contained secret or sensitive documents in its watertight safe. It was not long after the second letter arrived that Klatt was summoned to a meeting in Bonn, where he was told that a salvage operation on his former submarine was to be mounted by the government for reasons of 'ecological concern'.

As Horst Klatt was the only survivor of *U859* that Bonn could trace, and had confirmed his discovery of the consignment of mercury, he was asked to act as adviser to the expedition that would attempt to recover the flasks. And so it came to pass that, twenty-nine years after Oberleutnant Klatt had been plucked from the Straits of Malacca by those who had just sunk his submarine, he returned to the same waters in a bid to help his country retrieve a cargo of mercury. The operation, spread over several weeks during the winter of 1973, was a success, with some thirty of an estimated thirty-one tons of mercury being recovered and shipped back to Germany.

Horst Klatt, now, in 1973, fifty-one years of age, thought back to the perilous journey that had ended in tragedy so close to safety in

Penang, and wondered why the mercury had been so essential to Tokyo, and why its presence aboard *U859* had been such a closely guarded secret – so secret that even Korvettenkapitan Jan Jebsen's officers had not been told of it. He thought, too, of the ships *U859* had sunk and particularly of the *John Barry* and her supposed cargo of silver bullion. And he reflected on the strange twist of fate that both liberty ship and submarine should have been carrying silver at the time of their encounter in the Arabian Sea – the former silver coins for an Arab king and bullion for an unknown destination, the latter mercury, 'quicksilver', for a nation at war.

They were the same thoughts that the author of this book entertained twenty-one years later, in the winter of 1994, when, considering these facts, he reflected on the paths down which coincidence can lead. Indeed, it was this very coincidence that spurred me to investigate further the cargoes of the two vessels. It is well documented that Germany supplied armaments and raw materials – including mercury – to her Japanese allies. But the extreme secrecy attached to this consignment was intriguing.

And what of the silver coins, supplied to Saudi Arabia under the lend-lease programme, and silver bullion, shipped under the same arrangements and destined, as had been believed for fifty years, for British India, both of which consignments went to the seabed with the *John Barry*? The answer to such questions lay in the hands of Sheikh Ahmed Farid and his Ocean Group.

PART THREE

Chapter Nine

A Surfacing of Facts – A Dive to the Deep

The complexities facing the Ocean Group in its task of locating the *John Barry* and mounting a recovery operation on her waterlogged holds were many and varied. The most formidable foe, as ever, was the weather. For six months of the year, from May to October, the monsoon – the fabled Kharif – roars into the water of the Arabian Sea from the Indian Ocean. Consequently, any operations – a general reconnaissance, a surface survey, a submerged run over the wreck once located, not to mention any actual salvage attempt – were, and indeed remain, effectively restricted to six months of the year.

Then there was the problem created by the wreck's location. An operation of the kind that had to be carried out to salvage the *John Barry* required a range of support services that only a modern port would have available. With the wreck lying 127 nautical miles off Oman's eastern seaboard, even the well-equipped Mina Raysut, south of Dhofar's capital of Salalah, would be hard put to meet the needs of a heavy-lift recovery operation from depths which had never before been attempted. Much depended, of course, upon the goodwill and co-operation of the government of Oman, particularly in the supply of service vessels to the recovery operation once it were underway – the scale and quality of their assistance and encouragement was to prove absolutely crucial. And of equal importance was the availability, at the right time, of the specialist equipment and personnel that would play a fundamental role in the success of the overall operation.

Nor were the group's concerns confined to those of a sea-based nature. Indeed, within days of the transfer of the rights, in February 1990, Robert Hudson embarked on an extensive search through archival material, just as Brian Shoemaker had done before him, sifting through documents in London and Washington, adding to those already assembled by Shoemaker which he had made available to the Ocean Group. Given that much of the circumstantial evidence uncovered by Shoemaker indicated that the supposed cargo of silver bullion had been destined for British India, Hudson searched through the archives of the old India Office in London and through the declassified files of the Bank of England. While Robert Hudson was able, in some measure, to add to the circumstantial evidence compiled by Brian Shoemaker, he was obliged, in the absence of irrefutable documentary proof, to conclude by the time of the first reconnaissance over the presumed site of the *John Barry* wreck in November 1990 that it remained uncertain that her holds had been loaded with silver bullion.

As Master Joseph Ellerwald had recorded the position of the *John Barry* at the time of the attack – latitude 15° 10′N and longitude 55° 18′E – the initial reconnaissance was a relatively straightforward exercise. Indeed, within days of positioning the reconnaissance vessel chartered by the Ocean Group over what was presumed to be the site of the wreck, a sonar scanner, towed across the surface of the sea and known by deep-sea recovery operators as a towfish (a sophisticated piece of equipment of a type used to good effect some years earlier by Shoemaker for the United States Navy), transmitted back to the vessel images of a ship, in two halves, sitting on the seabed in 8,500 feet of water. The wreck of the *John Barry* had almost certainly been found.

The task of positive identification remained. It was not until the first week of March 1991 that the necessary equipment, a remote-operated vehicle (always referred to as an ROV) capable of transmitting pictures of considerable clarity, became available and was put into service above the site of the wreck. The ROV hired by the Ocean Group from the Florida-based Eastport International Company, which had established a sound reputation in deep-sea recovery operations, was set three priorities: to identify the wreck positively; to locate the principal fractures in the ship's structure, from which cargo could have spilled out on to the seabed; and, if at all possible, to inspect holds No. 2 and 3 for the existence of the silver riyal coins (which were known to have been stowed in hold No. 2, as we saw in Chapter Seven) and silver bullion which could have been loaded into hold No. 3.

On the morning of 6 March 1991 the ROV was lowered into the water and began its long descent to what it was hoped was the wreck of the SS *John Barry*.

The professionals from Eastport International, though hardened by previous experience, remember being particularly tense, with one member of the team commenting:

It was the mysterious reputation of the ship we were about to inspect that made this operation very special indeed. What were we about to uncover? Would we, within an hour or so, see any evidence of its controversial cargo? And, of course, uppermost in all our minds, was the wreck identified by the sonar scanned in November really the John Barry*?*

The men on the recovery vessel did not have long to wait. At 2.30 in the afternoon, as they sat in front of their monitor sets, what was almost immediately identified as the stern section of a wartime liberty ship came slowly into view. Although, in those early, exciting moments, no evidence came across the screen to prove that this was indeed the SS *John Barry*, there was no real doubt in anyone's mind.

The scenes being transmitted back up to the surface were remarkable. 'As the ROV made repeated passes and flyovers over the wreck, American World War II military vehicles came into view, together with gun turrets and stacked drill pipes. The sight was both eerie and wonderful,' an Eastport technician was later to comment.

The ROV's run over the points of fracture showed that the *John Barry* had broken in half across hold No. 3, prompting the question that, if bullion had been stored there, was it now lying on the seabed, covered by almost half a century of mud and silt? Consequently the ROV was sent tracking over the field of debris which had fallen out of hold No. 3. It worked the debris field in a box pattern and found steel plates, bent and twisted by the impact all those years before of *U859*'s torpedoes; drill pipes, scattered across the seabed as if by a giant's hand; a small diesel engine still lashed to its pallet; a lifeboat and an assortment of flotsam and jetsam, both great and small. But there was no trace of bullion. Another member of the Eastport team remembers:

It would have been extraordinarily fortunate to have found a silver bar so early in the search, but the hope was most certainly present. Had we done so it would have been sensational, for had there been just one, there surely would have been others!

The next day, 7 March, with the ROV having made its inspection of the stern and the debris field, it was directed to the bow section of the ship. The underwater scenes it recorded proved to be no less fascinating that those received on deck the day before.

'Out of the past came the liberty ship's forward guns, as if waiting still to discharge their fire, a US military jeep and a stack of oil drums,' relates a crew member of the reconnaissance vessel. 'It was a sad, grand sight.'

The ROV then turned its 'eye' on hold No. 2, making several passes over the deck above and discovering in the process a cargo hatch cover lying inside the hold itself. But whatever lay within the hold remained hidden from view by a mass of lumber, fallen masts, cables, trucks and other littered cargo. The whole wreck was a time capsule, a memorial to the extraordinary energy unleashed by man in a time of war.

While no evidence of substance had been uncovered that this was the *John Barry* (or that she had either coins or bullion in her holds), this stage of the reconnaissance concluded with the sure assumption that the wreck could be no other than that of the long-lost liberty ship. Indeed, this initial foray was judged by the Ocean Group to have been an outstanding success, principally because the clarity of the scenes transmitted back up to the reconnaissance vessel had established a scale of priority objectives for the next, more detailed survey. This would have to take place before any attempt could be made to penetrate the holds of the vessel, an operation which it was now believed would necessitate the use of high explosives. And, of crucial importance, the reconnaissance had proved that the wreck was indeed in two parts, with the bow containing hold No. 2 and a part of hold No. 3, and the stern containing the remaining, larger section. These facts would be vital to any eventual salvage operation, given that the coins were known to have been stored in hold No. 2 and that all available circumstantial evidence pointed to any bullion having been loaded into hold No. 3.

After this initial success, there was no doubt in Sheikh Ahmed's mind that Eastport International was 'the team for the job', even though, due to prior contractual commitments which kept the company's vessels and personnel in Europe for the following nine months, it was not possible to return to the Arabian Sea until January 1992. But on 10 January, Eastport's master survey ship *Deep Ocean Explorer*, attended by the company's support ship, *Valiant Service*, sailed out of Mina Raysut, Salalah, bound for the site of the wreck.

As in the survey of nine months earlier, a scale of priority objectives had been set down, namely to capture on video film the field of debris lying between the bow and the stern of the wreck, to film as much as possible of the contents of hold No. 1 and, again, the longed-for prize, if at all possible to recover at least one of the elusive silver bars. On this occasion, Eastport's ROV *Magellan*, a 'state of the art' remote-controlled deep-sea inspection capsule, was to descend on the wreck.

Moving slowly through the water like a giant fish, *Magellan* investigated the stern, which, in March 1992, had been identified as containing the greater part of hold No. 3. The pictures sent back to the surface proved beyond doubt that, with the exception of piles of drill pipe, this part of the hold was empty. *Magellan* then moved on towards the broken bow, and the remaining section of hold No. 3 and hold No. 2, crossing the debris field as it did so, recording on camera the detritus of war lying on the seabed. The ROV survey of nine months earlier had been hampered in its inspection of the remainder of hold No. 3 and hold No. 2 by a jumble of cargo lying across the deck. However, it was hoped *Magellan* would prove to be made of sterner stuff. The ROV nosed its way gingerly into the interior of hold No. 3. Yet its searchlight and camera revealed only stacked building supplies, believed to have been destined for ARAMCO in the oil fields of Saudi Arabia. Of silver bullion there was not the slightest trace. To add to the frustration now in the air came unseasonal weather, with roaring winds which generated 20-foot-high seas, forcing the Eastport team to make for sheltered waters.

On 14 February, however, the exercise was able to resume in a calm sea. Having failed to find any evidence of silver bullion in the two parts of hold No. 3, or in the debris field in between, the team decided to make a detailed survey of hold No. 2, in an attempt to locate the boxes of Saudi silver coins known to have been stowed there. With expectations on the *Valiant Service* high, the ROV *Magellan* began its probing search of the hold. But spirits were quickly to be dashed as it became apparent that the deck cargo, including two trucks, which had earlier prevented a detailed survey of this part of the wreck, were proving too much even for *Magellan*. Back up on deck, as the Eastport team sat in front of their monitors and surveyed the scenes of an impenetrable jumble of wartime cargo being transmitted by *Magellan*, a consensus opinion was quickly formed that this survey had gone just about as far as it could go. Indeed, without the use of explosives to blast away the deck cargo and, in the process, open up the hold, access was simply not going to be possible.

The return of high winds and mountainous seas soon made any further investigation out of the question; the decision was taken to abandon this phase of operations and, on 17 February, the *Valiant Service* sailed to Mina Raysut, with the Eastport professionals now convinced that the whole exercise of attempting to recover the controversial cargo from the *John Barry* would have to move to a new, pioneering stage in deep-sea excavation. For one fact was certain: if explosives were to be used, and no other method seemed likely to achieve the desired result, then it would be the first time a primed charge had been activated to open the holds of a steel-built ship at such a depth. It would, therefore, be an exercise of a highly delicate and experimental nature, for which very special abilities were going to be required. Sheikh Ahmed Farid al Aulaqi was in no doubt as to where a suitably professional and dedicated team could be found. The Ocean Group set about recruiting the services of the French International Maritime Institute – Ifremer.

While Ifremer had long been celebrated as an organisation of exceptional skill and innovation in marine recovery circles around the world, it was only in the early 1980s that it was catapulted to international prominence by locating the *Titanic* in the Atlantic Ocean. The wreck of the *Titanic* is, of course, classified as a grave, given the number of people who died when she sank, so there had never been any intention of excavating her hold and cabins. The *John Barry* would be a very different proposition.

One of Ifremer's Directors of Operations on the *Titanic* exercise had been Jean Roux. Upon being briefed on the complexities of the *John Barry* project he gave his opinion that the organisation's three-man miniature submarine *Cyana* would be ideal for a close-up reconnaissance of the wreck in order to establish at which points explosive could best be placed to open up hold No. 2. The explosives themselves, Roux proposed, would then be put into position by Ifremer's ROV *Scamp*, which, with its ability to carry out such a delicate manoeuvre to a one-metre target area, was all but purpose-built for the task. Even so, positioning the explosives by remote control at a depth of 8,500 feet would be 'analogous to attempting to place a marble hanging from a cotton thread 200 feet long into a match box'. The explosives would be linked to the surface vessel by an electrical detonation line and operated from there. Roux warned, however, that this initial operation would not be able to recover any substantial amount of cargo that might be found. Following detonation, *Cyana* would voyage down to the wreck to evaluate just what had been achieved, and uncovered, by the explosions. Any subsequent operation to recover a large quantity of coins or bullion would be a pioneering effort. Ifremer would have to develop special techniques and equipment to cope with the heavy-duty lift.

Two years had now passed since the Ocean Group had acquired the title rights to the liberty ship, and while the search for the wreck had been successful and the two subsequent surveys had clearly identified what needed to be done in order to retrieve the silver riyals and, if it was there, the silver bullion, the costs were mounting. Now, with the monsoon season approaching and the need for Ifremer to honour other commitments prior to being available to work with the Ocean Group, another nine-month wait was in view. Jean Roux's opinion that an Ifremer operation would have to be in two phases, with an intervening period during which heavy-duty lift equipment would be developed, meant still further delays. But the prospect of solving the mystery held a far greater appeal than the instincts of financial reserve. True to character, Sheikh Ahmed allowed the adventure to continue.

On 18 November 1992, Jean Roux and his Ifremer team assembled at Salalah to await the arrival of the Merchant Vessel *Castor*, which had been placed under contract to the Ocean Group for this new and most vital phase of the *John Barry* operation. During the nine-month wait for Ifremer personnel to become available, the decision had been taken to recruit the expertise of the British salvage operator Keith Jessop, who, in September 1981, had led a team that recovered £35 million of gold bars from the British cruiser *Edinburgh*, sunk by German action in the Barents Sea in 1941. Jessop's experience on the *Edinburgh* assignment – particularly his knowledge of the controlled use of explosives underwater – Sheikh Ahmed reasoned, could be put to good use on the recovery of cargo from the *John*

Barry. (Interestingly, the gold on board the British vessel was being sent by the USSR to the United States, via Britain, for payment of lend-lease supplies.)

So Jessop was in Salalah too, as was Brian Shoemaker, who had flown in from America to exercise the agreed 'observer rights'. While waiting back home for the latest phase of the operation to begin, Shoemaker had been far from idle. He had returned to Washington to pursue papers in the National Archives which might have been overlooked previously or might not have been fully evaluated during his earlier research. He knew that, as the time was fast approaching when the survey aspect of the *John Barry* operation would turn to salvage, any additional information he might uncover could well make a vital contribution to the possible success of the whole enterprise. He knew, too, that the results of his former trawl through the files, which he had made available to the Ocean Group, had been of considerable value to Robert Hudson in his own research efforts. If at all possible, he wanted to be able to report that no available paper on the *John Barry* had been left unturned.

While this latest foray into the files convinced Shoemaker that some of the *John Barry* papers had been pulled by Washington officials (including a rumoured secret manuscript stating that the liberty ship had been carrying silver bullion), he did uncover further documentation that prompted him to return to the belief that the precious metal loaded aboard the liberty ship had been destined for India. But that was not all. Like the Ocean Group, the John Barry Group had been disappointed that the surveys of the wreck had not uncovered evidence of bullion in hold No. 3, although Shoemaker himself harboured a belief that it could well have fallen on to the seabed when the vessel broke in two across the hold. But a nagging doubt had taken hold of him and he returned to his research with a mind open to the possibility of alternatives as to where on the vessel the silver may have been stowed.

On 28 October 1992, three weeks before leaving Oregon for Oman, Shoemaker felt justified in suggesting just such an alternative. Interestingly, he could also put forward an alternative to the port, Philadelphia, where he had always believed the bullion to have been loaded. Writing to Sheikh Ahmed, Brian Shoemaker set out highly detailed documentary evidence that in June 1944, 90 million ounces of fine silver, in bar form, had been assigned to India by the United States Treasury under the lend-lease programme and that plans had been made to ship such an amount between 17 June and the middle of July that year, a time scale that would have made the *John Barry* a probable candidate to carry some, if not all, of the consignment. The *John Barry* was in New York from 29 June to 5 July, and she sailed down the Hudson River and out into the Atlantic en route to Philadelphia on that day 'without cargo but in level ballast'. Both Shoemaker and Hudson had previously believed that, in the absence of any documentation confirming that cargo had been loaded in New York and given the existence of documentary proof that it *had* been loaded in Philadelphia, the latter port was the one to watch as they went through the files.

But now, as he reported in his message to Sheikh Ahmed, he had unearthed Treasury correspondence in Washington archives running from 21 June to 8 July 1944 which proved beyond doubt that the 90 million fine Troy ounces of silver in bar form, destined for India, had been taken from West Point, America's National Silver Bullion Depository, to the New York Assay Office, at 32 Old Slip, just one block away from the New York docks on the Manhattan side of the Hudson River, where the *John Barry* was to berth a few days later. In a letter dated 21 June, the Treasury Procurement Division in Washington advised the Director of the Mint, Nellie Tayloe Ross, that 'in connection with the requisition calling for approximately 90 million fine Troy ounces of silver in bar form for the government of the United Kingdom, to be transferred to the government of India, we have instructed Mr F.E. Johnson, our New York representative, to contract Mr Tabin at the Assay Office and arrange all details in connection with moving the bars from the Assay Office to the docks'. This letter, signed by the Director of Procurement, Clifton E. Mack, concluded by reminding Miss Ross of the necessary reference numbers to use for the transaction, 'when preparing your vouchers covering any expenses to be billed by our office against lend-lease funds'.

Nellie Tayloe Ross wrote the next day, 22 June 1944, to the Treasurer of the United States in comfortingly capitalist terms:

The silver, at the rate of $0.7111111111 per fine ounce, has a value of $64,000,000. This silver is carried in the Mint's accounts at $0.4666666666 per fine ounce – $41,999,999.99 – making a profit on the transaction of $22,000,000.01.

This businesslike approach was not without precedent. When, in December 1943, staff at the Foreign Economic Administration (the FEA – which had commenced its wartime existence as the more appropriately named Board of Economic Warfare) were conducting an in-house debate as to how the request for silver for British India could best be handled, Mr James Angell wrote an internal memorandum to his colleague, Mr Frank Coe, on the last day of the year:

My own disposition at present is to make the following recommendation . . . The transaction should be handled not through lend-lease but as a cash transaction through the United Kingdom and without any ounce-for-ounce return clause, in order to draw down UK dollar balances and draw down Indian sterling balances in London.

In making such a cold calculation, James Angell was doing no more that his political masters' bidding; as we saw in Chapter Three, on the first day of the year in which the FEA memorandum was written, President Roosevelt's administration had issued an edict that 'the United Kingdom's gold and dollar balances should not be permitted to be less than about six hundred million dollars, nor above one billion', a contrivance designed to keep Britain in a state of financial subservience to America and, in the process, compliant to Washington's political demands. The State Department was, at the time, insisting that the silver should be lend-lease on an exclusive United Kingdom requisition, a view that the US Treasury came to share. Following an inter-departmental debate, however, on 17 February 1944 the State Department advised Leo Crowley, the

FEA's Administrator, 'that the obligation for the return of the silver should be assumed jointly by the government of Great Britain and the government of India', an opinion which obviously prevailed and was confirmed in the letter of 21 June from the Treasury Procurement division to Nellie Tayloe Ross at the Mint.

Whilst such documentary evidence served to endorse what had long been a matter of open record, that the United States did supply lend-lease silver to India during the Second World War, with some 225,999,904 ounces having been shipped there between 1943 and 1945, Shoemaker had now confirmed through his own research that a request had been made to the New York Assay Office to arrange the transport of a consignment of silver bars, known to be India-bound, to the New York docks at a time when the *John Barry* would be at berth there. This fact, and this fact alone, while not previously authenticated by documentary evidence such as Shoemaker had now uncovered, had earlier given birth to the internationally held belief that the liberty ship was carrying 'Indian Silver', even though, as this book records, no evidence has ever been produced that she was scheduled to dock in the subcontinent. Further reinforcing Shoemaker's personal acceptance of this belief was his new discovery of two Treasury Procurement Division bills, one covering services rendered during the last week of June 1944, the other for the first week of July, for the transportation of the India-bound bullion from the West Point Silver Depository to the Assay Office at 32 Old Slip, New York. The first was for the transport of 19,180 bars – representing 19,996,153.98 ounces; the second for 65,760 bars – representing 70,003,846.02 ounces – amounting to the documented 90 million ounces precisely. Each bar, embossed with America's national emblem, the Bald Eagle, weighed between 1.020 and 1.090 Troy ounces, there being a slight weight differential between each hand-filled mould. The bars, stamped with the legend 'United States Assay Office, 1944', were 5½ inches by 11 inches at the base, 5 inches by 11 inches at the top and stood 3¼ inches in height. A treasury of silver bars indeed, but where, if not in hold No. 3, were they loaded into the *John Barry*?

That they were, Brian Shoemaker now had little doubt. In the light of the new evidence he had uncovered, and suspending his long-held belief that the bullion had been loaded in Philadelphia and stowed in hold No. 3, he outlined his new scenario to Sheikh Ahmed in his letter of 28 October 1992:

Several thousand tons of silver would have had to be stowed in one of the deep holds for two reasons. First, weight and balance; if stowed in an upper hold between decks, the ship would have been unstable. Second, following the loading rule of 'first on, last off', the cargo would have been loaded into a deep hold and kept there while the rest of the cargo was being loaded in Philadelphia and unloaded in Ras Tanurah. If it was in an upper hold then it would have had to be offloaded on the pier at Ras Tanurah in order to get at the rest of the cargo, which would not have made sense. Understanding these facts, that the ship sailed 'in ballast' from New York and that silver bullion would have had to be stored in a deep hold, the question is, where? Our most likely candidate is the deep tank under hold No. 1. The Liberty Ship Memorial Museum Staff in San Francisco assure me that the deep tanks were routinely used for cargo and only for water ballast if there was no cargo. The storage volume of the deep tank is 21,771 cubic feet. The space taken up by the silver bars would have been approximately 10,240 cubic feet. The top of the tank is steel, with two steel hatches. The hatches would have been bolted shut and the nuts possibly welded. In short, a ready-made vault that would have been a perfect place to prevent prying eyes and pilferage. If aboard, the bullion would have served as ballast between New York and Philadelphia and between the Gulf and India. The silver would have been secure in the deep tank from the crew and stevedores in Philadelphia and Ras Tanurah. The crew would have first learned that the silver had been aboard when the hatches were cracked in India.

Brian Shoemaker closed his letter to the Sheikh with these conclusions:

1. The silver bullion was shipped from the Port of New York aboard the SS John Barry.

2. The silver bullion was moved from New York Assay Office at 32 Old Slip and loaded aboard the SS John Barry *in Fletchers Dry Dock in Hoboken between crews. For secrecy, I assume that the Master was informed when he reported aboard, and possibly the Purser.*

3. The silver bullion is stored in the deep tank under hold No. 1.

Sheikh Ahmed wasted no time on receipt of this letter. On 31 October, aware that the latest phase of the *John Barry* operation would be underway in less than three weeks' time, he passed Shoemaker's submission to both Ifremer and Keith Jessop. Thus the news team assembled in Salalah on 18 November, awaiting the arrival of the MV *Castor*, were as well armed, both technically and with details of the latest research, as they could possibly be. All that now remained was for fair winds to attend them.

But the winds again blew strongly, impeding the progress of the *Castor*. Consequently, she did not arrive in Salalah until 20 November, two days behind schedule. It was not a good beginning, but on the 21st Dick Simmons stood on the dockside at Mina Raysut and bade farewell to Jean Roux, the Ifremer team, Brian Shoemaker and Keith Jessop. As the *Castor* disappeared over the horizon, Simmons reflected upon the twists and turns of the past three years.

They had entailed a considerable expenditure of human effort, ingenuity, boldness and cash – but not enough, he thought wryly, to lower his 'wreck fever' temperature. Surely, with the very best deep-sea technicians now part of the team and with Brian Shoemaker's recent research giving them a new hold upon which to pin their hopes, the mystery of the *John Barry* must be about to be solved.

Simmons' optimism was vindicated just two days into the attempt to penetrate the wreck and locate the cargo. The *Castor* had arrived over the site of the wreck on the afternoon of 22 November and the next day *Cyana* made her initial dive. Jean Roux and two of his Ifremer colleagues made up the submersible crew, which, in addition to taking a close-up video film of the wreck, hoped to obtain proof, although no real doubt had existed since the first reconnaissance of November 1990, that this was indeed the SS *John Barry*.

Such proof was quick in coming. While videoing the wreck's

superstructure, Jean Roux noticed the manufacturer's plate beneath the ship's bridge. *Cyana*'s exterior pincer arm plucked it from where it had been placed in February 1942, in the shipyard at Portland, Oregon. Back up on deck, the details on the plate finally removed all uncertainty. This was without doubt the American Second World War liberty ship; the SS *John Barry* had been found.

The next day, 24 November, Keith Jessop dived in *Cyana* with two of the Ifremer team. The previous day's excursion, in addition to locating the manufacturer's plate, had taken what Brian Shoemaker was to describe as 'outstandingly good' pictures, and much of this second close-up survey was used to obtain yet more film, a record that would not only determine the best points at which to place the explosives in the wreck, but reveal details about the vessel's final moments.

On 25 November the *Cyana* made her third trip to the bottom of the Arabian Sea, with Ifremer's Paul Henri Nargiolet accompanying the submersible's two pilots. The following day, the ROV *Scamp* was sent down to take yet more video films – a crucial reconnaissance, as it would fall to this piece of underwater wizardry to place the explosives that would lead the team to the elusive cargo.

It was this particular dive which, according to Brian Shoemaker, produced an astonishing overhead view of the entire wreck.

This was the first film which gave such dramatic and indeed moving scenes of the John Barry. *As the camera tracked the length of the wreck great detail had been recorded. Her decks were seen to be awash with timber, fallen masts, cables, trucks, jeeps and general cargo. The* Scamp *camera peered, as it were, into holds No. 1 and 2, with a Caterpillar tractor clearly visible in the latter. The truly amazing aspect of this particular film was the clarity of the pictures. The ship had obviously hit the seabed at full speed, the impact having ploughed a furrow about 15 feet high at the bow, which tapered back to the aft side of hold No. 2. The most dramatic evidence of just how hard the liberty ship had slammed into the seabed was revealed in the film, which showed that the bow section of the wreck had been driven about 15 feet into the seabed, an impact which had generated vertical compression lines, accordion lines, in the hull, and compound fractures.*

The film also confirmed Brian Shoemaker's earlier theory on what would have happened to the bullion had it been stowed in hold No. 3:

With the film showing in greater detail than ever before that the John Barry *had indeed broken in two across hold No. 3, and that the seabed was clearly very soft, with sand, sediment and mud, then the bullion it stowed would have fallen out on to the floor of the Arabian Sea and subsequently become buried.*

But this latest video film had confirmed another astonishing fact. If Shoemaker's current theory, that the silver bars had been loaded into the vessel's deep tank beneath hold No. 1, was correct, then, with the prow of the wreck some 15 feet into the seabed, the bullion could well be below the bottom of the sea. Of such a possibility Brian Shoemaker was now in no real doubt:

Given that the ship had obviously smacked into the seabed with such force, the silver, wherever stored, would, given its enormous weight, almost certainly have moved forward at the moment of impact. Consequently, if the bullion was in the deep tank under hold No. 1, it would have moved forward into the peak tank.

The film also suggested another possibility, that the bullion had not only careered forward at the moment of impact, tearing through the steel hulls as it did so, but that it had moved to the left. For the video revealed a large bulge on the port side of the forward section of the wreck.

'This carbuncle,' said Shoemaker, 'could also be the secret cargo. Indeed, the more the film was studied the greater became the awareness of the liberty ship's last moments. Even the upper decks gave evidence of the pressure that had been exerted when the ship struck the seabed. The film showed vertical hold ladders protruding though the upper decks, suggesting downward compression of about 10 feet.'

On the 27th, *Cyana* dived again, her fourth and final descent the liberty ship, this time carrying Ifremer's master engineer, Pierre Valdy, to whom would fall the task of deciding just where the RVO *Scamp* should position the explosives. It was on their run over the wreck that the bell of the *John Barry* was located, an evocative memento which, despite the repeated tuggings of the submersible's pincers, refused to come away. (Sadly, the bell was later lost during the series of explosions.)

Over the next two days, the *Scamp* was sent down to the wreck on 'dry runs' to test Pierre Valdy's judgement about the positioning of the explosives. Then, on 29 November, the *Castor* returned to Mina Raysut, to collect the explosives which had been flown into Oman on a chartered flight from Europe, together with the team that would handle them. The plan was that the *Scamp* would position 50kg packs of explosives at strategic points in the wreck and these would then be detonated in a series of carefully controlled explosions from the *Castor*. Due to the extraordinary depth at which the explosives would be detonated and the consequent pressure that would be exerted upon them, their effect would be limited, so Roux decided that *Cyana*, with her three-man crew, should undertake a close-up inspection of the results achieved by each series of detonations. Prior to the first detonation, Roux had also decided, given that the underwater film had shown the deep tank under hold No. 1 to be partly buried in the seabed, that the initial, target would be hold No. 2, into which it was at least known that the riyals had been stowed.

Following the first series of controlled explosions, *Cyana* dived on the wreck to survey the results. The images she transmitted were disappointing. The explosions had churned up the thick layer of silt, sand and mud which had been lying on the seabed, making visibility exceedingly poor. Hardly had this setback occurred than that old adversary, the weather, interrupted the salvage operation. Four days of ROV surveys were completely lost because of heavy seas.

When the rough seas abated, another series of explosions was detonated. But further disappointment followed. This time not only was visibility around the forward deck of the liberty ship reduced to all but zero, but *Cyana*'s camera began to malfunction. And then, with the weather conditions deteriorating, Jean Roux took the inevitable decision and the *Castor* was once again turned towards the shore.

But as the team sat in conference on the *Castor*, spirits rose. While no silver, either coins or bullion, had been seen, detailed knowledge of the disposition of the cargo had been gleaned, in particular of hold No. 2. Consequently, the team had a clearer idea of what would be required technically for the salvage of the wreck. As Jean Roux had earlier cautioned, there would, in any event, be an interval between the 'blowing' of the holds and the salvage operation, an interval during which the technicians at Ifremer would develop the equipment they believed would finally bring the elusive silver into the light of day.

Chapter Ten

Silver Galore!

When, some twenty-five years ago, John Gorley Bunker wrote, 'Somewhere in the Arabian Sea one of the richest treasures of all times waits, well protected by a mile of saltwater, for the future technique that may enable salvage crews to bring it up,' there were few who believed his prophesy would be fulfilled this century. Even those who expressed confidence that deep-sea technology would continue to develop apace, bringing the seemingly impossible within man's grasp, would hardly have conceived of the complexities that would attend a heavy-lift operation at 8,500 feet.

While Jean Roux, on his return to Ifremer's research and development centre at Toulon, remained cautiously optimistic that a refinement of the giant pincer 'grab' (an early type of which, known in marine circles as 'smash and grab', had been in use since the 1970s on deep-sea excavation projects) could be developed for effective operation on the *John Barry*, even he did not initially realise just how long it would take before such a revolutionary piece of equipment could be made ready, installed in a suitable recovery vessel and put on site over the wreck. Indeed, it was not until the fiftieth anniversary of the sinking of the *John Barry* by *U859* on 28 August 1944 that Sheikh Ahmed Farid al Aulaqi received word that the first salvage operation would definitely get underway in two months' time. Ifremer's development and testing of the steel 'grab' had been successfully concluded and it was on its way to Singapore, where a suitable salvage vessel, a former oil-exploration drilling ship, now renamed the *Flex LD*, was being refitted. Once in Singapore, the 'grab' would be put in place and then, prior to sailing to Salalah, sea trials would be carried out.

On board would be Robert Hudson – the first time that a member of the Ocean Group would be participating in any of the exercises above the site of the liberty ship. His considerable experience in marine matters was now to be put to good use; indeed, his designation on board the *Flex LD* was to be that of Salvage Master.

Members of the John Barry Group were to fly in from America to witness scenes which they hoped would vindicate their long-held belief that the ship whose name their group bore would prove to have been carrying, in the words of John Gorley Bunker, 'a fortune more fabulous than ever Ali Baba and his forty thieves could have hoped for'. Brian Shoemaker, Jay Fiondella, Herman McGuire Riley and Hugh O'Neill flew to Oman in order to witness what they and others believed would be the final chapter in the liberty ship's story.

On the evening of 19 October, the eve of the *Flex LD*'s arrival from Singapore and departure for the wreck site, Sheikh Ahmed gave a dinner party at Salalah's Holiday Inn for those who, like himself, had worked long and hard to bring about the recovery operation. Brian Shoemaker and Jay Fiondella, who had, arguably, started this greatest of treasure hunts, were their usual ebullient selves. Jean Roux and his Ifremer team were quietly confident. Richard Simmons, known to the team as 'Mr Fixit-Anchorman', was 'keeping his options open' on the question of success of the salvage operation, while Sheikh Ahmed, presiding over lobster fresh from the Arabian Sea and New York cut-steaks, told his dinner guests, 'Let's keep the whole operation in perspective. We all want to solve the riddle of the *John Barry*!'

The next morning, with the cameras of a London-based television documentary film company recording the scene, members of the John Barry and Ocean Groups stood on the quay at Mina Raysut as the 300-foot-long, orange-red *Flex LD* sailed into port. Robert Hudson went into conference with Sheikh Ahmed and Richard Simmons, while supplies for the planned four-week salvage operation were loaded aboard and new crew members were shown their cabins. Following a farewell lunch on board, Sheikh Ahmed and Richard Simmons left the *Flex LD* and returned to Muscat. A few hours later, the salvage ship passed out on Mina Raysut's breakwater and into the open waters of the Arabian Sea.

To Jean Roux, it must have seemed like a dismal rerun of two years earlier, when unseasonal high winds had also generated rolling seas, presenting his team with severe operational difficulties. To Robert Hudson, the frustration verged on the intolerable. The *Flex LD* had arrived over the wreck site on 21 October and since then the bad weather had made the planned deployment of the 50-ton 'grab' impossible. Unable to proceed until the weather improved, the team worked though a technical catalogue of 'dry runs', covering virtually every planned aspect of the operation. Yet the *Flex LD* remained awake twenty-four hours a day, with key technicians and supporting members of the crew working twelve-hour shifts.

As the waters around the ship continued to roll day after day, Hudson's anxiety increased. The cost of the operation had been budgeted at a daily rate of $30,000, so his dismay required little explanation.

For those not on duty, there was an extensive video library to dilute the tedium of life aboard a vessel anchored on the high seas, and the team spirit remained good. A rat, which was believed to have boarded in Singapore, was adopted by the team and named 'Ego'. And then, on the last day of October, fair weather returned.

As Ifremer's technicians began the laborious six-hour exercise of threading lengths of pipe, one by one, which sent the 'grab' out of its chamber in the centre of the *Flex LD*'s deck, down through 8,500 feet of water to the wreck, Jean Roux sat in front of the monitor on the vessel's top deck and studied the progress of his organisation's latest piece of revolutionary marine art, this most 'intelligent' piece of equipment. Based on the reconnaissance of November and December 1992, which had proved just how problematic any excavation of hold No. 1 and the deep tank beneath it would be, the decision had been taken to salvage hold No. 2, in which the silver coins had been stowed.

The decision was based on practical considerations. Following the exhaustive series of tests to which the 'grab' had been subjected in France, it was known that its hydraulics were capable of sweeping away the debris littering the deck above the hold, removing the military vehicles known to be lying in its mouth and, if necessary, peeling back the deck itself so as to gain access. It was further reasoned that much would be learnt during this initial excavation which could then be utilised in later, more difficult, exercises, such as breaking into hold No. 1 and the deep tank beneath.

At first, as was to be expected, considering that the deployment of the 'grab' was marine history in the making, there were difficulties. The 'grab', when directly over the wreck for the first time, did not always respond to the dictates of its remote-control operator and, to compound the difficulties, the pictures being relayed by its camera lacked the anticipated clarity. But perseverance paid dividends, and a modus operandi was eventually established between the 'grab' and those who had created it. To improve the pictures being sent back up to the surface, clarified water was pumped down to the wreck and then the 'grab' peeled back the deck of the *John Barry* above hold No. 2. It was now open and ready for excavation and the 'grab' set about rifling through the liberty ship's cargo.

Jean Roux, Robert Hudson, Brian Shoemaker and Jay Fiondella gathered round the 'grab' as it made its first arrival from the wreck. Herman McGuire Riley and Hugh O'Neill were ashore, waiting their turn to board the *Flex LD* as observers; a fifth American, Captain Alan Moore of the United States Coastguard Service, was also later to board the salvage vessel as Washington's representative. Members of the crew, having entered into the spirit of the exercise, were part of the excited circle. The film cameras were rolling. All eyes were focused on the pincers of the 'grab'. Only the protesting hydraulics could be heard as its steel claws slowly opened. The mud, splintered wood, sparking plugs and bagged cement which landed on deck were the ultimate anti-climax. As Brian Shoemaker told the camera of the documentary film crew, 'All we needed was one riyal coin. Just one. For if there was one, it would surely mean that there were 2,999,999 still below.'

The next day's exercise brought even greater frustration. The 'grab' was holding in its four hydraulic claws a giant gun it had snatched from within the hold and was slowly bringing it to the surface. Suddenly, one of the pipes hauling up the 'grab' buckled. The pincers momentarily relaxed their grip and the cannon plunged back down to the seabed.

Far in excess of the disappointment in losing such a relic was the dismay at the suspension of operations caused by the need to replace the damaged pipe. While the time taken for a replacement to be flown into Oman and then carried out to the *Flex LD* by a supply ship from Salalah was, in fact, minimal, the four days lost had eaten into the budget and poached time that Robert Hudson could ill afford to lose. For it was now 3 November, halfway through the planned time for the salvage operation.

Finally, the *John Barry* began to yield some of the silver cargo about which there had been so much speculation for over half a century. Robert Hudson was alone when the was made. The 'grab' was once more down in hold No. 2. As Hudson sat in front of the monitor on the top deck of the *Flex LD*, he noticed a glint in the silt surrounding the cargo. He called for Jean Roux to join him. The remote controls were activated and the 'grab' began its six-hour ascent to the surface.

And when, later that day, marine recovery history was made, it was a moment that Robert Hudson and the sixty-strong crew of the *Flex LD* will remember as a time of joint triumph for the rest of their days. As the 'grab' opened, releasing its treasury of silver coins, Hudson cried, 'We've hit the jackpot!' The coins clattered down upon the deck, the moment of impact being recorded by the camera of the documentary film crew on board – a scene which, a few days later, astonished television audiences around the world.

'When the "grab" opened it was like watching the world's biggest one-armed bandit,' Hudson said later. 'Silver rain fell out. Some black, some green, coated in silver sulphide, but the noise told us they were indeed coins. It was beautiful. We've pulled out about one and a half million. The rest aren't so easy to get at, so we have left them.' As to the silver bullion, Hudson was philosophical. 'No one is really sure if it's down there or not. There was documented proof that the coins were loaded into the *John Barry*, but following my own research I concluded that the bullion reached India aboard other vessels.'

In Arabia, there are many 'secrets', most of which have become public property before breakfast. Interestingly, the first leaks that a salvage operation was underway over the wreck of the liberty ship appeared in the British press. The Lloyd's List of 2 November 1994 was first to report the news, with a single-column story headed 'Silver Salvors seek *John Barry*'. Two days later, the *Independent* newspaper ran a story in its 'Pembroke' column under the heading 'The Adventure Lord Archer Turned Down', in which it quoted a Mr Simon Wharmby, a City stockbroker, who claimed that he had at one time attempted to interest the Conservative politician and novelist, Jeffrey Archer, in becoming an investor in the *John Barry* enterprise. Wharmby was reported to have told the *Independent* that he had been advised by Keith Jessop, who was not aboard the *Flex LD*, that the salvage operation was in progress. The article concluded by reporting Wharmby as saying excitedly, 'Last I heard they had dropped something on the seabed and clouded the water. But I'm expecting more news soon.'

These reports, while causing Sheikh Ahmed Farid mild amusement and irritation in equal amounts (the details in the Pembroke column, were, he said, 'news to me'), did prompt numerous telephone calls from around the world to his Muscat office. On one day alone, 8 November, his private office received over forty telephone calls from newspapers and radio and television stations asking for information on the salvage operation. It became apparent that the press were not going to go away and that a public statement had now to be made, even though the recovery operation was not at an end.

On 9 November Sheikh Ahmed instructed that a brief statement be issued through Reuters in Dubai, confirming that the recovery operation was indeed in progress and that some of the silver Saudi riyals had been brought to the surface. The statement generated an international storm of faxes and phone calls asking for permission to visit the site of the wreck, the majority of which laboured under the illusion that to reach the salvage vessel was a simple matter of a short excursion from Oman's shoreline, as opposed to a twelve-hour return voyage. Security demands on board the *Flex LD* prohibited visits by contingents of journalists and photographers, but Sheikh Ahmed's private office knew that some sort of press coverage had to be permitted. Consequently, under the terms of a 'world exclusive arrangement', the publication credited with having the globe's largest circulation, the London-based *News of the World*, sent Annette Witheridge to cover the story. Describing the opportunity as a 'reporter's dream', Annette flew out of London at twenty-four hours' notice and was joined on arrival in Muscat by her photographer colleague, John Ferguson, who had been taken off an assignment in Zimbabwe and diverted northwards to Oman. At dawn on 15 November these two representatives of the press sailed out of Mina Raysut aboard His Majesty Sultan Qaboos's warship *Al Batnah*, bound for the recovery site.

When the recovery of the coins was announced, press speculation as to their value ranged from $70 million to a quarter of that sum, with one report suggesting that the government of Saudi Arabia had made a handsome bid for the lot. Riyadh was reported to be embarrassed because while the coins were minted in America, the order had been given by King Abdul Aziz ibn Saud for them to be embossed with the legend 'Made in Mecca'. However, that biggest prize, the silver bullion, had eluded the efforts of the Ocean Group and Ifremer. But as Sheikh Ahmed Farid commented, 'This is not strictly a commercial venture. I want to solve the riddle. The *John Barry* is one of the great mystery ships of all time, because no one really knows what treasure she holds.'

And it remains so. Just two weeks after the 1.4 million coins had been brought to the surface, weighing in at 17 tons, Jean Roux and Robert Hudson took the inevitable decision to draw this first salvage operation of the *John Barry* to a close. As Hudson had told Annette Witheridge, the remaining 1.6 million coins were all but unsalvageable, and the budget for the operation was exhausted. While the bullion had eluded the collective skills of Ifremer and the former Royal Marine, the recovery of the coins represented an astonishing achievement, one from which all those associated with the operation could take both inspiration and encouragement for the future.

What the salvage operation had not delivered, of course, was any solution to the 'mysterious' and 'controversial' nature of the vessel and its wartime cargo. As late as 27 November 1994, at the press conference in Dubai which formally told the world of the recovery of the silver coins, the revolutionary means by which they had been retrieved and the fact that the bullion had not been detected, let alone brought to the surface, many myths about the *John Barry* continued to prevail. In the official information pack given to the press corps on that day, the silver bullion was described as being India-bound although, as Robert Hudson told Annette Witheridge, he had come to the conclusion, based on his own research, that all the silver lend-leased to India during the Second World War had reached the subcontinent and, therefore, it was most unlikely that there was any bullion in the wreck. On the other hand, he accepted, and continues to accept, that many questions on the nature of the cargo loaded into the holds of the liberty ship remain unanswered. Principal among them is, what was the *John Barry* carrying when, on 5 July 1944, she sailed from New York for Philadelphia 'in level ballast'? As we saw in Chapter Four, there is a distinct possibility that she sailed out of Philadelphia on 19 July 1944 with about 800 tons of cargo unaccounted for on the manifest. Given that the stowing of the coins was so well documented and their subsequent loss so well chronicled in America's archives, why, if indeed the bullion was also lost at sea, has the fact been suppressed by successive administrations in Washington during the last half-century? Or, as I put to the American Chargé d'Affaires in Oman, Roberta Chew, in June 1995, surely a state that can point to the precise positions held by its soldiers at the Battle of Chalmette (the Battle of New Orleans) on 8 January 1815 knows whether or not it loaded millions of dollars' worth of state silver into the holds of one of its own liberty ships during the Second World War and, if so, for whom it was intended?

Nor is this the only unanswered question. Indeed, during the research and writing of this book in the spring and early summer of 1995, many anomalies and coincidences became apparent. Important as pieces of declassified paper were, it was only as the fact that I was researching the story became known in circles inhabited by former diplomats and military and intelligence personnel, that people, often not wishing to be named, made contributions of crucial importance in the piecing together of the *John Barry* jigsaw.

Chapter Eleven

Secrets from the Top – Secrets from the Deep

The attempted unravelment of any conspiracy of state silence is, inevitably, attended by an army of theories and, over the years, the story of the *John Barry* has proved to be no exception. As research for this book progressed there were those who greatly assisted the writer by endorsing certain lines of enquiry. It has to be recorded, however, that one initiative, based on a remarkable claim about the liberty ship's cargo, yielded no documentary or indeed corroboratory evidence of any kind. But the claim intrigued.

London, 22 April 1995.
The hour was late, the transatlantic caller urgent in tone, claiming he knew the intended destination of the 'silver treasure' loaded aboard the *John Barry* during the summer of 1944. While he subsequently gave satisfactory answers that proved he knew the Gulf well and had served in an influential post there as late as the 1970s, I would not have pursued his claim at all but for one statement: 'Eddy fixed it all up.'

Colonel William Eddy was, in August 1944, suddenly appointed the American Minister in Jeddah, replacing the career diplomat James Moose. But Colonel Eddy was more than just a soldier turned diplomat. Indeed, his presence in the Kingdom of Saudi Arabia at the very beginning of America's assumption of its dominant role in the life of the country, principally though ARAMCO, cannot be regarded as a coincidence.

At the start of his administration, President Roosevelt sent 'Wild' Bill Donovan to London to study British Intelligence systems (he was, at Churchill's insistence, given unlimited wartime access to the code-deciphering school at Bletchley Park, with the view that on his return to America he would establish Washington's own intelligence service – the Office of Strategic Service, the precursor to the Central Intelligence Agency – the CIA). Donovan did this with exemplary efficiency. In the execution of his task, he demanded two strict conditions, both of which Roosevelt accepted: that he would have direct access to the President and that he could 'hand pick' his team.

Colonel William Eddy was a veteran of the First World War, a holder of the Congressional Medal of Honour, who, in the early years of the Second World War, played a pivotal intelligence role in the success of Operation Torch (when Allied troops moved into French North Africa, bringing an end to their Vichy regimes). He was also a fluent Arabic speaker and a lecturer, in Arabic, at Cairo University, which was where Donovan tracked him down and recruited him to his intelligence banner.

Roosevelt's decision, in July of 1944, suddenly to replace Moose with Eddy as America's representative in Saudi Arabia has never been explained, but the President had already decided that the Kingdom was to play a key role in his foreign policy strategy after the war. Not that there weren't problems. A 'Status of Nations' chart, issued as an Appendix to the President's 'Sixteenth Report to Congress on Lend-Lease Operations' on 23 August 1944, lists dates upon which governments considered eligible for lend-lease supplies became belligerents to the Axis Powers. Saudi Arabia enjoys the dubious distinction of being the only country on the list of which it was 'Uncertain' upon which dates either criterion – 'Earliest Date of Existence of State of War With Any Axis Power' and 'Earliest Date of Severance of Diplomatic Relations With Any Axis Power' – had been met. The Saudi King was very much his own man, an enigmatic figure, used to playing one side against the other, and Washington began to fret. Indeed, at the time of the fall of Berlin to the Allies, German archives contained evidence of how skilfully the Saudi monarch had played the role of the consummate politician with Hitler, with whom he had in July 1939 signed an agreement for the supply of small arms and ammunition and had commenced negotiations for the construction by Germany of a munitions production plant in the Kingdom. Well before the end of the war, Washington realised that King Abdul Aziz ibn Saud was a man to be watched and courted in this new sphere of American influence. The more so because of the monarch's appetite for arms, which, as Washington was well aware, he was passing to his fellow Arabs in Palestine, who were fighting what they saw as Britain's half-hearted attempts to stop the arrival of Jewish settlers. Yet Roosevelt knew that after the war America would be irrevocably committed to the creation of a Jewish state in Palestine, a policy he had to make acceptable to Saudi Arabia, with its vast oil deposits in which, through ARAMCO, Washington would have a vital stake.

It was a particularly difficult foreign policy objective and Colonel William Eddy, in addition to nursing ARAMCO in its infancy in the Kingdom, was the man best suited to achieving it. Eddy's role in the establishment of ARAMCO is beyond dispute; on occasion, even messages of state were relayed to him in Jeddah via the company's communication system. What is infinitely more difficult to prove are the details of his personal strategy, designed to persuade the Saudi monarch to accept the creation of an American-sponsored, Zionist Jewish state on what was then Arab land. It is known that Washington promised Saudi Arabia a $57 million inducement to be paid once the war was at an end, a staggering amount of 'aid' for the time, particularly for a country on the brink of untold riches from oil revenues. What precise role Eddy took in all this is not clear, although it is well established that he used his influence with the Saudi King to persuade him to meet personally with

Roosevelt in February 1945, after the Yalta Conference with Stalin and Churchill.

But of the Colonel's role in the *John Barry* affair, my midnight caller had no doubt. 'The silver bullion on the *Barry* was for Abdul Aziz, in exchange for not causing trouble for the Zionists in Palestine. It was to be the biggest bribe in history and Eddy fixed it all up.'

That is one theory. Here is another.

Joseph Giaconne of New York was, in conversation with the author, equally adamant in his version of the *John Barry* affair, and he was far more qualified to comment than the midnight caller, for in the summer of 1944 he was Able Seaman Giaconne and a member of the liberty ship's crew. Now in his eighty-eighth year, Giaconne's recollection of the loading of the *John Barry* remains sharply in focus and he, too, makes an astonishing claim. In every relevant detail but one, his version does not vary from that given to Brian Shoemaker by the former member of the Navy Armed Guard, Walter Nendza (see Chapter One), namely that the bullion, in boxes, was loaded into a specially built vault in hold No. 3, on the starboard side, but, Giaconne added, 'against the bulkhead of hold No. 2'. He also recalls the presence on board of armed FBI agents, one of whom 'challenged me on the bridge of the *John Barry*, even though I was a crew member'. But when asked what he believed the boxes to contain, Joseph Giaconne made the amazing reply, 'Gold!'

When asked where he believed the bullion was going he was enigmatic.

'That's a very sensitive question and none of us on the ship were meant to know. You'd better ask the US government.' Asking the US government, however, as many who have tried this approach over the years can bear witness, has always led to a dead end.

It has been a persistent belief that the *John Barry* was, on what proved to be her final voyage, bound for India. This was a long-held theory of Captain Brian Shoemaker. Yet, as we have seen, all available documentary evidence clearly establishes that the liberty ship was to discharge her cargo at Ras Tanurah, on Saudi Arabia's eastern shore (where the silver coins were to have been offloaded, together with materials for ARAMCO), the Gulf Island of Bahrain (where supplies would have been delivered for the Bahrain Petroleum Company) and the secret destination, not even identified to the vessel's Master, Joseph Ellerwald. The fact that the ship was to proceed to Abadan, at the northern end of the Gulf, has been proved conclusively, by the discovery of the US Navy's Intelligence Report of 3 September 1944, which not only identifies Abadan as a port of destination but confirms that the vessel's cargo included $26 million worth of silver. The secret state order for Ellerwald to make for Abadan, following the calls at Ras Tanurah and Bahrain, would have been contained in the steel box carried by the Navy Armed Guard Officer who, as we saw in Chapter Seven, threw the container into the sea following *U859*'s attack.

It has also been a long-held opinion that the supposed presence on board of bullion was, to a great extent, a result of shipboard speculation, 'crew gossip' inspired by the loading in Philadelphia of the silver coins from the American Mint. Indeed, the ship's purser, Gerald Richards, now of Independence, Missouri, has been quoted in print as having said in 1944 that bullion was on board. Today Mr Richards insists he was referring only to the loading of the silver coins.

But if rumours of silver bullion aboard the *John Barry* had been born of idle conjecture, why the persistent quoting of so precise a figure as $26 million? We now know, of course, that the figure itself is corroborated by an American Intelligence Report which was quite separate from statements taken from survivors of the liberty ship. It is this same report which confirms that the *John Barry* was not carrying water or sand in her holds to serve as ballast, but was loaded, proving that when she set sail from New York for Philadelphia on 5 July 1944, 'in level ballast', she was indeed carrying cargo of a considerable weight. This is also confirmed on the Vessel Performance and Cargo Report, which clearly indicates that no ballast was carried. It is this same document, with its many deletions and amendments, which carries the handwritten annotation against the section designed to show the port of discharge for 'Russian' cargo, 'Unk' – unknown

– and, then, 'Persian Gulf'. And, further still, it is this same Vessel Performance and Cargo Report which proves, as we saw in Chapter Four, that either the *John Barry* sailed with space to spare (which given her 461 tons of deck cargo is unlikely in the extreme), or she sailed with a possible 800 tons of cargo unaccounted for.

This fact alone serves to raise yet another questionmark over the curious conduct of the American state regarding the *John Barry* cargo. While, according to preloading state documentation, the USSR is clearly to be supplied with 'non-ferrous metals' or 'metals', the commodity is not shown in either designation on the cargo report. It has to be recorded that neither wee the coins listed on the report, although the transaction was minutely registered on state documents. This suggests not so much an 'on-off' love affair with secrecy as a studied attempt, in the case of the *John Barry*, to hide anything that may have attracted unwelcome interest. Indeed, as we saw in President Roosevelt's Congressional message, there was much about the arrangements governing lend-lease, including just who was getting what, which was available for public consumption. The existence of lend-lease to the USSR was internationally known, as was the fact that Abadan was a port of discharge of military hardware, which was then taken by road and rail through Iran into Russian territory. This openness about so many details is what makes the mystery surrounding the *John Barry*'s cargo so intriguing. And the veil of secrecy has remained drawn, with action being taken over the years to keep it that way. On 29 November 1967, Arthur Markel, General Manager of the Reynolds Sub-Marine Services Corporation of Arlington, Virginia, wrote to Mr R.T. Reckling, then Vice-President of Lykes Brothers, the company which managed the *John Barry* during the Second World War for the War Shipping Administration. Markel was at the time considering mounting a salvage operation on the wreck of the liberty ship. The second paragraph of his letter reads as follows:

In researching the Maritime Administration records, we find that the manifest contained building materials, but an annotation stated that a large quantity of silver bullion was also carried.

This manifest is believed to have disappeared from the archives shortly after Markel's letter; it is certainly not there today. However, other documents have survived the fifty-year-old campaign of secrecy, and the information they yield can be pieced together to form a fairly coherent narrative.

On 30 May 1944 Colonel Moore in the Washington office of the War Shipping Administration sent a teletype message to his WSA colleague in New York, Nick Larsen: 'John Barry to load New York to Red Sea account, British lend-lease.' While this is the first indication that the liberty ship would take cargo aboard in New York, it does raise the as yet unanswered question of why the arrangement should be charged to the account of 'British lend-lease', given that Britain had no cargo on board. Nonetheless, the crucial factor is that it confirms that the *John Barry* was to take on cargo in New York.

Then, as we saw in Chapter Five, there was the esoteric language employed by John Hutchins of WSA's Washington Office in a 'Secret' message to Nick Larsen in New York on 13 June. ('Proposed plan for July for friends . . . this would leave NY clear during the month for your special.') It is apparent that the 'special' was to be a consignment of considerable importance – witness the fitting of an extra 30-ton boom aboard the vessel, the crossing of the *John Barry* from the Hoboken side of the Hudson River to the Manhattan side (where it was just minutes away from the Assay Office at 32 Old Slip) and the constant use of the 'Russian Area' stamp on all internal WSA correspondence.

After the sinking, we come to the disappearance from the archives of Ellerwald's statement made in Khorramshahr, and the measure he took of making a statement independent of all authority, in which he records a total crew of forty-four as opposed to forty-two, as given on the Coastguard count, which supports the assertions by some of the crew that there were FBI agents on board, presumably to provide discreet security for the bullion.

Thus all available evidence suggests that the *John Barry* was prepared for the voyage in Hoboken and that, shortly after, in the absence of the Master and his crew, she was taken to the Manhattan side of the Hudson and there loaded with silver bullion from the US Assay Office. This strategy ensured maximum security, which, as the loading of the coins proved, would not have been possible in Philadelphia. This is also presumably why the coins for Saudi Arabia were not offloaded in the busier port of Jeddah, on the Red Sea, which would seem to have made more sense than taking them through the Arabian Sea and up into the Gulf to Ras Tanurah; in this tiny, more tightly controlled port (effectively managed by Americans anyway, through its use by ARAMCO), it was far less likely that attention would be drawn to the liberty ship.

It cannot be known for certain if Joseph Ellerwald, who boarded the *John Barry* for the first time on 3 July, was told of the special cargo in the holds of his new command in New York, or whether he only became aware of the secret consignment after the sinking of the vessel. But given that he was almost certainly unaware, at the time of sailing from Philadelphia, that one of his ports of destination was Abadan, it can be reliably assumed that he was ignorant of the special nature of some of the cargo.

Which brings us the pivotal point of the whole affair. For whom was the silver bullion intended? What hidden foreign policy initiative in the summer of 1944 prompted the government of the United States to send its treasure to an unlikely foreign field? President Roosevelt had, as we have seen, taken a special interest in his administration's lend-lease supplies to the Soviets. He had even taken measures to ensure that the third of the four protocols, which governed supplies to Joseph Stalin's regime, was amended to meet 'special circumstances', although it remains unclear just what he considered 'special circumstances' to be.

In the event, the discovery of the decisive clue to the mystery of the *John Barry* was almost routine. I approached the Russian Ambassador to Oman, Alexander Patsev, with a request for details of the Third Protocol, and the wheels of government in Moscow began to turn. In due course, the Director of the Ministry of Foreign Affairs Archives, Ivor Lebedev, advised that the schedules of the Third Protocol had indeed been extended, just as Roosevelt had told Congress on 23 August 1944, and they had included an agreement that the United States would provide the Soviet Union with materials of 'agreed specification'. As we saw however, in Chapter Four, the actual tonnages were 'approximate', being subject to fluctuation depending on the availability of goods at the dockside at any given time and also on the availability of suitable space aboard a vessel. I was also informed that the document included an appendix of goods supplied 'out of protocol' – that is under Roosevelt's secret extension, the details of which he did not divulge to Congress – and that precise terms were not always used. This seemed to me in keeping with American policy: it will be recalled that they used the vague 'non-ferrous metals' or 'metals' in other documentation concerning shipment to the Soviet Union. In the relevant section of the document held by Moscow, the even vaguer term 'equipment' is used. In addition, the Director of the Foreign Affairs Archives advised me that 'the agreed volume of goods to be supplied were not actually received'. This surely prompts the observation that at least some of those goods might well by lying on the bottom of the Arabian Sea.

Recognising how crucial all this information was, I requested sight of the Third Protocol itself, and on 8 July 1995 it was handed over to me at the Russian Embassy in Muscat. It proved to be an astonishing document. Running from mid-1943 to mid-1944, it was ratified at the Soviet Embassy in London on 19 October 1943; it was then taken to the Kremlin, since when it had not seen the light of day. It was signed on behalf of the Soviet state by F. Gusev and D. Borisyenko, with John Vaivant signing on behalf of Washington. Britain's witnesses were those Foreign Office mandarins of the time, Oliver Lyttelton and Alexander Cadogan, while Vincent Massie was the witness for Canada. While the British and Canadian representatives were not given access to the appendix designated 'out of protocol', they would have seen in the preamble that under its terms Washington was to supply Moscow with 5,100,000 tons of materials, 2,700,000 tons of which were to be carried on vessels flying the hammer and sickle and 2,400,000 tons under the Stars and Stripes. The routes to be followed, in the event of the Pacific Ocean route to Vladivostok remaining closed to America on account of the hostilities with Japan, would be via the Atlantic (to Murmansk) and the Persian Gulf (to Abadan). The goods and materials to be supplied under the Third Protocol alone represent an astonishing outpouring of American manufactures, as a brief example will confirm.

One thousand tanks, 24,000 jeeps, 12,000 motorcycles, 14,010 one-kilowatt radio stations, 100,000 mobile field telephones, 500 railway engines, 18,000 tons of leather with which to make military footwear, 3,600 pairs of army boots, 18 million yards of material with which to make army greatcoats, 25 million yards of cotton material with which to make army shirts and $12 million worth of medicines. And then, on page 24, come the goods to be supplied 'out of protocol'. These include, yet again, a cornucopia of material: 35,760 tons of aluminium, 4,032 tons of metallic magnium, 6,600 tons of nickel, 13,440 tons of zinc, 8,500 tons of cobalt and prodigious amounts of copper wire and pipes. And, at the foot of page 40, $2,400,000 worth of industrial diamonds that today would have a value of some $28 million. Whether or not they were carried to the Soviets aboard the *John Barry*, it is impossible to tell (but, like the bullion, they never reached Moscow).

But the *coup de grâce* delivered by the Third Protocol comes at the foot of page 35, sandwiched between the listing of utilitarian supplies. Under the subheading 'urgently required equipment' come two sparse lines: 'Requested – $60 million worth. Agreed to supply $25 million worth.' In view of the fact that, as we have seen, the supply of materials was approximate, the amount of $25 million is very close to the recorded value of the bullion carried by the *John Barry*, and is surely beyond the bounds of credible coincidence. The most telling aspect of this part of the hitherto secret Third Protocol is, of course, that in the preceding pages supplies of far lesser value are itemised to an almost laborious extent. Yet, quite suddenly, just three ambiguous words are deemed an adequate description for an item of enormous value. It leads inescapably to the conclusion that here at last is Soviet evidence that very special supplies, born of Roosevelt's 'special circumstances', were indeed expected by Moscow. As for the term 'equipment', Elmir Tagirov, Third Secretary at the Russian Embassy in Muscat, told me:

The way in which the word is used in the protocol, it is obviously meant to disguise. It could, in the context, mean just what those who wrote it wanted it to mean without giving too much away.

But again, the only conclusion that can be arrived at, on all the available evidence, is that such an unidentified value, worth today six times as much, must be the elusive consignment of bullion.

As to where the bullion was stored, it would seem, as Brian Shoemaker originally predicted, to have been in hold No. 3 even though Nick Larsen of the WSA ordered the installation of the 30-ton boom at No. 4, suggesting that cargo of considerable weight and secrecy was stowed there as well. This remains a mystery to be solved. If Stalin's silver *was* in hold No. 3, it seems highly likely that in excess of some 400 tons of it now rests in the sand and silt of the Arabian Sea, given that the ship broke in two across hold No. 3. The vast amount of debris discovered between the two parts of the wreck adds further weight to this view. It is a probability that will give Sheikh Farid's Ocean Group new challenges in any future salvage operation.

That President Roosevelt should have secretly sent bullion and diamonds to Stalin will generate yet further controversy about the nature of the relationship between the 'Big Three' – Roosevelt, Stalin and Churchill – during the final year of the Second World War. One historian who will not be surprised is Clive Ponting of Swansea University, who led the revisionist view of the so-called 'special relationship' between Britain and the United States, upon which this unravelment of the *John Barry* affair has, arguably, thrown additional light. Another will be Professor John Charmley, who has observed in print that 'Roosevelt spent the last two years of the war cultivating a special relationship with the Soviets', a relationship to which this book has hopefully brought a new dimension. Roosevelt's 'special circumstances' with Stalin amplify his well-recorded view of the political landscape of the post-war world, which he saw as being dominated by a form of co-existence between the United States and the Union of Soviet Socialist Republics. He understood well enough the difficulties he would have with his own electorate at being seen to accommodate Russia's grasp on Eastern Europe, but acknowledged that in light of the events of the Second World War, Stalin had to be given the territorial security he desired. Knowing equally well that the socialist state would be totally bankrupt at the end of the conflict, Roosevelt might well have thought that financial inducements would give him leverage to moderate Stalin's territorial ambitions and that from this influence a Moscow–Washington Axis might evolve.

Proof of this strategy may be drawn from Roosevelt's accommodation of Stalin at Yalta and his shock statement to Churchill that American troops would be repatriated from Europe just as quickly as could be arranged at the end of the war. Lend-lease, too, was to be abruptly terminated. The Yalta Conference, in effect, marked the end of the wartime 'special relationship' between London and Washington, with Roosevelt seeming anxious not to antagonise Stalin by keeping his forces of the continent of Europe. The widespread desire in Washington for a close working relationship between the US and the USSR to be forged after the war was emphasised by Roosevelt's former Vice-President, Henry Wallace. Writing in the influential publication *New Republic*, Wallace recorded the prevailing American view at the time that the centre of world power no longer resided in the capitals of Western Europe. Power, he wrote, was now in the hands of Washington and Moscow, with their respective leaders having much in common. Both believed, for example, that colonies belonged to the past. Both believed in the sovereignty of small states, even though both governments had 'occasionally stepped over the line' when the defence of their respective nations had been in question. Wallace also revealed that Britain had vetoed a resolution, proposed by the Russians at the 1943 Tehran Conference and supported by the United States, for the 'early liberation of the entire colonial world'. It was a strategy that Roosevelt's successor, Harry Truman, pursued through his many attempts to work with Stalin on arms control in the immediate post-war years, upholding his predecessor's opinion that the United States could indeed co-exist with the USSR.

Today, in the light of forty years of Cold War, it is, perhaps, too easily forgotten how popular the Russians were in the West at the end of the Second World War, principally because of the terrible sacrifices they had made during the conflict. Indeed, had it not been for the Red Army, holding down Hitler's troops, Britain could well have faced catastrophe before America entered the war. The post-war goodwill shown towards the Soviet Union was as much in evidence in America as in Europe, one of the reasons why Winston Churchill's speech in Fulton, Missouri, in March 1946 ('An Iron Curtain has descended across the Continent of Europe') – which is now seen as having kick-started the Cold War – was, at the time, widely regarded in America as an act of irresponsible, populist mischief. As to the consequent Cold War proper, that can be laid squarely at the door of Joseph Stalin's myopic view of the Western, capitalist world, and particularly his total misreading of the United States and his abiding suspicion and unrelenting hostility towards Washington and all its works. It was a situation that President Roosevelt had expressly sought to avoid, by means of a strategy in which the *John Barry* was used to play a potentially vital role.

The story of the *John Barry* thus retains a questionmark. Only the future and the resolve of the man who has carried the story this far will tell how long the world has to wait before the silver bullion finally surfaces. But, as Sheikh Ahmed Farid al Aulaqi remarks, 'The pursuit of the *John Barry*, the solving of this greatest riddle of the Arabian Sea, may still have surprises to spring.' Indeed. Stalin's silver? Gold and diamonds? The *John Barry* remains, until the next time, her controversial and mysterious self, and remains a magnet to those who abhor life without the dignity of danger.

Appendix I: The Significance of *U859*'s Secret Cargo

When I first discovered the coincidence that both the *John Barry* and *U859* were carrying 'silver', and embarked on the research which became this book, I was principally seeking to solve the mystery of the *John Barry*'s cargo. I did not anticipate that my research into the German navy's wartime strategy of despatching its submarines to the Indian Ocean would eventually lead to information every bit as controversial as the questions surrounding the liberty ship. However, after I made contact with a former naval intelligence officer who both endorsed and encouraged a line of enquiry I was already taking – that of seeking to establish the nature of the supplies that German U-boats carried to the Far East – it became apparent that *U859*'s secret cargo was not the only consignment of mercury that Berlin sent to the Japanese. Indeed, as 1944 wore on and the tide of war turned more strongly against the Axis powers, Tokyo applied increasing pressure on Berlin to send materials which could, hopefully, be used to turn events in Japan's favour. Mercury was not the only commodity the

Japanese needed. They also began to demand examples of Germany's scientific and technological advances – for Tokyo is said to have told Berlin that it would be necessary to develop 'special techniques' if the Japanese were to bring the conflict to a successful conclusion. This initiative, in tandem with Japan's conventional munitions programme, required large amounts of mercury – as we have seen, *U859* alone was carrying 31 tons of it.

Allied intelligence sources were well aware of these demands; they also knew that supplies were being delivered by U-boat – witness the pressure on the British navy to sink as many of them in the Indian Ocean as they possibly could. Not that this always prevented these increasingly urgent consignments from reaching Japan. One Far Eastern-bound U-boat carrying parts of the Messerschmitt ME163, an advanced rocket-propelled fighter, was sunk en route in 1944, but Berlin tried again, eventually getting technical drawings of the ME163 through to Tokyo. The Japanese developed the German blueprint as the Mitsubishi J8M1 and had manufactured five of them by the time they surrendered to the Allied forces in August 1945.

It is hardly surprising that Germany should endeavour to send supplies to its ally in the Far East, and some details of its consignments are well documented. Research for this book, however, uncovered at least one incident which for the past half-century has been concealed from the wider world.

In August 1944, two months after the Allied landings on the beaches of Normandy, *U195*, a U-boat of the IXD-1 class, was secretly loaded with a very special cargo in the submarine pens of Bordeaux, then under German control. The cargo was accompanied by a team of German technicians. The IXD-1s had originally been designed to carry fuel for their sister U-boats at sea and were, accordingly, fitted with six torpedo-boat engines, which gave a fast surface speed. For its special assignment, however, *U195* had her torpedo engines replaced with standard submarine diesels and her interior adapted to carry bulk cargo as opposed to fuel. On 20 August 1944, *U195*, under the command of Korvettenkapitan Steinfeld, left Bordeaux at the start of a long and hazardous voyage to Japanese-occupied Batavia (now Djakarta). She was carrying 250 tons of cargo, amongst which was another consignment of mercury, radar technology, optical instruments and, most dramatically of all, V2s, the rocket-propelled 'flying bombs' which were then, like the V1s before them, causing widespread death and destruction in British cities. The V2s were dismantled and packed in crates, and the accompanying technicians were to show the Japanese how to assemble the various parts and put them into service.

U195 had an uneventful run, arriving in Batavia in December 1944, four months after leaving Bordeaux. Her cargo was offloaded for onward shipment to Japan. She set sail for home on 17 January 1945, but six weeks later, on 3 March, she returned to the Batavian port of Tanjong Priok with engine trouble. When Germany surrendered two months later, the Japanese took over *U195*, giving her a new number, *I-506*, but never committing her to operations. Korvettenkapitan Steinfeld and his crew were interned.

Nor was this an isolated incident. Although details are hard to come by fifty years after the event, and many of those involved remain reluctant to talk about it, it is believed that at about the same time other U-boats were making similar long-haul 'dashes' carrying crated V2s – the most sophisticated and deadly weaponry then available to man. There is strong circumstantial evidence that *U180* and *U219* left Bordeaux with consignments of mercury and crated V2s shortly before the French port fell to the Allies. *U180* was destroyed not far into her voyage by an RAF-laid mine, while *U219* escaped an attack by an Avenger from an American escort carrier in late September and eventually arrived safely in Batavia. She, it is reliably believed, was also renumbered by the Japanese for placement in their service.

This bold strategy could have had fearful consequences for the Allies, and particularly for the Americans fighting in the Far East. According to a principal intelligence source to whom I imparted the above information, had the Japanese had time to mass produce the V2s, they could have inflicted great damage on the Allied cause, principally by using them for their primary purpose, as long-range offensive weapons, on the various islands in the Pacific held by the Americans. Yet, as my intelligence source remarked, 'Astonishingly, much remains clouded in secrecy, in both the West and Japan, on the various arms initiatives taken by the Japanese, particularly in the closing years of the war.'

It has been further established, however, that during the highly secret Operation Backfire, when American and British military personnel tested Germany's V weapons at their original place of firing just after the war, the question of the Third Reich sending the weapons to Japan during the closing stages of the conflict was briefly raised. Then, for unknown reasons, it was quietly dropped, as were enquiries by both British and American intelligence services, in the immediate post-war years, into Japan's urgent need for supplies of mercury in 1944. The only deduction arrived at during long conversations in England in April 1995 with a defence analyst and the one-time intelligence officer suggested that the Allies came to believe that the Japanese were developing a 'switching device' which, it is assumed, would have been used to trigger a detonation, possibly the warhead on a rocket-propelled weapon. Mercury would have played a fundamental role in any development and eventual manufacture of such a device. But there persist the clouds of secrecy to which my intelligence source referred, making verification of this theory impossible. As to any connection between the supplies of mercury and the V weapons, that too is a question which, it has been generally presumed, only the Japanese themselves can answer.

However, a select group of defence and intelligence analysts on both sides of the Atlantic have long believed that they know the truth. The information they possess is so astounding that in many a considered view it lessens the burden borne by President Harry Truman and, by implication, the American nation, for deciding to drop atomic bombs on the Japanese cities of Hiroshima and Nagasaki. The analysts believe – and all circumstantial evidence uncovered during the research which became this book supports their belief – that in those last months of the war Japan herself striving to produce an atomic bomb, which she would undoubtedly have used had she beaten the Americans in that most deadly of arms races.

The most dramatic evidence that Japan was developing an atomic bomb can be found in details of the highly secret voyage of *U234*, which sailed from Kiel, bound for Japan, on 25 March 1945, just forty-eight hours after the Allied armies had crossed the Rhine.

Like *U195*, *U234* had undergone major modifications to prepare her for this hazardous journey. She was a submarine of the XB class, originally designed to lay mines, but principally used to transport bulk cargo. The modifications entailed the removal of all but six of her mine tubes, which left large areas free for the stowing of cargo. The remaining six tubes were filled with specially crafted containers into which were stowed weapon blueprints, armaments and metals deemed to be of strategic value to Japan. Yet further modifications saw the welding of two steel platforms on both sides of the submarine's conning tower, to which were attached 20-foot-long metal cylinders. The loading of the 240 tonnes of cargo was overseen by a hand-picked task force, the Marine Sonder Dienst Auslands, and consisted of radar equipment, fuel-injection pumps, advanced radio systems, detonation fuses, optical instruments, vacuum tubes and boxes of anti-tank ammunition. The cargo also contained a considerable quantity of metals, which necessitated the removal of the U-boat's outer keel plates, permitting such materials to be loaded into the adjacent duct.

But it is the material stowed in the six mine tubes that is of most interest. For, in addition to further consignments of mercury, they held ten containers of radioactive uranium oxide (U235), an essential ingredient in the manufacture of an atomic bomb. Indeed, given the extreme secrecy that attended the shipment, it seems wholly legitimate to ask: if not an atomic weapons programme, what could the uranium have been for? All circumstantial evidence suggests that the voyage of *U234*, begun only two months before Germany's surrender, was a last desperate attempt by the Axis partners to snatch victory from the which jaws of defeat.

In the event, however, the Allied victory overtook *U234* in the course of her journey to Japan. While the U-boat was still in the Atlantic, her commander, Kapitanleutnant Johann Heinrich Fehler, heard on his radio news of his country's capitulation and the subsequent order, given on 10 May, for all German submarines to report their positions and then proceed to the nearest

Allied port. Kapitanleutnant Fehler had a crew of forty-four and a number of distinguished passengers, among whom was the Luftwaffe general Ulrich Kessler, who had been appointed Air Attaché to the German Embassy in Tokyo, and two senior Japanese navy commanders, Genzo Shoji, a distinguished designer of aircraft, and Hideo Tomonaga, a noted naval architect and engineer. When Fehler confirmed his decision to comply with the order to report his position and, in effect, place his craft under Allied control, the two Japanese committed suicide by drinking large quantities of luminal. On 14 May *U234* surrendered at sea to the USS *Sutton*, which then escorted her to the port of Portsmouth, New Hampshire, arriving there on 16 May.

The U-boat's cargo, including the radioactive uranium, was unloaded by American officials; much to German surprise, the manifest that Washington later produced amounted to only 162 tonnes, some 78 tonnes short of the amount which had been loaded two months earlier in Kiel. The Americans have consistently refused to comment on this discrepancy, or indeed to say to what use they put the uranium. The fate of *U234*, however, is well established. She was used for US navy experiments and then, in November 1947, taken off Cape Cod, on America's eastern seaboard, and sunk.

As with any subject even remotely connected with the *John Barry*, there remain many unanswered questions concerning the cargo the U-boats were carrying to their Japanese allies, and the use to which it was to be put on arrival. But it is intriguing to consider that the extraordinary facts related in this appendix should have emerged quite by chance from investigation of a strange coincidence – that two ships on opposing sides in the same conflict should both have been carrying secret consignments of 'silver' at the time of a fateful encounter in the Arabian Sea.

Appendix II: The Key Documents

ТРЕТИЙ ПРОТОКОЛ О ПОСТАВКАХ В СССР ИЗ АНГЛИИ, КАНАДЫ И США

19 октября 1943 г.

The title page of the Third Protocol, ratified in London on 19 October 1943.

APPENDIX II

потери судов, нарушение производственных планов или нужды других операций не позволят осуществить их выполнение, то возможно окажется необходимым программы поставок сократить. С другой стороны, если позволят условия, Правительства Соединенных Штатов, Соединенного Королевства и Канады будут рады пересматривать программы, от времени до времени с целью увеличения об"ема поставок.

В свидетельство чего нижеподписавшиеся, соответственно уполномоченные, каждый своим Правительством, подписали настоящий Протокол.

Настоящий составлен в четырех экземплярах на английском языке в г. Лондоне 19-го дня, Октября месяца, 1943 года.

За Правительство Союза Советских Социалистических Республик:

Ф. ГУСЕВ.

Д. БОРИСЕНКО.

За Правительство Соединенных Штатов Америки:

Джон Ж. ВАЙНАНТ.

За Правительство Великобритании и Северной Ирландии:

ОЛИВЕР ЛИТТЕЛЬТОН.
АЛЕКСАНДР КАДОГАН.

За Правительство Канады:

ВИНСЕНТ МЭССЕЙ.

The signatories of the Third Protocol.

ПОГРУЗОЧНЫЙ ВЕС ОБОРУДОВАНИЯ, ПОСТАВЛЯЕМОГО СОГЛАСНО СОВЕТСКИМ ЗАКАЗАМ ВНЕ ПРОТОКОЛА.

/Все веса в коротких тоннах/.

<u>РАЗЛИЧНОЕ ВОЕННО МОРСКОЕ ИМУЩЕСТВО</u> - Погрузочный вес I7,I00

МЕТАЛЛЫ, ХИМИКАЛИИ И ДРУГИЕ ПРОДУКТЫ.

/ Все веса в коротких тоннах/.

/ Поставка производится равными месячными количествами, насколько это осуществимо, за исключением случаев, оговоренных отдельно/.

/ Количества, предложенные ниже, включают то количество материала, которое должно быть поставлено в течение Третьего Протокольного Периода по новым заказам и по старым заказам недопоставленным к 30-му Июня I943 года/.

<u>ДЮРАЛЮМИНИЕВЫЕ И АЛЮМИНИЕВЫЕ ОТЛИВКИ</u>.

<u>Запрошено</u>: 80,640 тонн

<u>Предложено</u>: 35,760 тонн

I8,000 тонн должны быть поставлены другими участниками протокола.

/ Подлежит пересмотру в сторону увеличения, насколько позволят обстоятельства/.

<u>МЕТАЛЛИЧЕСКИЙ МАГНИЙ</u>.

<u>Запрошено</u>: 4,032 тонн

<u>Предложено</u>: 4,032 тонны

<u>Н И К Е Л Ь</u>.

<u>Запрошено</u>: 9,408 тонн

<u>Предложено</u>: 6,600 тонн

3,600 тонн в чушках.
600 тонн в монель-ломе.
2,400 тонн максимально содержащегося в изделиях из стали и цветных металлов.
I,800 тонн в чушках должны быть поставлены другими участниками протокола.

<u>МОЛИБДЕНОВЫЕ КОНЦЕНТРАТЫ</u>.

<u>Запрошено</u>: 4,480 тонн

<u>Предложено</u>: 4,000 тонн

The start of the secret appendix: 'Goods to be Supplied Out of Protocol'.

APPENDIX II

ЭЛЕКТРОЛИТИЧЕСКАЯ МЕДЬ.

Запрошено: 134,400 тонн

Предложено: 134,400 тонн максимум.

	Тонн, Максимум.
Медь в медных сплавах	75,264
Медь в прокате желтой меди	15,000
Медь в медном кабеле и медной проволоке	20,000
Медь в подводном кабеле	50
Медь в силовом кабеле	21,395
Медь в морском кабеле	465

Ц И Н К. /В чушках/.

Запрошено: 13,440 тонн.

Предложено: 13,440 тонн.

К О Б А Л Ь Т.

Запрошено: 161 тонна.

Предложено: 80,5 тонны.

/ Должно быть поставлено в первые шесть месяцев.

Другие участники протокола восполнят остальное.

К А Д М И Й.

Запрошено: 224 тонны

Предложено: Должно быть поставлено другими участниками протокола.

МЕДНЫЕ СПЛАВЫ. /Латунь и бронза/.

Запрошено: 107,520 тонн

Предложено: 107,520 тонн.

МЕДНЫЕ ТОВАРЫ И ТРУБЫ./Прокат из латуни/.

Запрошено: 16,128 тонн

Предложено: 15,000 тонн.

МЕДНЫЕ ПРОВОДА И ПРОВОЛОКА.

Запрошено: 33,600 тонн /неизолированная медная проволока/.

Предложено: 20,000 тонн

An example of some of the materials to be supplied, including cobalt and nickel, with tonnages specified.

На I2,000,000 долларов автоблокировочных систем, из старых заказов, недовыполненных на 30-ое Июня I948 года. / Предложение предоставляет 8,000 км. Определение приоритета, который должен быть дан, будет эквивалентно потребителям собственной страны, которым предоставляется подобное оборудование/.

НА 36,500,000 долларов вспомогательного промышленного оборудования, оставшегося от старых заказов, недовыполненных на 30-ое Июня I948 года. В дополнение к вышеуказанному предложению на вспомогательное промышленное оборудование на 30-ое Июня I948 года останутся недопоставленными по предварительной оценке старые заказы на сумму в 64,000,000 долларов. Эти заказы предлагается подвергнуть тщательному рассмотрению на предмет отмены тех из них, которые уже не являются необходимыми. Те же из них, которые отменены не будут, останутся в производстве в порядке существующей системы приоритета и оборудование по ним будет поставлено, как только закончится его изготовление.

<u>СИЛОВОЕ ОБОРУДОВАНИЕ, ВКЛЮЧАЯ ОБОРУДОВАНИЕ И КОТЛЫ ДЛЯ СУЩЕСТВУЮЩИХ СТАНЦИЙ</u>.

<u>Запрошено</u>: На I35,000,000 долларов.

<u>Предложено</u>: На 75,000,000 долларов.

На 57,000,000 долларов - новые заказы.
На I8,000,000 долларов, старые заказы, недопоставленные на 30-ое Июня I948 года. / Предположительно/.

<u>ЭЛЕКТРО-СИЛОВОЙ КАБЕЛЬ</u>.

<u>Запрошено:</u> I2,000 км.

<u>Предложено</u>: I2,000 км.

<u>КОНТРОЛЬНО-ИЗМЕРИТЕЛЬНЫЕ ИНСТРУМЕНТЫ И ИСПЫТАТЕЛЬНЫЕ МАШИНЫ</u>.

/ Точные измерительные и испытательные машины и инструменты/.

<u>Запрошено:</u> На 2,000,000 долларов.

<u>Предложено</u>: На I,700,000 долларов.

На 840,000 долларов - новые заказы.
На 860,000 долларсв - старые заказы, недовыполненные на 30-ое Июня I948 года. /Предположительно/.

<u>СРОЧНО НЕОБХОДИМОЕ ОБОРУДОВАНИЕ.</u>

<u>Запрошено</u>: На 60,000,000 долларов.

<u>Предложено</u>: На 25,000,000 долларов срочно необходимого оборудования.

Page 35 of the Protocol: the bottom item is the ambiguously styled 'Urgently Required Equipment', now believed to be silver bullion. The entry explains that Moscow had requested $60 million worth but that Washington committed to sending 'approximately' $25 million worth.

2. Танки. - I,000 танков /ВАЛЕНТАЙНОВ/. Запчасти на I2 месяцев будут поставлены и для танков и для танковых пушек в соответствии со шкалой с наиболее полной нормой, базирующейся на опыте нормальной потребности и в возмещении соответствующих частей.

3. Порох. -

а/ Типа - 2,250 коротких тонн в течение первых шести месяцев в дополнение к приблизительно 2,500 коротких тонн, которые не были отправлены к I-му Июля I943 года.

б/ Типа М.OI7 - I,600 коротких тонн, которые не были отправлены к I-му Июля, а также тот излишек, который изготовлен до момента окончания производства.

4. Авиационный бензин.- I0,000 тонн в месяц будет предоставлено в Абадане в соответствии с соглашением с Правительством Соединенных Штатов, по которому последнее предоставит подобное же количество Правительству Соединенного Королевства из количества ациационного бензина, которое должно быть поставлено Правительством Соединенных Штатов Правительству СССР.

ГРУППА II. - РАЗЛИЧНЫЕ МАТЕРИАЛЫ -

I. Олово. - 6,000 тонн /Минус любое количество сверх 6,000 тонн, получаемых СССР из Китая/.

2. Свинец. - I2,000 тонн из Австралии.

3. Быстрорежущая сталь. - 60 тонн при условии согласования спецификации.

4. Кобальт. - 72 тонны во вторые шесть месяцев.

5. Промышленные алмазы. - На 2,400,000 долларов, при условии согласования спецификации.

Page 40: the bottom item records the agreement to supply $2,400,000 worth of industrial diamonds. This consignment, which would today have a value of approximately $28 million, never reached Moscow.

Mr. Frank Coe December 31, 194

James W. Angell

Provision of 100 Million Ounces of Silver to the Government of India

I attach a preliminary memorandum on the above question. I have not yet completed discussions with our British Empire people, and if any important new considerations arise from these discussions, I will so inform you.

My own disposition at present is to make the following recommendations:

1. The requested silver should be sent to India.

2. The transaction should be handled not through Lend-Lease aid but as a cash transaction through the U.K. and without any ounce for ounce return clause, in order to draw down U.K. dollar balances and to draw down Indian sterling balances in London, and in order to reserve Lend-Lease aid for purposes more closely connected with the war.

3. Before going further with these recommendations the ground should be explored with the British and with the Senate silver group.

. tt.chment 5

JWAngell: ea

An internal memo between two members of staff at the Foriegn Economic Administration in Washington, providing evidence of the US policy of keeping Britain's dollar reserves low. The year, obscured on this copy, is 1943.

APPENDIX II

JUNE 13, 1944

<u>VIA TELETYPE</u>

SECRET

MR. N. N. LARSEN – WAR SHIPPING ADMINISTRATION – NEW YORK, N. Y.

PROPOSED PLAN FOR JULY FOR FRIENDS IS AS FOLLOWS: FOR YOUR SPECIAL 12 SHIPS IN GROUP 300 BERTHING NEW YORK JULY 3. OF THESE 8 WOULD LOAD TO 937.5 tons each + 1,875.00 tons each 7,500 TONS AND 4 TO 7,100 TONS. 8 SHIPS IN GROUP 301 BERTHING AT NEW YORK JULY 11. OF THESE 6 SHIPS AT 7,500 TONS, 2 SHIPS AT 7,100 TONS. TOTAL PROGRAM IS THUS 20 SHIPS.

WE NOW HAVE 33 SO-CALLED JULY SHIPS FOR THE REGULAR ROUTE AND WE WILL HAVE TO CUT THIS NUMBER TO 20. WE ARE THEREFORE PROPOSING TO CANCEL THREE SHIPS IN N.Y. IN GROUP 48, 5 SHIPS AT NEW YORK IN GROUP 49 AND 3 SHIPS AT NEW YORK IN GROUP 50. ALSO ONE SHIP AT PHILADELPHIA IN EACH OF GROUPS 48, 49, AND 50, THUS MAKING A TOTAL OF 13 CANCELLATIONS. THIS WOULD LEAVE NEW YORK CLEAR DURING THE MONTH FOR YOUR SPECIAL.

IT IS POSSIBLE THAT ONE OR BOTH OF THE SUGAR SHIPS MAY BE SHIFTED TO NORTH ATLANTIC LOADING FOR THE SAME DESTINATION AS NOW SCHEDULED.

WILL BE GLAD TO GET YOUR COMMENTS ON THIS PROGRAM AND WILL TRY TO REACH YOU BY TELEPHONE.

HUTCHINS

John C. B. Hutchins/lb
cc: Captain Conway
Mr. Donald

DECLASSIFIED
Authority NND730046
By LAG NARA Date 4/13/90

Special Note:
Box 68 HAS oversize CHARTS of P.6 Shipping including 2 on J. BARRY

The message from John Hutchins to Nick Larsen of the War Shipping Administration, dated 13 June 1944, detailing measures to be taken to keep New York 'clear during the month for your special'. Note the obscure opening words: 'Proposed plan for July for friends'.

June 22, 1944

Treasurer of the United States
Treasury Department
Washington, D. C.

Attention: Mr. W. J. Weber

Dear Sir:

For your information, in connection with Lend-Lease to the Government of India of 90,000,000 fine ounces of silver, as referred to in the directive from the Acting Secretary of the Treasury, dated June 20, 1944, there is enclosed herewith a copy of a telegram which has been forwarded to the Superintendent of the United States Assay Office at New York, New York.

The above-mentioned silver, at the rate of $0.7111111111 per fine ounce, has a value of $64,000,000.00. This silver is carried in the Mint's accounts at $0.4666666666 per fine ounce - $41,999,999.99 - making a profit on the transaction of $22,000,000.01. As in prior similar cases, we understand that your office will arrange for issuance of a Certificate of Deposit covering the latter amount into the Treasury as a miscellaneous receipt. It is requested that this office be provided with two copies of the Certificate of Deposit inasmuch as it is necessary for us to return one to the Division of Disbursements with the Schedule of Collections.

Check No. 474,347, dated June 22, 1944, drawn to the order of the Treasurer of the United States, in the amount of $64,000,000.00, is enclosed herewith.

Very truly yours,

(Signed) [illegible]

Director of the Mint

Enclosures - 2
FWT:MB

The letter from the Director of the US Mint, Nellie Tayloe Ross, to the US Treasurer, dated 22 June 1944, detailing how a profit of $22 million and one cent was made on a single transaction for the supply of lend-lease silver to British India.

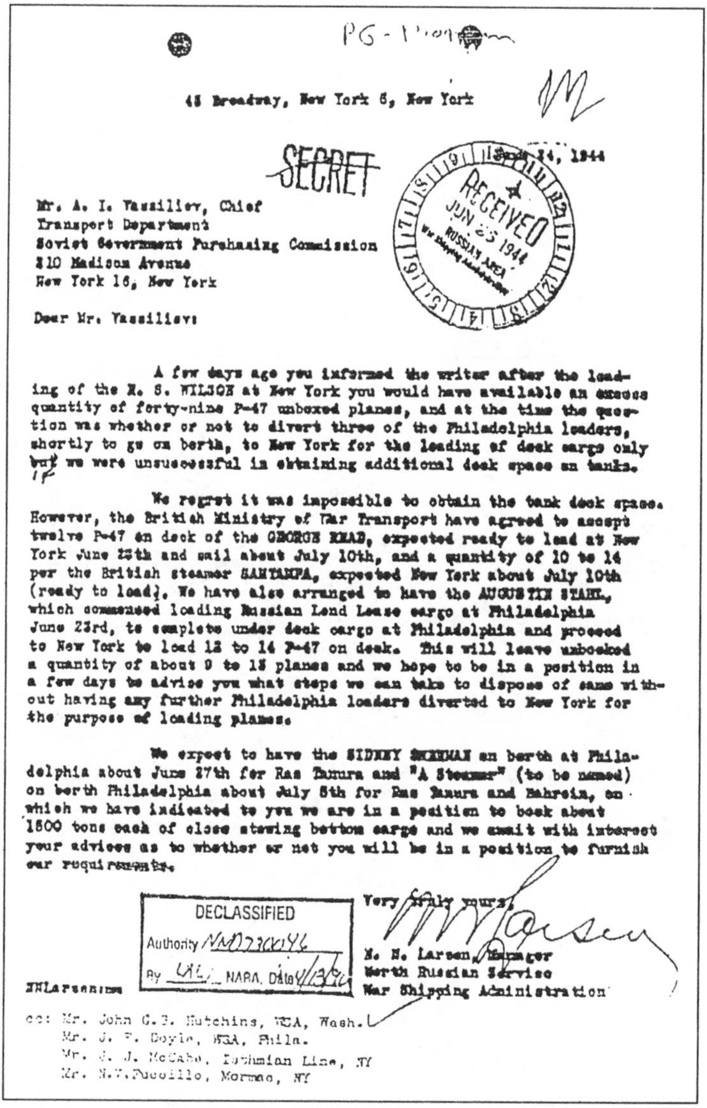

45 Broadway, New York 6, New York

SECRET

June 24, 1944

RECEIVED
JUN 25 1944
RUSSIAN AREA
War Shipping Administration

Mr. A. I. Vassiliev, Chief
Transport Department
Soviet Government Purchasing Commission
310 Madison Avenue
New York 16, New York

Dear Mr. Vassiliev:

A few days ago you informed the writer after the loading of the H. S. WILSON at New York you would have available an excess quantity of forty-nine P-47 unboxed planes, and at the time the question was whether or not to divert three of the Philadelphia loaders, shortly to go on berth, to New York for the loading of deck cargo only but we were unsuccessful in obtaining additional deck space on tanks.

We regret it was impossible to obtain the tank deck space. However, the British Ministry of War Transport have agreed to accept twelve P-47 on deck of the GEORGE MEAD, expected ready to load at New York June 25th and sail about July 10th, and a quantity of 10 to 14 per the British steamer SANTAMPA, expected New York about July 10th (ready to load). We have also arranged to have the AUGUSTIN STAHL, which commenced loading Russian Lend Lease cargo at Philadelphia June 23rd, to complete under deck cargo at Philadelphia and proceed to New York to load 12 to 14 P-47 on deck. This will leave unbooked a quantity of about 9 to 13 planes and we hope to be in a position in a few days to advise you what steps we can take to dispose of same without having any further Philadelphia loaders diverted to New York for the purpose of loading planes.

We expect to have the SIDNEY SHERMAN on berth at Philadelphia about June 27th for Ras Tanura and "A Steamer" (to be named) on berth Philadelphia about July 8th for Ras Tanura and Bahrein, on which we have indicated to you we are in a position to book about 1500 tons each of close stowing bottom cargo and we await with interest your advices as to whether or not you will be in a position to furnish our requirements.

Very truly yours,

N. N. Larsen, Manager
North Russian Service
War Shipping Administration

DECLASSIFIED
Authority NND73C0146
By [illegible] NARA, Date [illegible]

NNLarsen:mm

cc: Mr. John G. B. Hutchins, WSA, Wash.
Mr. J. F. Doyle, WSA, Phila.
Mr. J. J. McCabe, Isthmian Line, NY
Mr. N. V. Fuccillo, Mormac, NY

The letter from Nick Larsen of the WSA to the Soviet Government's Purchasing Commission in New York, marked 'Received June 25 1944', offering '1,500 tons of close stowing bottom cargo' on a vessel now known to have been the *John Barry*.

"John Barry"

. B 311 CARGO ALLOCATION SHEET # 1 JULY 5, 1944
BASE AND FINISH at PIER 84 NO. SIDE
PORT OF DISCHARGE A PERSIAN GULF PORT

	COMMODITY	TONS	CUBIC
	BAHREIN AND RUSSIA		
	RUSSIAN CARGO ALLOCATED NOT ON HAND		
20	HALF TRACKS	180	21000
12	TRACTORS	144	7200
	TELEGRAPH WIRE	50	2000
	CANNED MEAT	300	15000
	DRY EGGS	50	5000
	TIRES AND TUBES	50	8000
	RUBBER GOODS	25	1750
	ELECTRIC POWER EQUIPMENT	100	6000
	INDUSTRIAL EQUIPMENT	100	6000
	CABLE	200	10000
	TELEPHONE WIRE	60	4200
	TRUCK SPARES (2ND YEAR) (58 TONS ON HAND)	150	9000
	RUSSIAN CARGO ALLOCATED ON HAND		
144	STUDEBAKER 2½ TON TRUCKS	742	66604
	PIPE	99	3960
	MACHINE TOOLS	93	5049
	COTTON CLOTH	58	3501
	RUSSIAN WAR RELIEF	22	3023
	CUMENE-NO LABEL BY LIGHTER FROM ATLANTIC REF.	400	22000
	ETHYLENE GLYCOL (NO LABEL)(451 ON HAND)	600	33000
	RADIO EQUIPMENT	45	3500
		3468	235787
	BOTTOM CARGO		
	STEEL SHEETS	175	
	STEEL BILLETS	42	
	RAILS	819	
	METALS TO ARRIVE	464	
		1500	
	TOTAL:	4968	235787

STEVEDORE: LUCKENBACH
CLERK: JIM CARNEY

The Cargo Allocation Sheet of 5 July 1944, with its handwritten annotation 'John Barry', showing 'bottom cargo' of 1,500 tons. Note the item 'metals to arrive – 464 tons'.

CONFIDENTIAL

This form must be filed at the FINAL port of clearance in Continental United States, and in Alaska, Hawaii, and Puerto Rico with the Collector of Customs for transmittal to the War Shipping Administration before midnight of the 4th day after such clearance.

shoe

Date of departure 7-19-44 (Month, day, year)

Port of departure Philadelphia

743-744 (Do not use this space)

VESSEL PERFORMANCE AND CARGO REPORT
(VESSELS DEPARTING FROM UNITED STATES PORTS)

Punch No. 4

DECLASSIFIED
E.O. 12356, Sec. 3.3

THIS REPORT MUST BE FILED WITH THE COLLECTOR OF CUSTOMS FOR:

I. Every vessel engaged in foreign trade of the United States upon clearing with cargo or in ballast (1) from a continental port of the United States, or (2) a port of noncontiguous territory of the United States (viz., Alaska, Hawaii, and Puerto Rico).

II. Every vessel engaged in the noncontiguous trade of the United States with cargo or in ballast (1) departing from ports in continental United States for ports in Alaska, Hawaii, or Puerto Rico or (2) between noncontiguous ports (viz., Alaska, Hawaii, and Puerto Rico).

1. Name of vessel: S.S. JOHN BARRY 2. Flag American 3. Type Freight (Freighter, tanker, etc.)

1063561 (Do not use this space) 00 (Do not use this space) 2 (Do not use this space)

0110000

VESSEL PARTICULARS, OWNERSHIP AND SERVICE

4. Gross tonnage 7176 tons
5. (normal) 11 knots
6. Type of engines (kind) Reciprocating
7. (a) Load line applicable to this voyage: Summer (Winter, summer, etc.)
(b) Draft at this load line 28' 4¼" feet
8. Deadweight applicable this voyage 11200 tons
9. Total bale cubic capacity of vessel 499816 cu. ft.
(a) Refrigerator space cu. ft.
(b) Chilled space cu. ft.
(c) Deep tank capacity 41135 cu. ft.
10. Passenger capacity (all classes)
11. Owner Maritime Commission
Nationality American

12. Name of any government agency (civil or military) controlling use of vessel W.S.A. (Br. Min. W.T., WSA, Army, Navy, Neth. Ships and Trading Committee, etc.)
13. (a) Charterer Lykes Brothers
Nationality American
(b) Type of charter G.A.A. (Time, voyage, BB, etc.)
14. Operating agent Isthmian Steamship Company
15. Agent at port of departure Isthmian Steamship Company
16. Name of line Isthmian Steamship Company
17. Nationality of line American
18. Employment for this voyage: (Check / Approx. cargo Tonnage)
(a) Carrying U.S. Army cargo
(b) Carrying U.S. Navy cargo 246
(c) Carrying Lend-Lease cargo 1093
(d) Carrying commercial cargo 6894

ITINERARY (United States Ports)

Port of call	(19) Name of Port	State	(20) Date of Arrival Mo.	Day	Yr.	Departure Mo.	Day	Yr.	(21) Days delayed Awaiting cargo Number	Awaiting crew Number	Awaiting start of repairs Number	Otherwise Number	(22) Cargo tons of 2,240 pounds unloaded	(23) Cargo tons of 2,240 pounds loaded
1st	Philadelphia	Pa.	7	6	44	7	19	44						8233
2d														
3d														
4th														
5th														
6th														
7th														
8th														
9th														
10th														

The Vessel Performance and Cargo Report compiled at Philadelphia after the *John Barry*'s departure. Note the handwritten annotations of the final page – 'unk' for 'unknown' and the vague 'Persian Gulf'.

Cargo carried shall be listed in such detail as to show the quantity (in long tons of 2,240 pounds, shipping weight, including tare, if any) of each commodity or general cargo carried between each port of lading and each port of discharge. *Number of units and description of each type as well as long tons, including tare, is to be shown for* (1) locomotives (steam, diesel, etc.); (2) freight cars (box, gondola, etc.); (3) motortrucks (light, heavy, etc.); (4) passenger automobiles; (5) airplanes (pursuit, bomber (light, heavy), etc.); (6) military tanks (light, medium, heavy, etc.); (7) tractor cranes (crane capacity). *The 10-ton minimum does not apply to these commodities.*

Commodities in quantities of less than 10 tons each may be combined and designated "General cargo." No commodity shall be included in general cargo unless the total quantity of such commodity on board is less than 10 tons.

FREIGHT				PORTS OF—				
		Cargo		Lading			Discharge	
Code	Commodity (For instructions at top of page)	Number of units	Tons of 2,240 pounds	Name	Date	Code	Name	Code
	[illegible]							
6145	Steel plates		566	Philadelphia	7/19	143	Bahrein	141118
4229	Clay		9					
1141	Firebrick		85					
6153	Steel Pipe		239					
7021	Steel Tanks		29					
6169	Pipe, Pipe Fittings		11					
6151	Structural Steel		37					
7213	Gas Engines		15					
6156	Sewer Pipe		84					
7369	Gray Towers		66					
1	Smokestacks		16					
7331	Crane KD (1)		12					
4241	Asbestos Material		18					
0953	Beer		18					
7011	Exchangers Heat		39					
9091	General		384					
			~~1620~~					
	Tanura							
329	Doors, sashes		29				Ras Tanura	141810
1091	Iron Valves		26					
7331	Hoists		9					
1141	Steel Bars		206					
7333	Mixers		14					
4341	Firebrick		35					
1819	Tires, tubes		15					
6151	Structural Steel		182					
4331	Cement		54					
2119	Lumber		700					
6153	Pipe 83/4		700					
7421	Generators		33					
9079	Transite		238					
6159	Pipe Fittings		152					
4299	Vermiculite		46					
9077	Somastic Pipe		532					
4229	Slay Cinders		96					
3321	Furniture		7					
6152	Bare Pipe		144					
4321	Conduit Cement Pipe		45					
3022	Cedar Poles		6					
9077	Field Material		105					
1136	Steel Wire Mesh		169					
082	Asphalt		13					
299	Wool Cement		60					
0893	Concrete Water Reducing compound		18					
6153	Pipe		652					
7331	Erection Equipment		48					
6153	Pipe 12 3/4		307					
4331	Cement		600					
5393	Water Reducing Compound		25					
			~~5266~~					
	U.S. Army							
7223	Auto Parts		11				Persian Gulf [illegible]	179399
8735	Weapon Carrier		39					
7814	Trucks		65					
7331	Cranes		108					
7215	Tractor Crawler		23					
			~~246~~					
	Russian							
6 3	Wrought Pipe	~~[illegible]~~	~~0959~~ 199				"	
6157	Asco Steel Rails	~~[illegible]~~	753					
6157	O.H. Steel Rails	~~[illegible]~~	~~65~~ 141					

JUL 21 1944

APPENDIX II

Commodity (See instructions at top of page 1)	Cargo: Number of units	Cargo: Tons of 2,240 pounds	Landing: Name	Landing: Date	Landing: Code	Discharge: Name	Discharge: Code
Brought forward:							
Bahrein		1628					
Ras Tanura		5266					
U. S. Army		246					
Russian		918.3					
		8058.3					
O.H., H.R. Structural Steel Sheets		174.5					
TOTAL		8232.8					

OUTBOUND CARGO LOSS REPORT
(To be stapled to cargo report and sent to Tabulating Section)

Tabulating Section: Punch tonnage and commodity loss cards for the attached cargo report in same way as ordinary tonnage and commodity cards except as follows:

1. Do not punch any cards for passengers.
2. Do not punch any cards for any items markod "Not Lost".
3. Punch the following additional information

Col. 73, on tonnage card only (political control) 2
Cols. 74-79 (date of loss) 5/25/44
Col. 80 (Cause of loss) 4
Col 71, on tonnage card only (type of attack) 1

RECEIVED

	Measurement of cargo in cubic feet	Measurement of cargo in cubic feet	Long tons	Long tons
24. Total underdeck cargo		~~419136-0~~ 4191		7772
(a) Cargo carried in refrigerator space				
(b) Cargo carried in chilled space				
(c) Cargo carried in deep tanks (dry cargo vessels only)	10610		175	
25. Total deck cargo		~~52561~~ 526		461
26. Total cargo (item 24 plus 25) on board at the time of clearance including cargo in transit, if any		~~471697-0~~ 4717		8233

27. (a) Total deadweight capacity reserved for use of bunkers on this outbound voyage .... Long tons 1297

(b) Bunkers actually on board departing United States — Check: Coal ☐; Fuel oil ☒; Diesel oil ☐ — 2037 1297

28. (a) Water, stores, dunnage, armament, and defensing, on board clearing United States 740

(b) Ballast loaded for this voyage ....

29. (a) Deadweight tons available for cargo (subtract total of items 27 (a) and 28 (a) from item 8) 9163

(b) Deadweight capacity unused (subtract item 26 from item 29(a)) 930

(c) Percent of deadweight unused to deadweight available for cargo (item 29 (b) divided by item 29 (a)) .... 10% %

30. Cargo tons loaded at United States ports to be discharged at foreign ports of call or ports in noncontiguous territories of the United States:

	Names of foreign and noncontiguous ports	Country	Long tons
1st	Bahrein		1628
2d	Ras Tanura		5266
3d	~~U.S. Army~~ Umk	Persian Gulf	~~246~~ 1339
4th	~~Russian~~		~~3093~~
5th			
6th			
7th			
8th			
9th			
10th			
	Total cargo tons loaded at United States ports		8233

In item 30 "Cargo loaded at United States ports to be discharged at foreign ports of call" should be shown the total cargo tons loaded at United States ports (in cargo tons of 2,240 pounds) regardless of kind, class, or destination

31. Cargo tons on board arriving in the United States, or in noncontiguous territory, for discharge in a port of a foreign country or in another noncontiguous territory (in transit cargo) .... (Name of Country) .... Long tons

32. (a) Bale cubic available for cargo .... Cubic feet ~~475043~~ 471

(b) Broken stowage and/or unused space (subtract item 24 from item 32 (a)) .... ~~55907~~ 5

(c) Percent of broken stowage and unused space to bale cubic available for cargo (item 32 (b) divided by item 32 (a)) .... ~~11.7~~ % 1

Comments on voyage: (Remarks explaining delays and suggestions on how to improve turn-around time, stowage of cargo, etc., will be appreciated. Indicate nature of any repairs made and time involved at United States ports).

I HEREBY CERTIFY that this is an accurate and complete report of the lading of this vessel at her final United States port of clearance for this voyage.

Balance - Philadelphia (Signed) William M...

(Title) ....

APPENDIX II

C.J. Ship File

ISTHMIAN STEAMSHIP COMPANY

L1 - 24

71 BROADWAY

NEW YORK 6, N.Y.

ARCHIBALD E. KING
VICE PRESIDENT

MM

RECEIVED
JUL 21 1944
RUSSIAN AREA
War Shipping Administration

SECRET - REGISTERED

July 20th 1944

Mr. John B. Hutchins
Persian Gulf Section
Div. of Shipping Services
War Shipping Administration
Washington 25, D. C.

Att: Mr. H. N. Higinbotham

SS "JOHN BARRY" WSA V-6

Dear Sir:

The subject-named vessel recently departed from the port of Philadelphia - having loaded cargo under our berth agency - destined for the ports of Ras Tanura, Bahrein and 'a port in the Persian Gulf'.

Yours very truly,

THE UNITED STATES OF AMERICA
WAR SHIPPING ADMINISTRATION
by: ISTHMIAN SS CO., Agents

A. E. King

Vice President

CEM/ec

cc:
Lykes Bros. SS Company
17 Battery Place
New York 4, New York
Att: Mr. R. F. Rader

The letter dated 20 July 1944 from Archibald King of the Isthmian Steamship Company reporting the sailing of the *John Barry*. Again, note the vague expression 'a port in the Persian Gulf'.

CONFIDENTIAL Declas by Navy Auth Intelligence Report

ENEMY ATTACK ON MERCHANT SHIPS

From U. S. NAVAL OBSERVER At ADEN, ARABIA Date 3 September, 1944

Subject: MERCHANT SHIP SINKING BY ENEMY SUBMARINE.

Name of Ship S.S. "JOHN BARRY" Flag U. S.

Type
(1) Tanker ☐
(a) Single Bulkhead ☐
(b) Twin Bulkhead ☐
(c) Summer Tank ☐
(2) Cargo ☒
(3) Passenger ☐
(4) Passenger-cargo ☐

Gross Tonnage 7172 Whether Armed Yes ☒ No ☐

Date of Attack 28 August, 1944 Position at Attack 15 deg N 54 deg 55 : E.

Whether Sunk ☒, Damaged ☐, Captured ☐, or Escaped ☐

PARTICULARS OF SHIP AND VOYAGE

Questions	Answers
1. (a) Port of Departure	Aden, Arabia.
(b) Date of Sailing	26 August, 1944.
(c) Destination	Abadan, Iran.
(d) Route Instructions	Zig Zag singly to 57 deg 30 min E. thence GAC thence FOR [illegible].
2. Name of Owners and Charterers (if any) (If on Government Service the fact should be stated)	Lykes Bros. S.S. Co., New Orleans, La. Carrying Lend-Lease cargo on Government service.
(1) Cargo (a) Loaded or in ballast (type of ballast)	Loaded.
(b) General description and weight of cargo	General Cargo. $26,000,000 in silver
(c) Deck load (give distribution)	Not known.
(d) When a tanker give distribution and amount of liquid cargo or ballast	
3. Full Christian Name, Surname and Nationality of Master	Joseph [illegible], U. S. Citizen, German born.

(Page 1)

Enclosure (A) to Serial No. 01011016

11

The US Navy Intelligence Report made out at Aden on 3 September 1944. This dramatic piece of evidence established for the first time that the *John Barry* had been destined for the port of Abadan and that her cargo included $26 million worth of silver.

APPENDIX II

SWORN STATEMENT
Joseph Ellerwald
Master
SS JOHN BARRY

STATE OF NEW YORK)
COUNTY OF NEW YORK). ss.

I, Joseph Ellerwald, being duly sworn, depose and state:

My address is ——————,
. I have held a Master's license, unlimited, since 1942 and I joined the SS JOHN BARRY as Master on July 3, 1944 at New York. The last Articles were opened on this vessel on July 7, 1944 at Philadelphia. We sailed from Philadelphia on July 19 to join a convoy in Norfolk. On leaving Philadelphia our cargo consisted of 8,233 tons of general; the crew on leaving Philadelphia comprised 44 men, including myself; in addition, there were 27 Navy gunners aboard.

We left Norfolk in convoy on July 24, bound for Ras Tanura, Arabia via Suez; upon reaching Port Said, we proceeded on alone. We stopped at Aden on August 26 for a few hours to receive naval instructions. There were no changes in our crew from the time we left Philadelphia.

At 10 p.m. ship's time, August 28, 1944, the SS JOHN BARRY was struck by two torpedoes. The first torpedo hit in the after part of #3 hatch, starboard side and one-half hour later a second torpedo struck the vessel in the way of the engine room, starboard side.

When the first torpedo hit us, I was in my office and the concussion threw me from the chair. I immediately went out on the bridge; the general alarm had been given by the Mate on watch and I know that the Radio Operator sent off an SOS call. The engines were ordered stopped. At the time the torpedo struck us, our position was 15°10'N - 55°18'E. There was a west northwest wind at the time, about force 6; the sea was rough and the visibility poor.

As the vessel was going down by the head rapidly, I ordered the crew to abandon ship. The JOHN BARRY was equipped with four lifeboats and four square rafts. All of the rafts were tripped, but two of the lifeboats were rendered useless; #3 lifeboat had been blown on the after deck by the concussion and the forward starboard lifeboat had been blown off the ship. About 10.10 p.m. the crew started to leave the vessel; at 10.20 p.m. I went over the side into #2 lifeboat and the Chief Engineer and the Radio Operator followed soon after. In lowering #2 lifeboat, it was capsized, and some of the men who were in her swam either to a raft or to the remaining lifeboat which had already been launched.

The independent statement made by the *John Barry*'s Master, Joseph Ellerwald, in New York on 17 October 1944. It is most interesting for the details Ellerwald chose not to record.

SS JOHN BARRY
Joseph Ellerwald, Master - p. 2

The Chief Engineer and the Radio Operator jumped over the ship's side soon after I had gotten into the swamped lifeboat and joined me there with other members of the crew.

About 10.30 p.m. August 28, while #2 lifeboat was standing off the vessel at about 300 ft., the second torpedo struck the JOHN BARRY in the way of the engine room, starboard side. The ship immediately broke in two and sank, her bow and stern being the last to sink beneath the surface of the water. We stayed in the swamped lifeboat that night and at dawn it was bailed out.

Because of the direction of the current, I knew that we were in a sea lane and would probably be picked up shortly by some vessel appearing in the vicinity so both the lifeboats that had got clear of the ship put out sea anchors. At 10 a.m. August 29, a vessel was sighted on the horizon and we signalled her by a radio which we had saved. At 1 p.m. August 29, the men in #2 lifeboat were picked up by the SS BENJAMIN BOURN; there were 28 in all, including myself. I later learned that a Dutch tanker, whose name I do not know, had picked up the remaining members of the crew from the remaining lifeboat and the two rafts about 1/2 hour before we were picked up. These men were taken to Aden and when the SANTA BARBARA, the vessel on which I was repatriated, arrived at Aden on September 16, I learned these crew members had been taken aboard the Dutch tanker and landed there.

As a result of the torpedoing and sinking of the JOHN BARRY, two of the crew are missing. They are:

1. GORDON W. LYONS, Chief Off. I believe this man was in his quarters at the time we were torpedoed. I had not seen him since 8.30 that night. I questioned members of the crew and two of them, the Chief Cook and the Bosn., said that they thought this man was on the boat deck shortly before the vessel sank. When questioned further, both the Chief Cook and the Bosn. admitted they were not sure that it was the Chief Officer they saw on deck.

2. TAN SEE LEE (JEE), Messman. I questioned members of the crew and none of them had seen this man after the vessel was torpedoed.

We arrived at Khorramshahr on the BENJAMIN BOURN on September 5; 29 of the crew, including myself, were repatriated on the SANTA BARBARA, leaving Khorramshahr

APPENDIX II

SS JOHN BARRY
Joseph Ellerwald, Master - p. 3

on September 9 and arriving in New York on October 15. The two following men were injured:

1. GEORGE WILCAS, A.B. This man was standing on the boat deck at the time #2 lifeboat was swamped. The forward davit broke off and the end hit him on the head and he was left in the hospital at Khorramshahr.
2. WILLIAM WATLER, Ch. Eng. This man suffered a leg injury.

One man, Rucker, Messman, suffered an injury to his side when he fell on the dock at Khorramshahr.

As a result of the torpedoing and sinking of the JOHN BARRY, the crew lost all of their personal effects. As to the disposition of the lifeboats, two were lost by the torpedoing and the remaining two were abandoned when the men were taken aboard the rescue vessels.

Joseph Ellerwald
Joseph Ellerwald, Master

SUBSCRIBED AND SWORN to before me
this 19 day of October, 1944
A. W. Paulsen

NOTARY PUBLIC, KINGS COUNTY NO. 424
CERT. FILED IN NEW YORK COUNTY NO. 517
COMMISSION EXPIRES MARCH 30, 1945

STATE OF NEW YORK)
COUNTY OF NEW YORK) ss.

I, William Watler, being duly sworn, depose and state:

My address is
I was Chief Engineer on the SS JOHN BARRY when this vessel was torpedoed and sunk on August 28, 1944. I have read the statement made by Captain Joseph Ellerwald of the JOHN BARRY and the contents contained therein are true and correct.

William T. Watler
William Watler, Ch. Eng.

SUBSCRIBED AND SWORN to before me
this 17th day of October, 1944
A. W. Paulsen

NCG [illegible]

CONFIDENTIAL

UNITED STATES COAST GUARD

REPORT ON U. S. MERCHANT VESSEL WAR ACTION CASUALTY

To: Commandant, U. S. Coast Guard, Washington, D. C.

Ship S/s JOHN BARRY Service OCEAN FREIGHT

Owner W.S.A. Operator LYKES BROS.

Information furnished by MASTER. Date 23 MARCH, 1945

Line No.	Questions	Answers
1	Year built and propulsion	Built 1941 Propulsion STEAM
2	Tonnage	Gross 7172 Net 4375
3	Draft loaded (maximum allowed)	Fwd 27'(M) Aft
4	Draft when attacked	Fwd 26' 3" (M) Aft
5	Cargo on board (any deck)	Nature GENERAL + $26,000,000 IN SILVER BULLION Tons 5200
6	Voyage	From ADEN To RAS-TANURA, PERSIAN GULF
7	Were routing orders followed	YES
8	Any criticism of orders	NO
[illegible]	Weather at time of attack	Weather CLEAR Sea ROUGH
10	Was enemy sighted? When	NO
11	Any friendly ships in sight	NO
12	Were navigation lights on	NO
13	Date and time of attack	Date 8-28-44 Time 2200
14	Position	Latitude 15° 18'N Longitude 55° 18'E
15	Nature of attack (Give data)	TORPEDOED
16	Number of hits	2
17	Location of hits (Mark diagram)	1-FOR'D; 1-AFT-[illegible] [illegible]
18	Effect of hits	SANK SHIP.
19	Was ship armed? What type	YES
[illegible]	Was armament used? State result	NO
21	Any explosions or fires*	Ship NO Cargo NO
22	Was deck ruptured	YES
23	Did ship break in two	YES
24	Was SOS sent	YES - FROM LIFEBOAT.
25	Ship's speed	Normal 11.5 When attacked 12.0 When abandoned STOP
26	Time abandoned, sunk	Abandoned 2215 (15 min.) Sunk 2240 (40 min.)
27	Was ship reboarded	By whom NO When —
28	Was ship brought in	How NO Approximate damage SUNK

*Fill in this diagram to show attack hits, fires, etc.

(OVER)

14

The statement made by Ellerwald to the US Coastguard on 23 March 1945. This is the first written evidence that he had known all along, or had come to know after the sinking of the *John Barry*, that his vessel had been carrying silver bullion. Note his handwritten response to question 5.

APPENDIX II

Indicate by star (*) rafts, floats, or suits used as temporary refuge in water before rescue by lifeboats.

Line No.	QUESTIONS	ANSWERS
29	Lifeboats	Number carried 4 Which used 2
30	Lifeboats	Number lost 2 How TORPEDO EXPLOSION.
31	Life rafts	Number carried 4 Which used 2 + 1* = 3
32	Life rafts	Number lost 1 How ~~NOT NEEDED~~ TORPEDO EXPLOSION
33	Life floats	Number carried 3 Which used 2*
34	Life floats	Number lost 1 How NOT NEEDED
35	Lifesaving suits	Number carried 74 Number used 0
36	Were boats, etc., attacked	Attacked NO Casualties 0
37	Time in each boat, raft, etc.	2 Boats 14 hrs. 2 Rafts 14 hrs. — Float — Boat — Raft — Float
38	Rescued by and where 28P7R	By ALLIED SHIPS Where NEAR SCENE
39	Number of gun crew carried (military)	Officers 1 Enlisted men 26
40	Number ship's crew carried	Officers 10 Radiomen 2 Unlicensed 29
41	Number passengers and others carried	Passengers 0 Others 0
42	Total on board	68
43	Number gun crew injured (military)	Officers 1 Enlisted men 0
44	Number ship's crew injured	Officers 1 Radiomen 0 Unlicensed 1
45	Number passengers and others injured	Passengers 0 Others 0
46	Number gun crew lost (military)	Officers 0 Enlisted men 0
47	Number ship's crew lost	Officers 1 Radiomen 0 Unlicensed 1
48	Number passengers and others lost	Passengers 0 Others 0
49	Total casualties	Injured 3 Lost 2
50	Persons lost by (Specify)	Drowning 2 Fire 0 Shell or torpedo 0 Other causes 0
51	Total rescued	Gun crew 27 Officers 9 Radio operators 2 Unlicensed 28 Passengers 0 Others 0 Total 66
52	Persons saved by	Boats 35 Rafts 31 Floats 0 Suits 0 Preservers 0 Other means 0 No aid 0
53	Engineering watch below	Number on watch below 2 Number lost below 0
54	Number of look-outs	9
55	Any defective material	NO
56	Any personnel fault	NO

COMMENTS, CRITICISMS, AND RECOMMENDATIONS

The comments, criticisms, or recommendations of survivors with respect to safety of seamen and ships involved in war actions are earnestly solicited by Headquarters in order that the fullest provision possible may be made for the safety of American ships and seamen.

U. S. GOVERNMENT PRINTING OFFICE

JHJ.

15

November 29, 1967

Mr. R. T. Reckling
Vice President - Operations
Lykes Brothers Steamship Co.
P. O. Box 50990
New Orleans, Louisiana 70150

Dear Mr. Reckling:

In your absence this date I conversed by telephone with Mr. M. G. Bulloch concerning a U.S. vessel named the JOHN BARRY operated by Lykes Brothers for the War Shipping Board during WWII. This vessel was sunk by enemy torpedoes on 28 August, 1944 in very deep water in the Gulf of Aden.

We are attempting to verify a cargo of silver which was carried on this vessel in order that we may make a decision concerning salvage.

In researching the Maritime Administration records, we find that the manifest of this vessel contained building materials but an annotation stated that a large quantity of silver bullion was also carried. We assume that the latter was carried under some secrecy order. The Maritime Administration is presently researching this vessel as are the State and Treasury Departments in order to ascertain the amount of silver and the ownership.

We would sincerely appreciate it if you could research your files on the subject as an additional verification. Thank you for any assistance you may be able to give us.

Sincerely,

Arthur L. Markel
Vice President &
General Manager

Rosslyn Bldg., 1901 N. Fort Myer Drive, Arlington, Va. 22209 Phone: (202) NA 8-5886 or (703) 524-

The letter from Arthur L. Markel to R. T. Reckling of Lykes Brothers which suggests that up until November 1967 Washington's archives had contained a manifest recording the presence of silver bullion aboard the *John Barry*. That manifest is not in the archives now.

Index

Abadan 112, 113, 115, 175, 176, 178, 179, 206
Abdul Aziz ibn Saud, King 4, 12, 115–16, 119, 120, 167, 173–4
Active, HMS 89
Adamant 136
Aden 37–8, 39–41, 44, 82, 101, 103, 106, 108, 112, 114
Al Aulaqi, Sheikh Ahmed Farid 4–5, 7, 9–11, 31–4, 147, 149–50, 152, 155–6, 161–3, 166–7, 183
  biography 40–46
Al Aulaqi, Saleh 42
Al Harthy, Sheikh Zaher Hamed 28
Al Khaleej 5
American Bureau of Shipping 78
Angell, James 153
Arabian Sea 82, 100, 106, 117, 121, 143
ARAMCO 78, 114, 118, 148, 172–3, 175, 178
Archer, Jeffery 166
Asharq al Awsat 9
Atlantic Ocean 82, 88, 90–1
Atlas of Ship Wreck and Treasure 3
atomic bomb 188, 189
Australia 56–7
Awe, HMS 123

Bahrain 69, 77, 80, 81, 175
Bahrain Petroleum Company 78, 175
Baker, James 30
Barth 100
Base Poula 124–8
Batavia 186–7
Bell, D.W. 68–9, 79, 80
Benjamin Bourn, SS 102–3, 107, 108, 122
Berwickshire, HMS 126
Bletchley Park 59, 91, 172
Bolt, Rating 97
Bordeaux 186–7
Borisyenko, D. 179
Braynard, Frank 72
Britain
  lend-lease to 51–61, 154, 177
  US and 49–55, 59–60, 119, 153, 181–2, 196
  World War II 49–50, 53–8, 85
British Admiralty 118
British Empire 37, 40–1, 49, 55–6, 59–60, 119
Bunker, John Gorley 9, 19, 21, 22, 71, 74, 161, 162

Cadogan, Alexander 179
Cambridge University 28–9
Cape of Good Hope 88–9, 95, 99
Careless Word...a Needless Sinking (Moore) 21, 72
Cargo Allocation Sheet 79, 80–1, 200
Caster, MV 150, 156, 159–60
Cavalcante, Bernard 22–3
Certificate of Abandonment 17, 23
Chariot attack 131
Charmley, John 49, 63, 181–2
Chew, Roberta 168
Churchill, Winston 51–5, 59–61, 172, 181–3
Code and Cipher School 91
codes 59, 90–1, 98–9, 132
Coe, Frank 153
Cold War 67, 182
Coliu 95
Conrad, Lieut. Barbara 107, 109, 110, 114, 115
Crowley, Leo 153
Cyana 149, 156–7, 159

Daily Express 9–10
Daronia 126
Deep Ocean Explorer 147
Der Spiegel 10
Devoy, Vice-President 75
Dhofar War 38–9, 43–4
Diver 9
Doenitz, Admiral Karl 88–9, 98
Dole, Robert 33–4
Donovan, 'Wild Bill' 59, 172
Doyle, J.F. 81–2
Dubai press conference 1–11, 168
Dunn, David 31

Eastport International 145–9
Eddy, Col. William 117, 171–4
Edinburgh, HMS 3, 150
Ellerwald, Joseph 7, 76, 79, 81, 82, 106–7, 144, 175, 177–8
  deposition 101–4, 108–11, 114–15, 207
  statement to US Coastguard 111, 210
Enigma code 59, 90

Fafalios 126
FBI 26, 174, 177
Fehler, Johann Heinrich 189
Ferguson, John 167
Fernanders, Jesse 29
Fiondella, Jay 18, 21–2, 24, 27, 30–1, 33, 162, 164
Fletchers Dry Dock 76, 156
Flex LD 5, 6, 10, 162–5, 167
Foreign Economic Administration (FEA) 116, 153–4, 196
Foreign Office 119
Frankfurter Allgemeine 10
French International Marine Institute *see* Ifremer
Fukutome, Admiral 87

Gehlen, Dr Hans von 92, 97–8
Germany 85, 92, 137
  Navy *see* U-boats
German War Graves Commission 138
Giaconne, Joseph 174
Glomar Explorer 20
Gopal, Neena 2
Gorch Foch 92
grab 6–7, 20, 161–4
Gulf News 2, 3, 11
Gusev, F. 179

Halifax, Lord 53
Hart, Parker T. 13, 26, 115, 116–18, 121, 124
Hessler, Gunter 89, 91
Hezlet, Arthur 129–37
Hitler, Adolf 85–6, 88, 99
Hoboken 76, 77, 79, 156, 177
Hudson, Robert 5, 10, 31–2, 36, 38–9, 45–6, 144, 151, 152, 162–5, 168
Huff-Duff 59, 90, 129
Hutchins, John 69, 77, 78, 81–2, 177, 197
Huthi, Sayid Sami 117

Ifremer 5, 149–50, 156–7, 159–63
Independent 166
India 4, 9, 26–7, 151–4, 168, 174, 198
India Office 144
Indian Ocean 86–92, 100, 126, 185–6
Intrepid, USS 19
Iran 13, 176
Isthmian Steamship Company 75, 77, 81, 205
Italy 92, 98, 100

Jabbar, Abul 3
Jannucci, Captain 98–9
Japan 49, 53, 87–8, 91, 132, 137–9, 185–90
  Navy 87–8
Jebsen, Jan 7–8, 86, 92–100, 104–6, 121, 125–30
Jeddah 115, 117–19, 172–3, 178
Jessop, Keith 3, 9, 150–1, 156–7, 166
John Barry, SS
  bid invitations 11–13, 23–4, 26, 28–30
  cargo 4, 9, 10–13, 23, 25–7, 74, 77, 78–81, 109, 111–13, 115–16, 139, 144–5, 154–6, 160, 168–9, 171, 176, 180, 200, 206
  Cargo Allocation Sheet 79, 80–1, 200
  crew of 81, 83, 101, 110, 177
  last voyage of 82–3, 101
  manifest 12, 168, 176–7, 212
  salvage operation 4–6, 143, 149–51, 161–8
  secrecy over 4, 12, 28, 75, 77–9, 81, 108–11, 116, 151, 168, 171–83
  ship's log 76–7
  sinking of 4, 7–8, 72, 74, 102–15, 122
  survey of wreck 144–8, 156–60
  Vessel Performance and Cargo Report 79–80, 175–6, 201
  wartime service 74–6
John Barry Group 18, 30, 32–3, 151, 162
Johnson, F.E. 152
Jordan, Stanley 119–20

Kaiser, Henry 73–4
Kessler, Ulrich 189
Key West 19
Khorramshahr 103, 106, 107, 108, 111, 114, 177
Kiehn, Oberleutenant 92
Kiel 8, 86, 92, 93, 126, 188, 190
King, Archibald 81, 205
Klatt, Horst 7–8, 10, 93–9, 104–6, 108, 110, 115, 121–2, 124–5, 127–30, 134–9
Klein Smartfish 20

La Corona 113
Larsen, Nick 68–9, 75, 77–9, 81–2, 177, 181, 197, 199
Lask, Lieut. 97, 127
Lebedev, Ivor 178–9
Lebkicher 117, 118
lend-lease 26, 63, 115, 172, 176, 182
  to Britain 49, 51–61, 153, 177
  to India 9, 26–7, 152–4, 168, 8

INDEX

reverse 55–8, 66–7
to Saudi Arabia 116, 119, 172–3
to Soviet Union 64–70, 80, 151, 176, 178–81
Third Protocol 67–9, 178–80, 191–5
Liberty Ship Memorial Museum 155
liberty ships 2, 71–4, 83
Liberty Ships (Bunker) 19, 21, 71, 74–5
Lloyd's List 166
'Lost Squadron' 21
Lothian, Lord 51
Lykes Brothers 75, 176, 212
Lyons, Gordon W. 103
Lyttelton, Oliver 179

McDermott, Will and Emery 33
McGuire Riley, Heman 29–31, 33, 162, 164
Mack, Clifton E. 152
Magellan, ROV 147–8
Malacca Straits 8, 118, 129–30, 135
manifest 12, 168, 176–7, 212
marine-recovery operations 19–21
Maritime Administration 33
Archives 12, 22, 176–7, 212
bid invitations 11–13, 23–4, 26, 28–30
Markel, Arthur L. 176–7, 212
Marks, Sally 24
Massie, Vincent 179
Mayboom, A.W. 113
media coverage 9–10, 166–7
Merchant Marine Veterans 25
mercury 125, 128, 137–9, 185–9
Mina Raysut 143, 147, 149, 156, 159, 162–3
Montgomery, Cran 24
Moore, Captain Alan 164
Moore, Arthur 21, 22, 72
Moore, Colonel 75, 177
Moose, James 115, 116, 119, 172
Morgenthau, Henry 26, 50–1, 53
Muscat, Russian Embassy 179, 181

Nagumo, Vice-Admiral 88
Nargiolet, Paul Henri 157
National Liberation Front 41–2
Naval Arctic Research Laboratory 20
Naval Institute 22, 92
Naval Intelligence report (Aden) 110, 111–13, 115, 175, 206
Navy Historical Centre 22
Nendza, Walter 25, 174
New Republic 182
New York 75–7, 78, 152, 154, 155, 168, 175, 177, 197
Assay Office 152–5, 177–8
New Zealand 56–7
News of the World 10, 167
Norfolk, Va 81, 82, 101, 110
North Yemen 39

Ocean Group 4, 11, 31–4, 38, 45–6, 143–5, 147, 149–51, 162
Oesten, Korvettenkapitan 126, 128, 134
Office of Strategic Service 59, 172
Oldney, Lieut. Cdr John 114
Oman 35–6, 38–9, 43–5, 143
Exclusive Economic Zone 23, 30
and salvage operation 11, 24, 28, 30–4, 144
O'Neill, Hugh 28–33, 162, 164
Operation Backfire 187
Operation Dolphin 90
Operation Drumbeat 88
Operation Drumroll 89
Operation Torch 172
Oregon Shipbuilding Corporation 75

Palestine 173–4
Patsev, Alexander 178
Patton, Boggs and Blow 31
Pearl Harbor 18, 53, 72
Penang 8, 90, 124–9, 133, 135, 137
Persian Gulf 71, 81
Persian Gulf and Red Sea Naval Reports 122
Philadelphia 25, 27, 77, 79–82, 101, 151–2, 155, 168, 175, 178
Phillips, Sir Frederick 50–1
Phuket 131
Pokryshkin, Alexander 66
Ponting, Clive 181
Port Said 82, 101
Portland, Maine 75, 76, 77
Portland, Oregon 75, 157
Portsmouth, New Hampshire 190

Qaboos bin Said al Said, Sultan 5, 35–6, 38, 43

Ras Tanurah 12, 26, 80, 81, 82, 114, 115–16, 155, 174, 178
Rashwan, Asem 5
Reckling, R.T. 176, 212
Red Army 64–6, 183
Reynolds Sub-Marine Services 176
Richards, Gerald 175
Riyadh 13, 26
Robert E. Peary 73
Roosevelt, Franklin D. 50–61, 63–8, 71, 79, 116, 119, 153, 172–4, 176, 178–9, 180–3
Ross, Nellie Tayloe 152–4, 198
Roux, Jean 5–7, 149–50, 156–7, 159–65, 168
ROV 145–9, 157, 159
Royal Navy 117, 121, 186
Intelligence 113–14
pursuit of *U859* 118, 121–4, 128, 131–4
Royal New Zealand Naval Reserve 114
Rucker, Messman 103

Salalah 143, 147, 150–1, 156, 162
San Diego 19, 21
Santa Barbara 103
Saudi Arabia 4, 5, 13, 24–6, 42, 114, 115, 118, 167, 172
lend-lease to 116, 119–20, 172–3
Scamp, ROV 149, 157, 159

Shabwa 40, 41, 42, 44
Shoemaker, Brian 18–34, 144, 151–2, 154–8, 162, 164–5, 174, 181
Shoji, Genzo 190
Short, Livingston 115, 116
Sidney Sherman, SS 117
silver: bullion 4, 8–9, 11–12, 19, 22–3, 25, 27, 74, 79, 109, 111–13, 115, 139, 144–5, 151–6, 158–9, 166, 168, 174–8, 180–1, 194, 206, 210
  coins 4–7, 11–12, 24–6, 115–16, 118–19, 139, 145, 159, 164–8, 178
Simmons, Richard 31–3, 36–9, 45–6, 156, 162–3
South Africa 52, 54
South Yemen 36, 41–5
Soviet Union 181–3
  Air Force 66
  and *John Barry* cargo 9, 13, 79–80, 112, 114, 176
  lend-lease to 64–70, 151, 176, 178–81
  Purchasing Commission 68–9, 79, 199
Stalin, Joseph 63, 178, 181–3
Steinfeld, Korvettenkapitan 186–7
submarines *see* U-boats
Suez Canal 82, 100
Suleiman, Sheikh Abdulla 117
Sunday Telegraph 49, 63
Sunday Times 137
Sunetta, SS 108, 112–13, 122
Sutton, USS 190

Tabin, Mr 152
Tagirov, Elmir 180
Tan See Jee 103
Tanjong Priok 187
Tay 100
Tehran Conference 182
Third Protocol *see* lend-lease
Thompson, J.L., & Sons 73
Titanic 2, 6, 149
Tizard, Sir Henry 59
Tomonaga, Hideo 190
Toulon 5, 161
towfish 144
Trenchant, HMS 8, 118, 129, 131–7
Trincomalee 129, 131, 136
Troilus, MV 121, 123
Truman, Harry 182, 188

U859 7–8, 70, 83, 86, 118
  maiden voyage 92–100, 121–8
  mercury cargo 125, 128, 137–9, 185–6
  pursuit of 118, 122–4, 128–9, 132–4
  salvage attempt 137–8
  sinking of 89–90, 118, 130–7
  sinks *John Barry* 74, 104–6
U861 125–6, 128, 134
U-boat War in the Atlantic (Withers) 90–1
U-boats 85–100, 121–35, 185–90
Ultra detection system 90–1
United Arab Emirates 39
United States 4, 11–13, 17, 23, 33, 62
  and Britain 9, 49, 51–61, 119, 153, 181–2, 196
  and Saudi Arabia 119–20, 172–3
  and Soviet Union 63–70, 181–3
  see also lend-lease
uranium 189, 190
US Assay Office 152–4, 156, 177
US Coastguard 22, 25, 110, 111, 114, 164, 210
US Merchant Marine 72
US Mint 22, 23, 25, 152, 154, 175, 198
US National Archives 12, 22, 24, 26, 151
US National Silver Bullion Depository 152, 154
US Navy 18, 19, 144
  Armed Guard 25, 82–3, 110, 113, 174
Chief of Naval Operations 107
  Judge Advocate General of 23
  Naval Research office 20
US State Department 22, 23, 25, 26, 27, 30–1, 116, 153–4
US Treasury 22, 23, 26, 152, 153
Procurement Division 152, 154
USSR *see* Soviet Union

V2 rockets 186–8
Vaivant, John 179
Valdy, Pierre 159
Valiant Service 147–9
Vassiliev, A.I. 68, 79
Versailles Treaty 85–6
Vessel Performance and Cargo Report 79–80, 175–6, 201

Wallace, Henry 182
Walter, William 110
War Shipping Administration (WSA) 68–9, 75–8, 80–2, 176–7, 181, 197, 199
Watler, William 103
Wenneker, Admiral 88
Wharmby, Simon 166
Wilgas, George 103
Wilkinson, Tim 10
Witheridge, Annette 10, 167–8
Withers, Lieut. Cmdr Andrew 90–1
Woods, Lieut. Cdr 114–15
World War I 49, 85
World War II 55, 72, 92, 181
  Britain and 49–50, 53–8, 85
  Japan and 53, 87–8, 91, 185–90
  merchant shipping 71–2
  Soviet Union and 64–6, 183
  submarines 85–100, 121–37, 185–90

Yalta Conference 182
Yamomoto, Admiral 87
Yousuf bin Alawi bin Abdullah 30

Zionism 173–4